Jules Didiot

The Religious State According to the Doctrine of St. Thomas

Jules Didiot

The Religious State According to the Doctrine of St. Thomas

ISBN/EAN: 9783743369160

Manufactured in Europe, USA, Canada, Australia, Japa

Cover: Foto ©Lupo / pixelio.de

Manufactured and distributed by brebook publishing software (www.brebook.com)

Jules Didiot

The Religious State According to the Doctrine of St. Thomas

RELIGIOUS STATE,

ACCORDING TO

THE DOCTRINE OF ST. THOMAS.

BY

JULES DIDIOT,

Honorary Canon of Bayeux; Doctor of Divinity; late Professor of Philosophy and Dogmatic Theology.

(Translated from the French.)

LONDON:
BURNS & OATES, 17 & 18, PORTMAN STREET,
W.;
And 63, PATERNOSTER ROW, E.C.

Printed by W. Davy & Son, Gilbert Street, London, W.

TRANSLATOR'S DEDICATION.

To the dear Nuns of the Assumption, whose edifying lives, great kindness, and watchful care first dispelled my ignorant prejudices and instilled into me respect and affection for this holy "*Religious State*," I gratefully dedicate this translation, and hope that it may assist them in teaching others that which they taught me.

Feast of the Assumption,
    15th August, 1874.

PREFACE.

THIS treatise *on the Religious State* forms one of *a series of ascetical works embodying the doctrine of St. Thomas of Aquino.* As such, we confidently present it to all true theologians, who will appreciate the utility of an exact commentary upon the text of the Angelic Doctor, even though we may not have succeeded in giving it either the marvellous depth or the charm of novelty we find there. We offer it with still greater confidence to those souls who have vowed religious perfection, persuaded that the voice of him who was both the most sublime Doctor of the schools, and one of the most admirable religious of the middle ages, will not fail to give powerful encouragement to the virtues and works of the religious life. This great man, and still greater Saint, cannot fail to have fathomed the principles from which he daily derived the rules of his conduct, and which became the fruitful source of his sanctity. Who, then, could more ably develope these principles than one so devoted to his profession and so inflamed with the desire of promoting the spiritual progress of his religious brethren?

If the world is now tottering to its fall from the want of principles in the intellect and of strength of will; if Catholics, and more especially religious, are the only labourers who can strengthen our shifting ground and rebuild our ruined walls; and if the time favourable for restoration has come, when we may hope that the Vatican Council will again bring us the miracles of sanctity, of apostleship, education, and Christian science, which were the result of the Council of Trent, can we doubt that the study of St. Thomas' ascetic theology must prove both very beneficial and necessary for us?

This teaching succeeds better than any other in giving to the mind a spirit of rectitude, fortitude, and intelligence. It places man in the full possession of his reason and faith, delivering him from that narrowness and those vain fears and errors which paralyze so many souls called to the performance of great works. For when a ray of the Angelic Sun has lit up the mind, it endows the heart with a rare consistency and an indomitable energy; it helps us efficaciously both to will and to persevere, because it places us really upon the supernatural ground of the Roman Church, in the sight of God, under the direct impression of His grace, in the calm of a conscience which joyously sacrifices all its possessions to that only Good who alone deserves to be loved without measure, and who alone can be adored without remorse.

And with this before us, why tremble at the task which God has confided to us, or grow fainthearted at the sight of those evils which He sends us to remedy? Why not deliver up oneself entirely to the practice of religious perfection, when it is one's calling? And then, why should not the happy success of the holy Council be secured in every soul, in every society, and even in the most desperate affairs of this world which it has to save?

It is this Christian ambition and these fond hopes, already justified by the esteem and devotion with which St. Thomas' teaching inspires so many excellent minds, that have dictated this book on the *Religious State*, wherein will be found a constant exposition of the precepts and teaching of the Angel of the Schools. He will often speak to us himself, without his words undergoing any change save that of translation. When his exalted thoughts would seem to transcend the bounds of ordinary minds, then we shall try so carefully to explain them, that they may be food for the unlearned and the simple. Further, his theories will be adapted to the usages and requirements of our day. But whatever the expression, it will be always he who instructs us. The commentator is merely a humble student, seated lovingly at his master's feet, transcribing his teaching for other disciples, often farther advanced in wisdom than himself. Doctor, Master, and Angelic Guide, you know that I have desired faithfully to reproduce your brilliant words! But in my unskilful hands, what will become of their precious substance? Will they still possess that power they had on your own pure lips, when, in that prison where you were detained as a martyr to the religious life, they converted to the love of heavenly things and to spiritual perfection your young and noble sisters, who had become to you apostles of worldly vanity and agents of your persecutors?

The religious state is the sole object of this treatise; the doctrines common to all Christians, such as perfection in general, the theological virtues, and prayer, will be dealt with in other works. And since this one is exclusively ascetic, it would be unreasonable to expect to find in it those magnificent and most excellent teachings of St. Thomas which relate either to the canonical position of Regulars or to the defence of their institutions against the attacks of their enemies. We have also omitted to give the Latin text of the holy doctor, or any other quotations than those he himself alleges, either from Scripture or from the Fathers. A different method might have displayed more erudition, but would not have been so well adapted to our purpose and principal end. In fine, this work is in substance taken from the *Summa Theologica*, II^a II^æ, q. 183—189, and from the *Summa contra Gentes*, book 3, chapters 130—139.

Wishing to explain the first principles of the religious state, we shall not enter into the detail of exercises of piety, practices of mortification, and works of zeal, which have a real but at the same time secondary importance. Many valuable works, above all the *Lives of the Saints*, and the traditions which form the treasure and heirloom of every

Community, fully dispense us from thus entering into so long a task. Further, it was more befitting one of little spiritual knowledge to follow closely an acknowledged authority in the Church, by writing a short and simple *Introduction* to all those rules and books which are the inexhaustible and wholesome food of religious life.

The very plan of our treatise is taken from that of St. Thomas of Aquino. After a preliminary study of the nature of the religious state, we shall see in the evangelical counsels, considered first generally, then in particular, three powerful helps and three efficacious virtues, which Our Lord recommends to those who desire to attain to perfection. The theory of the vows will explain how the observance of these divine counsels constitutes a state properly so called in the Church. We shall then examine the nature of the sins committed by religious. The divers forms of regular life, and its most important works, will be the subject of the following chapters;

and after having considered the religious state in its essence, means, and action, we end, like the Angelic Doctor, with the important doctrine of Vocation, which could not be rightly understood, unless some definite notion of that state to which God is pleased to call His chosen friends had already been acquired. Although the end of each chapter will be followed by a brief, but at the same time, substantial *résumé*, the conclusion of this book will present a synoptical view of the numerous passages from the works of St. Thomas, wherein he describes the religious state. A steady and sustained attention will, it appears to us, be the duty of the reader, who would meditate over these pages, and derive from them nourishment for his soul. Asceticism is in fact a science, which cannot be acquired without labour, and which withholds its secrets from inattentive and heedless minds. However we may endeavour to facilitate this study, the necessity of application, in order to sound its principles and draw from them logical conclusions, can never be dispensed with. This spiritual science can in no wise be transformed into a series of bright pictures and vivid delineations, with the idea of rendering it easy and intelligible at first sight, or after a hasty perusal. We do not believe that piety can be solid when made easy, or that an ascetical book can be of much use when it can be pleasantly and fully taken in at a first reading.

Our aim is that this book should be clear, for such as will be at the pains of reading it more than once, and of analysing and comparing its different parts. It has even the pretension, which our readers will not refuse to pardon, of proving that the religious state is not a mere matter of sentiment, but a sacred art having a positive groundwork, fixed laws, regular means, and requiring a severe apprenticeship; in fine, that it must be cultivated with the patience, application, and length of time at least equal to, if not greater than that given to the attainment of any human art.

If, therefore, the following chapters exact from the reader some thought and meditation, we shall consider it no matter for regret, confiding in the good sense of those Christian souls, who, inspired by God's grace, clearly see that spiritual progress is well worth the care and labour they bestow on it, and that they must judge of the solidity of such progress, rather by the depth of conviction from which it proceeds, than by the number or brilliancy of its works.

This work bears the imprimatur of the Bishop of Verdun.

CONTENTS.

	PAGE
CH. I. Nature of the Religious State	1
CH. II. The Evangelical Counsels	15
CH. III. Religious Poverty	27
CH. IV. The domain of Holy Poverty	58
CH. V. Religious Chastity	83
CH. VI. The Privileges of Virginity	102
CH. VII. Religious Obedience	130
CH. VIII. Religious Vows	150
CH. IX. The Holocaust and Consecration	168
CH. X. Sin in the Religious Life	202
CH. XI. The Forms of the Religious Life	226
CH. XII. Works of the Religious Life	273
CH. XIII. The Entrance into Religion	309
CH. XIV.—CONCLUSION. The Religious	357

THE RELIGIOUS STATE.

CHAPTER I.

The Nature of the Religious State.

ON the Feast of St. Thomas of Aquino, the Church's office instructs us to ask of God the grace to understand fully the teachings of this incomparable master. The author begins this book by addressing the same prayer to our Divine Lord, begging for his readers and for himself a ray of the light divine, which may reveal in all clearness to their minds the simple yet deep thoughts of the Angelic Doctor. Let us devoutly enter his school, and hearken to his teaching concerning the nature of the Religious State.

Whenever one and the self-same perfection is common to a multitude of objects, though in divers degrees, and with varying intensity, it is usual to attribute it specially to that object which shares it most largely and possesses it *par excellence:* thus the name of *fortitude* is exclusively given to the virtue that keeps the soul firm and unshaken amid considerable difficulties, whilst the name of *temperance* is reserved for the virtue which regulates and moderates the appetite for sensual gratifications; even though the overcoming of slight obstacles may claim to be called fortitude, and though there be a certain degree of temperance in the moderate enjoyment of the most common and unattractive pleasures of life.

This law of speech and thought, which is a real homage we pay to the most noble traces of the Creator's hand in the beings He has made, will help us to explain the name and nature of the religious state. True it is that the virtue of *religion*[1] leavens in a way every act whereby we do God service and pay Him due worship, whence every man is necessarily *religious* if he devote but a minute to the

---

[1] The virtue of religion is the disposition which divine grace, seconded by our endeavours, implants in the soul, in order to incline the will to the faithful performance of the worship due to God, consisting as it does in sacrifice, adoration, devotion, vows, oaths, &c. The virtue of religion excludes impiety, indifference, superstition, blasphemy, perjury, &c.

worship of God. The same is yet infinitely more true of the Christian who is exact in the fulfilment of the precepts concerning the honour, adoration and praise we owe to the King of kings. But the glorious names of *Religion* and *Religious* mainly apply, and with far greater accuracy and truth, to souls who devote themselves wholly and for ever to God's service, and, so to speak, offer themselves as a holocaust to His Sovereign Majesty, as may be gathered from the following description made of such by St. Gregory:[2] "Some there are who keeping nothing for themselves make a sacrifice to the Almighty of their senses, their tongue, their life, and of all other gifts vouchsafed to them."

And because this *religious* self-immolation is not a merely passing tribute, or temporary loan to God, but a consecration which definitively separates us from the world, a holocaust leaving us nothing of our former independence, an immolation extending to all the powers and acts of our life, it results in a permanent *state*, a new and enduring *life;* in other words, in the *religious state*, the *religious life*.

[2] Homily XX. on Ezechiel.

Hence the religious state may be described as the highest excellence of the virtue of religion, whereby it becomes, so to speak, incarnate in a man and living in him, inspiring and guiding every other virtue bestowed by the Divine bounty, bringing into captivity all his bodily and spiritual powers, and binding them by gentle ties to the service and honour of God, rendering his every action, be it what it may, an act of religion,[3] transforming his life into a hymn of adoration, a continual

---

[3] Even as vices and sins may be subordinated to each other, and so work up to one common end; as, for instance, with the profligate who steals in order to gratify his lust; so too, may the several virtues afford each other mutual aid for God's glory and the welfare of man. Besides the acts it may claim as its own, such as worship, vows, &c., the virtue of religion can stimulate hope and charity to elicit unto God's honour acts proper to themselves, which will thus bear the twofold impress, of hope, or charity, and of religion. Acts thus originated serve as means and instruments whereby religion attains its special ends. This supremacy of one virtue over another, the government and influence it thus exercises in the soul is an important fact of spiritual life, more especially of the religious state which derives therefrom that unity of purpose and of action so essential to solidity and permanency.

sacrifice: so that he is no longer merely chaste, humble, obedient, or charitable, but is so by the constant inspiration of the virtue of religion; he is not merely a Christian, or even a saint, but a *religious;* in a word, his life is not only a life of good works, but a *religious* life, in the deepest and fullest sense of the word.

The religious is thus wholly penetrated and transfigured by the virtue of religion, exalted to the rank of those objects which are absolutely, unreservedly, and irrevocably dedicated to the Divine service, like the chalice, or the ciborium, freed from the claims and power of the world; belonging but to God, in whose honour they are consumed even till their latest breath, like the hallowed incense slowly burning in the fire of the sanctuary, and exhaling its last perfumes at the foot of the tabernacle.

This supreme, unceasing, and irrevocable influence of the virtue of religion over the life and actions of a Christian is what constitutes the essential and distinctive character of religious life. This is not to be found only in community life, nor in its regular practices, nor in virginity, in voluntary poverty, nor in obedience, for without being a religious one may acquire and make profession of these virtues. But the religious life is intrinsically constituted and radically distinguished from the clerical or secular life in that it is the result of a sacrifice, the outcome of a holocaust; in a word, it is a new life which has its source and inward principle in the virtue of religion.[4]

Never forget this, ye happy victims of this mystic immolation; consider of what spirit ye are, in order to live in accordance with its sacred inspirations; look upon yourselves as bound to the praise and service of God before and above aught else, and study diligently the virtue of religion, in itself, and its workings, in the perfect model thereof presented you by Jesus Christ, the true and everlasting High Priest, by Holy Church, that living and spiritual harp whose ceaseless strains go up before the Lord in canticles of love, in

---

[4] This interpenetration of religious life by the virtue of religion is so absolute, that religious orders are styled "religions;" thus we speak of entering religion, we talk of the "religion of Malta," or "of St. Benedict." Hence the term "religious life" is more significant and fuller than that of "regular life," which has direct relation but with one of the means of practising religion, viz., the *rule*.

supplication and thanksgiving. Let your hearts be moulded into an exact conformity with its wondrous liturgy, and let your daily conversation show it forth, even as our temples are the instruments and symbols thereof; scrupulously observe its rules, uphold its magnificence, and spread the relish of its beauty. "Behold, now bless the Lord, all ye servants of the Lord, who stand in the house of the Lord, in the courts of the house of our God. In the night-time lift up your hands to the holy places and bless ye the Lord" (*Psalm* 133). Let this motive rule all your works and virtues, that you may escape the frequent and fatal danger of gliding insensibly from the high position on which Providence has placed you, so as to lapse into that imperfect and everyday life of Christians living in the world.

From this notion of religious life, our Angelic Doctor unhesitatingly concludes that it is in reality *a state of perfection.*

Virtuous and religious acts are doubtless indispensable for salvation, since none can hope to attain heavenly bliss without paying to God, while this life of trial lasts, the homage due to His infinite Majesty. This obligation is common to all mankind, and its fulfilment is far from establishing them in a state of perfection, for perfection consists not in merely avoiding mortal sin. But the religious life far transcends this necessary degree of religion. It dedicates the whole man to the glory of his Lord, and with him all his possessions; his outward belongings by poverty, his body by chastity, his will by obedience. It enables him to say with St. Paul: "Brethren, I do not count myself to have apprehended; but one thing I do, forgetting the things that are behind and stretching forth myself to those that are before, I press towards the mark, to the prize of the supernal vocation of God in Christ Jesus. Let us all, then, as many as are *perfect*, be thus minded" (*Philip.* iii. 13—15). The highest perfection of man on earth, the most sublime degree it is given him to attain, consists in his cleaving unreservedly to God and the things of God. Wherefore the religious state is a state of perfection,[5] not indeed the only one, or even the most exalted, yet unquestionably is it the safest, the best fur-

---

[5] See further on the chapter on *Obedience*. It follows from this that the religious life has no *exclusive* claim to be called "a perfect life," or "a state of perfection."

nished with efficacious means for maintaining us in the right path, for encouraging our progress therein, and preventing our being weighed down by the burden of our natural inclinations into those darksome and narrow ravines where we can scarce breathe the air of heaven, or be reached by the radiance of the Sun of Justice.

Not that the mere fact of entering religion makes us perfect. Perfection in its actuality and completeness is neither the lot nor the duty of every Religious; nor should devout souls be unduly alarmed at their faults and shortcomings, as if by the very fact of their imperfection they were wanting to the most essential duty of their condition. The religious state, it is true, has for its distinctive aim, the attainment of perfection; this is its immediate end, to which it naturally aspires; but to this very tendency it is that it owes its name of a *perfect state*. It is in no wise required that he who strives for an end, should have already attained it, so as to need to devote his efforts but to maintaining himself in the joyful possession of his prize. All that is required of him, and is sufficient is, that he really intends to reach the object he aims at and proves by deeds the sincerity of such intent. Now, as perfect union with God, or in other words, the perfection of charity is the special *end* of the religious state, though not the indispensable condition of its existence, it follows that Religious are bound not indeed to be perfect in charity, but merely to direct their efforts to that end, and to endeavour to become so. Hence, in entering religion, a Christian makes no profession of actual perfection, but binds himself to be earnest in striving after its acquirement: even as when we go to school, we make no pretence of being learned, but apply to study for the purpose of acquiring knowledge. Thus, too, does the Religious resemble the Greek philosopher Pythagoras, who, as St. Augustine relates, refusing to be called *wise*, styled himself a *lover of wisdom*.[6]

Such, likewise, is the teaching of the Ancient Fathers. In the conferences of Cassian (Conference I, Chap. 7), Abbot Moses addresses religious as follows: "We must apply

[6] Book VIII., Chap. ii., on the City of God. Philosopher means a lover of wisdom, and was substituted by Pythagoras for the title of "Sophos" or "wise," which, properly speaking, belongs only to God.

to fasting, manual labour, to poverty, to reading, and to other virtuous exercises, that so we may ascend as by so many degrees, to the perfection of charity." And the Pseudo-Dionysius in the sixth chapter of the *Ecclesiastical Hierarchy* says, that it is "by serving God and worshipping Him with all purity of soul, that they who are called God's servants attain the perfection which He loves." The Religious is, then, bound to *ascend* to perfection, and to cleave thereto ever more closely, but he is not blameworthy for not having yet attained it. He is like the pilgrim who must unceasingly go forward to his journey's end, without pitching his tent by the roadside, yet is he not expected to reach in a single day, and as it were by a leap, the distant shrine to which his vow directs him. Wherefore Origen, in his eighth Treatise on St. Matthew, makes these observations on the words of our Lord (Matthew xix. 21), "If thou wilt be perfect, go, sell all that thou hast and give it to the poor." "He that exchanges wealth for poverty, in order to become perfect, will not become so the very day he distributes all his property to the poor; but from that time forth, divine contemplation will begin to guide him in the way of all virtue." And thus, St. Thomas adds, all who are in religion are not perfect, but some are mere beginners, while others are advancing in that holiness on which they have already entered.

It must, however, be borne in mind that it were an inaccurate view of the religious state to consider it, either exclusively, or mainly at least, as a life of penance and expiation. As a special state, as a mode of life penance can be but a kind of preparation for the religious state, a preliminary process whereby the soul is cleansed of its stains, and set free from the occasions of sin, but which does not contemplate growth in virtue as its immediate object.

The religious life is then better, nobler, and easier than the condition of the mere penitent,[7] yet does it afford the fullest scope to the virtue and practices of penance. According to the Angelic Doctor the exercises of the religious life aim principally at removing the impediments to perfect charity, and still more

---

[7] This will be still more obvious, if we compare the religious life with the *public penance* practised in the early Church, and which constituted among the faithful a distinct order, a particular condition.

at the suppression of whatever may wholly destroy divine charity, to wit, mortal sin, and the occasions of deadly transgression. Now penance has precisely the same end, as every endeavour is directed to the uprooting of the miserable causes of guilt. This being the case, nothing can be easier than to combine the penitential with the religious state, so that the former may serve the latter as an instrument for attaining the purity of conscience, which is the first and indispensable degree of Christian perfection. A good Religious must needs be a sincere penitent, and something more besides. Tears, sorrow, the task of atoning for days spent in sin must not make him lose sight of the essential character of his profession. It is not enough that he tremble under the strokes of Divine Justice, that he bow down in dust and ashes; he must enlarge his soul and run in the way of the Lord; he must take wings to himself, and with eagle flight soar up to the divine Sun, which is the source of all light, purity, joy, peace and perfection. In the cloister, penance, like all other virtues, must be transformed by religion into a spiritual holocaust to be immolated to the praise of God; it must look to the future, to the perfection to be attained, rather than to the past and to the guilt demanding expiation. Thus will penance rise to a degree higher than that which is usual in secular life; it will be *religious* and hence *perfect* penance.

We will now briefly sum up the teaching of our Angelic Master concerning the essence of religious life. It is a state of entire consecration to God, of the immolation of self and all its belongings, to the honour of the Divine Majesty; it is therefore a state of perfection, and to a certain extent, of penance. We will now go more deeply into the study of the perfection peculiar to religious, and examine the divinely instituted means whereby it may be attained.

CHAPTER II.

The Evangelical Counsels.

THE end proposed by the religious life is the most excellent that it is given to man to conceive; namely the cleaving of the soul to God and to divine things. St. Thomas considers it an impossibility for us to occupy ourselves thoroughly and successfully with things of a different nature at the same time, which of course is still more true of undertakings at cross purposes with each other. In order that the human mind might be more freely raised towards Heaven, Our Lord has given to us in His Holy Law three precious *counsels*, the observance of which releases us as much as is possible from the necessary occupations and burdens of our pilgrimage in this world. This, indeed, is not yet the complete liberty of the children of God, the absolute freedom of the elect who are established without fear, without hesitation, and without division in the contemplation and possession of the infinite Good. Yet, thank God, it is the life of Angels in a burdensome and corruptible flesh.

This happy state is not however so indispensable to sanctity that we cannot be just until we have embraced it. Virtue and justice can exist in the midst of this world; they do not exclude even a goodly and extensive use of earthly and corporal things, provided man observe therein the moderation and order indicated by right reason. Therefore the admonitions by which the Divine law engages us to sacrifice all our worldly possessions are called *evangelical counsels*, and not *precepts* or *commandments*, because God *counsels* man, but does not oblige him to abandon the lesser goods of this earth for others more considerable.

These counsels are written in the law, they are not the law itself, still the law could not be complete without them, because they are both its ornament, its fruit, its perfection, and the most certain and powerful means of its fulfilment. They radiate from all the commandments; but especially from the first as from a centre of love and religion. If we must adore the Lord our God in spirit and in truth, if we must serve Him and Him alone, if we must love Him with all our heart, soul and strength, if we be truly called upon to establish some proportion between our homage and His glory, between our love and His goodness, or to speak more exactly, between our works and our duty, is it not evident that a generous soul when vividly enlightened by grace, will joyously renounce all that would lessen its worship, repress the transports of its love, or cool the fervour of its service and zeal? Now, if we examine the habitual course of human life we discover three principal causes of solicitude and embarrassment, three things which imperatively claim man's thoughts and labours, which disquiet, trouble, and fatigue him, and which thus prevents his complete union with God.

Firstly, *his own person.* We generally busy ourselves a great deal as to how we shall use our capabilities both physical and intellectual; in what place we shall live, how we are to get through this world, and what is to be the object of our life. This search after an advantageous and agreeable position; after a dwelling adequate to the requirements of both body and soul, is not the least source of our perplexities. The responsibility of our undertakings, the obscurity of the ways which we must incessantly pursue, the oft recurring desire to better our state is an incredible torment, in an age and a society so agitated as our own.

Secondly, *persons who are dear to us*, principally one's wife and children. How to love them, how to provide for them, how to govern them, how to accommodate oneself to their dispositions, to deal gently with their weakness, restrain their inclinations and solve with prudence the great problems, first of their education, then of their vocation! How to be able to direct the lives of others, when one has so much difficulty in regulating one's own, to share their sorrows, their anxieties, their dangers, and alas too often their errors, what a task, and at times what a torment!

Thirdly, *exterior goods*, which one needs to sustain life, namely, food or clothing, a dwelling or a shelter, the possession of riches, the desire of a legitimate éclat and of an honourable position in the world, and besides this, so much vanity, ambition and imperious passion enthral man in every way, each one of which would of itself absorb a thousand times every resource of the mind, the whole energy of the will, and courage of the heart.

With such hindrances how is it possible to give oneself entirely to God? Divine mercy counsels us then to escape this threefold and tyrannical solicitude. To deliver us from the first, which is the care of our own person, God gives to us the counsel of *obedience*, by which man leaves in the hands of his Superior the entire disposition of his actions. This is the exhortation that we read in the Epistle of St. Paul to the Hebrews, " Obey your prelates, and be subject to them, for they watch, as being to render an account of your souls."[1] To the second, which is that for one's family, God approves the counsel of *virginity* or of *continence*, and this is why the Apostle tells us, " Now concerning virgins, I have no commandment of the Lord; but I give counsel as having obtained mercy of the Lord, to be faithful;"[2] and he then adds in explanation of his motive, " And the unmarried woman and the virgin thinketh on the things of the Lord; that she may be holy both in body and spirit. But she that is married thinketh on the things of the world, how she may please

[1] Heb. xiii. 17. [2] 1 Cor. vii. 25.

her husband."[3] Finally, as to the third, which concerns exterior things, the divine law gives the Christian the counsel of *poverty*, exhorting him to cast off all that which would burden his mind with cares, or trouble it by disquietude. Thus our Lord has said to us, "If thou wilt be perfect go sell all that thou hast and give to the poor, and thou shalt have treasure in heaven: and come, follow me."[4] These are three fundamental counsels, which cannot be ignored, without our being entirely absorbed by the cares of this world! They are essential to the sacred liberty of the cloister, and all religious are absolutely bound to observe them. And apart from this threefold and holy observance, there is no perfect consecration to the Lord; none of that excellency of religion, nor of that energetic tendency towards sanctity, nor finally of that sublimity of mortification which constitute the religious state; but in the divine law we find other and less essential counsels, the practice of which can be freely omitted, without our life being overburdened by worldly cares and business, and in regard to these, it is not absolutely necessary that a religious

[3] 1 Cor. vii. 32, 33.   [4] St. Matt. xix. 21.

should observe them all. The acts which they recommend to us are really meritorious, for example: the care of the sick in hospitals; or visiting the poor and imprisoned. But as they are not necessary to the freedom of the soul, their omission does not intrinsically vitiate the nature of the religious state. St. Thomas compares them to the different remedies which a physician may use for the cure of one complaint, all of which he certainly does not prescribe at the same time. For the same reason, the religious is not obliged to perform all the exercises which lead him to perfection, but only the three counsels, which are the foundation of his state, and those which, though secondary, are determined and prescribed by the rule of which he has made profession. Others, though assuredly most useful in themselves, are nevertheless for him acts of supererogation, because he has not bound himself in a general and indefinite manner to follow all the practices of perfection, but only a certain number of them: and therefore the others are not obligatory to him; for no one is bound to works of supererogation except inasmuch as he has personally pledged himself to them.

Thus counsels prescribed only by the constitutions peculiar to each order are simply accessory and accidental to the religious state, whereas those of *obedience, chastity* and *poverty*, are its essence, its life, and necessary elements. These three virtues should consequently predominate over all secondary virtues, which converge towards them as towards their centre—at the same time threefold, yet one—resting upon them as on their foundation and corner stone. Neither the care of the poor nor of the sick; the instruction of children and of the ignorant, manual or intellectual labour, should ever induce the religious to forget that the three great counsels of the Gospel claim his most constant and serious attention, and that his worthiness of his sublime vocation will ever be proportionate to his *poverty, chastity* and *obedience.*

Let us however place all things in their natural order. There is nothing more conducive to making solid progress in virtue, nor is there anything dearer to our Angelic Doctor than that rational arrangement which allots to all creatures the just and exact rank to which they have a right. Now poverty, chastity and obedience, from which as from deep roots rises the mystic tree of religious life do not constitute Perfection, they only form its conditions and instruments, its effects and signs.

Perfection consists in the union of the soul with God, and on that we must constantly fix our eyes, and towards that we must continually direct our efforts. It will avail us little to be humble, pure, or disinterested, if we do not unite ourselves by means of these virtues to the supreme source of all holiness. The true spirit which should inspire these religious acts consists in following faithfully the evangelical counsels, in order, by so doing, to honour, praise, and serve the Sovereign Master, and thus to attain to that perfect chastity, which unites in such close intimacy the all powerful Creator with his weak creature. Lift up your hearts! To be freed from all worldly attachments, to be above all its petty ambitions is assuredly an incomparable enjoyment! But we must aim still higher; let us not be satisfied with hovering, so to speak, on the white wings of the dove in the bright area of the spiritual world. Let us forget ourselves, and using our virtues as a mystic ladder, mount towards God alone! May the cry of our souls ever be that of St. Ignatius of Loyola; to be obedient; chaste, poor and religious, all *to the greater honour and glory of God.* Our Lord himself teaches us that these three virtues are not yet perfection, but only the dispositions which prepare us for it. He said with regard to poverty, "If thou wilt be perfect, go sell all that thou hast and give to the poor, and come, follow me." Even the sacrifice of everything is not sufficient; perfection consists in following Our Lord.

But these same virtues are at once the *effects* and the signs of perfection. When the soul is strongly possessed with the love or desire of any object, by a natural consequence, it eagerly avoids all that does not appertain thereto. If then the heart of man is drawn towards divine things by fervent love and desire, he will not fail to reject all that could delay his flight towards God. He will forsake the care of earthly goods, sacrifice all human affections and all family ties, and he will even divest himself of himself. This is the signification of the following words from Holy Writ: "If a man should give all the substance of his house for love, he shall despise it as nothing."[5] "Again, the kingdom of heaven is like to a merchant seeking good pearls, who, when he had found one pearl of great price, went his way, and sold all that he had and bought it."[6] "But the things that were gain to me, the same I have counted loss for Christ. Farthermore, I count all things to be but loss, for the excellent knowledge of Jesus Christ my Lord; for whom I have suffered the loss of all things, and count them but as dung, that I may gain Christ."[7] O sweet and holy consolation! it is then true that the religious life is not only a constant tendency to perfection, but that it is likewise the result and the token thereof. It is the fruit of charity, a holocaust consumed by divine love, an eternal testimony that one day heavenly grace raised this feeble and languid soul and cast it upon Jesus Christ our Lord with an irresistible force and a superhuman power. It was already the perfection of charity. And in future darkness and anguish and spiritual desolation, its remembrance will remain as an ineffable joy and a

---

[5] Canticle viii. 7.   [6] St. Matthew xiii. 45, 46.
[7] Philipp. iii. 7, 8.

vivifying light. The humbled and crushed soul will hear within herself this word of life, and will bless God for having revealed to her this threefold renouncement, the sure token of a love stronger than death.

Our Lord in his charity for men has deigned to call them to be perfect, even as His Heavenly Father is perfect. Three means are peculiarly efficacious to raise them to this incomparable height: poverty, chastity, and obedience. All do not hear, nor are all called to hear this word, which is but a counsel. Religious, however, who are desirous of being entirely consecrated to the service of God, and thus to reach perfection, cannot be excused from making these counsels the constant rule of their lives; and in embracing this life they show that their ambition is not only to become saints, but that they already obey the impulse of perfect charity.

Such is the substance of the chapter we have just read; it is now necessary to consider successively each one of the three virtues which correspond with the three evangelical counsels.

CHAPTER III.

Religious Poverty.

THE evangelical counsels are the express words of God, excellent amongst all others which fell from the lips of incarnate Wisdom, words addressed to men whose only desire was to reach the highest possible point of perfection, words of sovereign justice and supreme goodness addressed to those Christians who were not content with ordinary justice and common sanctity. Thus the free acts, by which one endeavours to fashion oneself on this celestial ideal and these divine counsels, are necessarily *acts of virtue*, that is to say, actions which are just, right and good.

And because the all-powerful hand of God operates in hearts faithfully corresponding with His grace, that which His infinite wisdom has prescribed and counselled; and since it is a necessity of our nature that we possess faculties in accordance with and in proportion to each kind of action which we are called upon to exercise; our Lord places in souls, piously submissive to the rules of the religious state, three faculties, three supernatural powers, three *virtues* corresponding with three series of works which He has recommended to them as most conducive to perfection. These are the *religious virtues* of poverty, chastity, and obedience.[1] We already know their necessity and efficacy as regards regular life; and will now insist thereon still more, and bring out more clearly their tendency and their real spirit, so as to take the measure of their extent, tendency and spirit, and thus arrive at the thorough knowledge of that miracle of grace and of divine mercy which is styled the religious, or a voca-

---

[1] According to the strict sense of theological expression, voluntary poverty is not a *virtue* but only a *beatitude* resulting from the *virtues* of temperance and humility, and from the *gift* of the Holy Ghost, which is the fear of God. However, as these virtues and this gift unite their influence to produce holy poverty, we may consider them as a *moral* virtue, which we name religious poverty. Chastity and obedience are equally moral virtues; that is to say, supernatural qualities which incline our will to the constant practice of a good proposed by God to our reason. And all these virtues are here directed and inspired by the virtue of religion.

tion to a religious life. Let us begin by contemplating with respectful love His privations and utter destitution, recalling to us the glorious poverty of Bethlehem.

It would be impossible for man to consecrate himself wholly to the divine service, and to attain the perfection of charity and religion if he did not thoroughly detach himself from worldly matters. "O Lord," says St. Augustine, "he does not love Thee enough who loves anything except in Thee and for Thee;"[2] and again: "Charity increases when cupidity lessens, and the former is perfect when the latter is destroyed."[3] It is then evident that in religious orders, in these schools where one learns the art of perfection, in these spiritual camps where one is trained by combat to take heaven by storm, one must necessarily extirpate from one's heart all ambition and affection for worldly honours and possessions.

Now from the fact of our possessing any portion of these exterior riches, our mind gets naturally influenced by their charms, fascinated by its brilliancy, and thus drawn to love them. The great doctor of Hippo, who had a long

[2] Confessions, Book x. ch. 9.
[3] Book of 83 Questions, Question 36.

and sad experience of this, wrote thus to two Christians of his day: "Earthly goods are loved more when the possession of them is actual, than when they exist only in our desires: for, behold in the case of the young man who came to our Lord to be made His disciple, was it not on account of his worldly goods that he went away sad and sorrowful? It is one thing not to desire that which is wanting, and another thing to wrest from our bosom that which, so to speak, already forms a part of our own being. The one is more easily sacrificed because it is foreign to us, whilst the other is like a limb which requires violent and painful amputation."[4] St. John Chrysostom, in like manner, remarks that actual possession of riches kindles a fiercer flame and gives a greater strength to the attachment for them.[5] If then a man would acquire perfect charity, the first condition he will have to fulfil will be voluntary poverty. He must be resolved to live henceforth without corruptible treasures, without exterior riches, and removed from the honours of the world, according to this counsel of the Lord,

[4] 34th Epist. of Paulinus to Therasia.
[5] *On St. Matthew*, ch. 64.

"Wilt thou be perfect, go sell all thou hast, give it to the poor, then follow me."[6] Like the Prophet Eliseus, he will go for the last time to his dwelling on the day when the divine love began to inflame him with the desire for heavenly things; he will arm himself with a sword for the sacrifice, he will slay his oxen, which in the mystical language of Holy Writ are symbolical of the abundance and fatness of the earth; he will use them to feed the poor; and then, freed from all perishable ties, he will return to the contemplation of the imperishable treasures which God has in store for those who love Him alone.[7]

From that time forth he will be reckoned amongst the number of those "just ones" of whom St. Gregory speaks, and "who wishing to attain the summit of perfection, longing to possess in the recesses of their heart more sublime wealth, abandoned all outward possessions."[8]

A thousand-fold blessed are they who can thus enter into themselves, and find there with holy poverty the unspeakable riches of

---

[6] St. Matt. xix. 21.
[7] St. Ambrose, *Officio*, Book I., ch. 30.
[8] *Moralia super Job*, Book VIII.

the kingdom of heaven. They will be almost wholly freed from the attacks of that most common and tyrannical passion, which pushes men and urges them on with such madness to striving after empty riches, to that unbridled pursuit of pelf and place, to sordid avarice, to gnawing envy, to excess and ruinous ostentation, and often to the lowest infamy or to the darkest despair. They will not be subject to those perpetual temptations which are so fatal to divine charity, and which enervate it when they do not stifle it altogether; those temptations which the Christian living in the midst of this world is sure to feel, both in his conscience, lured on by the bait of worldly enjoyments, and grandeur; and in his honour, daily exposed to these vile bargains wherein virtue is bartered for gold; and in his innocence, threatened with the deprivation at least of that respectability, rank and position to which he so unhappily clings, if not with the immediate loss of the bread necessary for his livelihood. If even a Christian be stronger than the temptation, if he remains victorious in these ever-reviving contests, yet it will be next to impossible for him to divest himself entirely of all attachment to and anxiety for worldly goods. However temperate and prudent he may be, he is obliged to watch over his fortune, preserve and augment his family resources, and defend his interests against unjust pretensions; and his heart thus divided between heaven and earth, thus tossed about by so many cares, cannot, unless by a miracle, arrive at the summit of perfection, which is at the same time the supreme happiness here below, and, according to St. Paul, the pledge and earnest of eternal bliss.

Oh! how much more independent, happy, free, and indeed how much more fit to possess those interior and durable possessions is the man who has become voluntarily poor; how much more easily can he consecrate himself to the service of the altar, to be there enchained by the sacred ties of religion, to find in his soul an incessant hymn to the glory of the Divine Redeémer, and on his lips those pure and harmonious strains in which the angels love to join.

It has always been a test of good sense and sound reason to renounce all wealth and terrestrial honours in order to apply oneself exclusively to the contemplation of natural truth, or to the research of created infinite wisdom. Profane antiquity praises this disinterestedness in several of its philosophers, as, says St. Jerome, in "Crates, of Thebes, once of great wealth, who when about to depart for Athens, where he intended to devote himself to the study of philosophy, generously threw away a large sum of money, deeming it impossible to unite virtue and riches."[9] But how much more reasonable is it to strip oneself of these transitory goods, of this human power which is so soon shattered, this splendour so soon extinguished, and of this abundance so soon exhausted, in order to follow our Lord perfectly. Thus we shall be able to hear the infinite Word, in whom are contained every divine idea, and all the knowledge of God, the word which imparts life, strength and beauty, and finally to possess eternal and substantial Wisdom. In this school the soul learns that true philosophy, that science of sciences, a single ray of which is more brilliant than all the coruscations of human intellect or genius. Let the religious joyfully practise that which the hermit of Bethlehem recommended to the monk Rusticus : " Christ lived destitute of human riches ; to become His

[9] *Letter to Paulinus.*

disciple, do thou imitate in thyself His holy poverty."[10]

Voluntary poverty is not only a powerful remedy against covetuousness and the love of external goods, an efficacious preservative against the allurements of human honour and glory, and finally, an excellent disposition for receiving the lessons of our Divine Master, but it is also a most perfect work of religion and charity. Even a simple alms distributed now and then, though sometimes very small and almost insignificant, such as a glass of cold water or the widow's mite, is nevertheless a deed of the highest worth and most pleasing to God. "It is," says St. John Chrysostom, "the most efficacious remedy that the penitent can oppose to sin."[11] Now, according to the Angelic Doctor, the absolute renouncement of riches professed by religious, far from detracting from the merit gained by other Christians in almsgiving, surpasses it in value inasmuch as the universal surpasses in extent the particular; and as the holocaust excels in efficacy and mystical signification a common offering or ordinary sacrifice. Let us

[10] *Letter* of St. Jerome *to Rusticus.*
[11] IX. Homily upon the Epistle to the Hebrews.

listen to the words of St. Gregory the Great: "Those who distribute to the poor some portion of their abundance offer a mere sacrifice; because in immolating to God a part of their substance they reserve the other for themselves; but those who retain nothing, offer a holocaust far superior to the sacrifice."[12] And St. Jerome, in reply to an objection Vigilantius had made against monastic poverty: "As to your pretending that it is better to retain wealth so as to distribute its produce from time to time for the relief of the poor, need I answer this myself, seeing that our Lord has thus expressed Himself, '*If thou wilt be perfect go sell* ALL *that thou hast;*' that which you approve is only the second or third degree of perfection, assuredly much to be applauded, but provided we forget not to prefer the first degree to these which are inferior."[13] This same error of Vigilantius is condemned also in the book of *Ecclesiastical Dogmas:* "It is good to distribute successively one's goods to the poor, but it is better to give them all at once, and by so doing to follow the Lord thus to be delivered

---

[12] XX. Homily on Ezechiel.
[13] *Against Vigilantius.*

from the solicitude imposed by them, and to share the poverty of Jesus Christ."[14]

This indisputable superiority of voluntary poverty over the most munificent liberality, is of itself sufficient to make us esteem and cherish these invisible but incorruptible riches of religious poverty far beyond all the goods of this world. To be poor with Jesus, to be perfect with Him, to possess in an eminent degree all the graces and merits promised so often to the giver of alms by Holy Writ, what consolation, what joy, and what strength is not this for the soul!

This teaching sheds also a new lustre on that special character of the regular life, which as we have already shown consists in realizing completely and in personifying the virtue of religion. Poverty willingly embraced and forming a substantial groundwork to the state of perfection, is not a commonplace or superficial offering, it is the sacrifice of all exterior goods; it is the holocaust, in the flame of which the victim is entirely consumed; it is annihilation unto dust and ashes, proclaiming with an unparalleled eloquence the infinite existence and majesty of that great God, in

[14] Chapter 71.

whose eyes we are as nothing. Yes! when I behold in the streets of Assisi that poor beggar, barefooted and bareheaded, miserably clothed, drenched with blood from the wounds in his hands and side, it appears to me that through the veil of this wondrous poverty I see the heavens opened and gaze at the eternal and indescribable splendours of the King of kings.

But this religious poverty must be real and spontaneous, embraced with love and kept with jealous care. It would be dangerous were it involuntary, or if there remained at the bottom of our hearts some desire of acquiring for ourselves temporal wealth. We should then fall into many grievous sins, according to the Apostle: "For they that will become rich, fall into temptation, and into the snare of the devil."[15] Religious should therefore be still more faithful to the spirit, than to the exterior forms of detachment. These forms may be more or less rigid, more or less severe, but the spirit should always remain entire and immovable. The better to distinguish these two elements of the virtue of poverty, and to exaggerate nothing in this difficult matter, we

[15] 1 Tim. vi. 9.

will dive, with the Angelic Doctor, still deeper into that knowledge which we have already acquired of worldly riches and of holy and religious poverty. Let us compare them therefore respectively with that notion of *happiness*, which is the final end to which we direct all our efforts, and consequently the supreme rule after which all is measured in this life, whether deeds or conditions, ends or means.

Riches of themselves are neither beneficial nor injurious, being as indifferent to our happiness as any metal stored away in the most remote regions of the heavens, and to be discovered only by the analysis of philosophers or by the calculation of astronomers. Like everything external to us, they cannot exercise influence on man's happiness unless they assimilate themselves, as it were, with him. For happiness unfolds itself in the very centre of our being and in the marrow of the soul, it is there that it manifests its presence, and buds and blooms in a mysterious sanctuary unapproachable to all save God and oneself. How then are these outward and material things to penetrate so deeply within us? Will their substance be mixed and moulded with our own? And shall gold be transformed into our flesh, and circulate through our veins and be identified with our blood? But these are but the mad day-dreams of the miser, who recognising with consternation that riches are not happiness because they are external to him, would fain be clothed therewith and be wrapt up in them, and wholly buried in them; but in vain, for his *heart* remains void and consequently unhappy. The goods of this world cannot then penetrate into us, and therefore cannot directly make us happy. They need then to have recourse to an intermediary or agent existing within us, and upon which they may be brought to act. This precious medium is perfection. It is from this that we derive all our feelings of joy, all the pleasure we experience, and all the happiness which we possess. It is within ourselves, it subsists in us, it is the blossom and fruit of our faculties, of our efforts and of our deeds.[16] At the same time

[16] Assuredly besides these perfections and *acquired* virtues of which we speak, God himself bestows upon us *infused* virtues, which are the most fruitful source of life and supernatural happiness. But it is not on those that exterior agents exercise their chief influence; they contribute only to their growth, and not to their first production.

it is connected with that which is without; its acquisition and its development are subject to exterior conditions. It meets in the surrounding world with many obstacles and also numerous enemies; but yet in this world it finds vast and powerful aid, most efficient to promote its growth, and by a natural consequence to promote our happiness. Riches when wisely employed, and used as a means towards that perfection and happiness which we may wish to attain, may become good, and consequently deserve their name of *goods*. They constitute then a *means* which is good, but which derives all its goodness from the end to which they are directed. If we discard this end and search after riches for their own sake, or even desire them for any other purpose than our "perfection," we immediately divest them either wholly or partially of their useful character, of their goodness, and of their right to esteem. Still more pernicious do they become when they impede perfection, when they diminish or destroy it, and thereby mar our happiness.

Our perfection comprises several degrees, the least and lowest is that which is perceived by the senses, and is inherent to the body;

this is the degree of merely material well being. Above that comes the intellectual and moral degree, which embellishes and perfects the mind, without exceeding the limits of its nature, and this is the degree of purely human virtue. Higher still there is the supernatural, which brings us into close communion with divine nature; and this we call the degree of grace and Christian virtue. Finally at the summit of this golden ladder reigns that complete perfection, which consists in the entire possession of God, who is present to the mind of His elect, as truth and knowledge, as the justice and sanctity of their hearts, and as the light and strength of their redeemed bodies; and this last is the state of glory. To this hierarchy of perfection there is a corresponding hierarchy of happiness, which also possesses its gradations, first of all, well being, which is merely animal; then purely human happiness; after which, and above all, the happiness of a Christian life, which finds its fulness and its reward in the happiness of eternal life, in the beatific vision. It is obvious that the higher superior degrees of this twofold series of perfection and beatitude are superior to the inferior degrees, in proportion as they are the more noble and exalted; and further that all use of earthly goods which indulges the senses to the detriment of the soul, or which flatters human reason to the disadvantage of supernatural virtue, is culpable and utterly incapable of producing real happiness.

It is quite true that exterior riches aid us to sustain that corporal life which is itself a visible and necessary condition of progress in virtue and supernatural life, but it is no less true that they enervate the body, encourage the attacks of those passions of which they are the favourite food, and multiply both the occasions and means of sin.

It is true also that they may help us to acquire science, and arts, and the natural virtues, but how often do they not engender pride, vanity, and even impiety, in such a way that in order to enjoy the dim coruscations of their purblind minds men lose for all eternity the dazzling and infallible light of the Spirit of God.

It is also true that they enable us to relieve the wants of our needy neighbour and thus to advance in the virtue of charity which is the fulness of earthly perfection, but they have nevertheless deserved both the blame and condemnation of our Lord, for if sometimes they are instruments of charity, they are one of its most cruel enemies. Their general effect is to weigh down the soul, and thus prevent its mounting towards the sacred heights of divine love, and this for the three principal reasons mentioned above, but which it may be useful to repeat in the exact words of our doctor. *Firstly*, they bring with them great anxiety and care: "And the care of this world, and the deceitfulness of riches choketh up the word, and he becometh fruitless," [17] says Jesus Christ; and, according to the Commentary of St. Gregory, "riches prevent good desires from penetrating into our hearts, and shut its doors to the breath of life." [18]

Secondly, the enjoyment of riches frequently increases that natural inclination and affection which we already have for them; and that is why our Divine Master tells us: "Amen, I say to you, that a rich man shall hardly enter into the kingdom of heaven," [19] which must be understood of him who possessing earthly goods yet strives to be so detached from them

---

[17] St. Matt. xiii. 22.   [18] XV. Homily on the Gospel.
[19] St. Matt. xix. 23.

as to remain faithful to virtue; for as to him who bestows his whole heart upon them, St. John Chrysostom declares that our Lord has taught that it will be *impossible* for such to enter heaven: "And again I say to you: It is easier for a camel to pass through the eye of a needle, than for a rich man to enter the kingdom of heaven."[20] *Thirdly*, exterior riches create in the soul much pride, disdain, vain glory and contempt for others, according to this verse of the Psalms: "They that trust in their own strength, and glory in the multitude of their riches."[21]

Perfect charity cannot therefore without great difficulty, be united to the possession of great worldly wealth, or to a brilliant fortune, or to high honours and exalted rank. Thence the title of "blessed" in its full meaning is not given to the rich man in Holy Writ, but is attributed to him who has been found without blemish, "that hath not gone after gold nor put his trust in money or treasures;" happy is he because he has done that which was almost incredible, and the inspired writer, transported with admiration for him, asks immediately after, "Who is he, and we will praise him?

[20] St. Matt. xix. 24.   [21] Ps. xlviii. 7.

for he hath done wonderful things in his life."[22] Surrounded by riches as in the midst of flames, he has not been consumed by the fatal love of them. In respect therefore to that perfect felicity which we look forward to in our heavenly country, worldly riches are rather an impediment to it than a means of attaining thereto, since they are dangerous to that charity without which man is spiritually dead, and is unable to obtain eternal life.

Let us however suppose, and by a miracle of Divine grace that this supposition is at times realized, let us suppose that the wealth of this world does not prevent our soul's being perfect in charity, or being happy with that incomplete yet real happiness that falls to the lot of the friends of God. Would it thence follow that the advantages of riches are universal, applicable to all states, equally so for every virtue, and in such wise that escaping from the evils which they generally bring in with them as their dangerous and fatal train, all Christians would be equally certain to derive from them solid advantages? But such is not the case. St. Thomas, of Aquino, distinguishes two kinds of true happiness on

[22] Eccles. xxxi. 8, 9.

earth, the happiness of the active and that of the contemplative life. The first is that intimate joy and contentment of heart which is the result of exterior works of charity, zeal, benevolence, and devotedness towards one's fellow man. It corresponds with the virtues and perfection which we acquire, or which God bestows on us in order to glorify Him exteriorly before the eyes of men, who will thereby be assisted, edified and drawn to love and serve their heavenly Father; and unquestionably riches are a most effectual and most powerful means for the attainment of this end. The greatest of the ancient Greek philosophers says, "We accomplish a great many things by our friends, by our riches and by our political power, as by so many organs and instruments."[23] And in truth how could we relieve the indigence of the poor, assist the orphan, found schools, build churches, or endow hospitals, if we had not recourse to those goods which our Lord has recommended us to employ in order to make friends for ourselves in the eternal dwellings? They contribute, therefore, considerably to the bliss of the active

---

[23] Aristotle's Moral, Book I.

life which is represented in the person of holy Martha, the elder sister of Lazarus.

But it is not so in the contemplative life, which is the most blessed and most perfect. In that, after the example of Mary Magdalen, man chooses the better part, namely, an uninterrupted meditation and enjoyment of divine things, and disengages himself entirely from creatures to unite himself solely and completely to the Creator. This contemplative life consists in the exercise of virtues wholly spiritual, it has no requirements, save the scanty pittance which is absolutely necessary to sustain nature. And we here contemplate one of the most beauteous features, and one of the highest perfections of this life. God becomes the only object of thought and care! and hence there can be no great advantage in the possession of riches, which would prove a clog and a hindrance in that, on account of the anxiety of which they are the inexhaustible source, they disturb the recollection and inward calm so needful for contemplatives. The philosopher whom we have quoted above, saw as much by the mere lights of his unaided reason. Exterior works require great exterior means, and those exterior means must be proportionate to the greatness of the exterior work. But he who has embraced a contemplative life, has no further need of external resources for the accomplishment of his undertakings; rather would he find them to be an obstacle and a hindrance. Bare necessaries are sufficient for him.[24] "Having food," says the great Apostle St. Paul, "and wherewith to be covered, with these we are content."[25] We may in very few words define the part which worldly goods are to play on the stage of our spiritual life; they are of undoubted help to the active life, but are pernicious to that more favoured and perfect state of contemplatives, and become dangerous to eternal life and supreme beatitude! Will any one then still insist, that they constitute real happiness, or that they are its chief source?

Poverty, on the contrary, when voluntarily embraced, frees man from all those vices which riches produce; it delivers him from those superfluous anxieties, and inordinate cares which throw the mind into a state of perpetual confusion and dissipation; it

[24] *Morals*, Book X.   [25] 1 Tim. vi. 8.

permits him to devote himself more freely to meditation, the love of God, and to the search after heavenly goods. It therefore very efficaciously aids the immediate attainment of charity, and hence the ineffable joys of our true home, for such is the promise of our Lord himself, "go sell what thou hast and give to the poor, and thou shalt have treasure in Heaven."[26]

Religious poverty appears to us in all its glory, when we consider it as indispensable to the exercise of the contemplative life, in which is to be found the greatest happiness we can enjoy during our earthly pilgrimage, or as eminently favourable to the progress of the virtues of religion and charity, and consequently to the acquisition of that inheritance reserved for us by our divine Father. It is evident that poverty contains greater riches than all exterior wealth, is preferable to all perceptible goods, and that it is more powerful than all the honours and resources of the world. But it is not however, in itself, absolute perfection, independent of all subordination to a superior end. Whether

---

[26] St. Matt. xix. 21.

we consider *poverty*, or riches, or other exterior goods, or anything in fact in the possession of man, it does not derive its value from itself, it has therefore no claim upon our esteem by the simple fact of its existence, and its praiseworthiness is not always in proportion to its rigour and austerity. It becomes truly a blessing when it assists the development of virtue, and deserves our consideration according to the measure of its co-operation with the fulfilment of this purpose. Therefore should it wholly hinder our spiritual progress or even retard it, poverty would cease to be beneficial, and would even become absolutely pernicious. Reason has therefore the right to assign to it limits which cannot be overstepped without injury to our spiritual interests.

Involuntary poverty is often the occasion of robbery, lying and perjury, says St. Thomas, and St. Gregory adds, spontaneous poverty sometimes, even when it effectually relieves a man from the troubles which accompany riches, may engage him in far more perilous occupations: "Those who would have led a useful life in the enjoyment and cares of human things, find that repose destroys them with its murderous sword."[27] And so again poverty may be an evil inasmuch as it prevents us from relieving the temporal misfortunes of our neighbour, unless this evil be compensated by a greater good, as in the case of those religious of whom we shall speak later, who can render more real service to the poor and to society by prayer, by the adoration and worship of God, by study, by tuition, and by preaching, than by the most generous liberality. Finally, poverty would be an absolute evil, and one for which nothing could make amends, if it deprived man of the means of sustaining his existence, for there is no advantage the pursuit and desire of which can justify us in retrenching that, which is indispensable for the maintenance of our physical life.

It is necessary then that religious poverty be sincerely desired and never forced. It must also be so associated with serious occupations as to preserve it from the dangers of idleness. It must have assured and lawful means of providing for our necessities; and here the Angelic Doctor teaches us that it

---

[27] *Morals*, Book VII.

will be so much the more perfect as it allows the heart to be the less troubled about providing the absolute necessaries of life; for calm of mind will enable the heart to turn more easily to God. And, without exposing ourselves to strange and ridiculous errors, we cannot forget that all search after, and all possession of worldly goods, however trifling they may be, must necessarily involve some distraction of the mind, and more or less anxiety. But if one confines oneself to that moderate portion of these material things requisite to lead a simple and mortified life, the spirit of prayer and of detachment will not suffer much by the use of them. To seek that which is necessary, without troubling about that which is superfluous, is not contrary to the perfection of religious life.

The souls most devoted to poverty, the consciences most timorous in the observance of the precepts and Evangelical counsels should never forget that our Lord has not forbidden to them "*all*" solicitude, but that only which is superfluous and dangerous. As in this passage of holy Writ, " Be not solicitous for your life what you shall eat;" which St. Augustine interprets as follows; " The Lord does not forbid our acquiring these things inasmuch as they are necessary to us, but He forbids us to make them the end of our works, and as it were the motive of our zeal, in preaching the gospel."[28] As to this other word, "Be not therefore solicitous for the morrow;" St. Anthony shows us that it would be perilous to draw from it the conclusion that we should reserve nothing for the future. "As to those," he says, "who insist upon practising the abandonment of all temporal wealth to such an extent as not to allow themselves a provision of food for a single day, nor the possession of a mere mite, nor of any other object equally insignificant, let them be cautious, for we have often seen such people fall suddenly into great delusions, disabling themselves from the fitting accomplishment of that which they had rashly undertaken."[29] St. Augustine also says: "If these words of our Lord Jesus, '*be not therefore solicitous for the morrow,*' were to be understood in the sense of reserving nothing for the morrow, how would those manage who separate themselves

---

[28] *Of the Sermon on the Mount*, Book II. ch. 25. *Works on the Monastic life*, ch. 26.

[29] *Conference of the Fathers.*

for several days from the society of men in order to apply with greater energy to prayer?"
. . . . . But our Lord Himself retained some money during the days of his ministration, and in years of scarcity the Apostles always took care to send in advance the alms necessary for their Churches.[30] " This is what our divine Master would teach us: "When we do any good let us do it not for time, which is justly symbolized by the morrow, but for eternity."[31] St. Jerome—the fervent lover of monastic poverty—sets forth this comment on the same text; " The thought of the present day suffices for us; as for the things to come, and which are uncertain, let us confide in God."[32] St. John Chrysostom says: "Content yourselves with the work you perform, to gain that which is necessary for you; and do not engage in superfluous works for the acquirement of things equally superfluous."[33] Finally, our Angelic Doctor thus sums up and completes the doctrine of the Fathers as to the solicitude of earthly possessions: "The Lord has not

---

[30] *Works on the Monastic life*, ch. 23.
[31] *Sermon on the Mount.* Ibid.
[32] *Commentary on St. Matt.*, ch. 6.
[33] *Commentary on the same chapter.*

forbidden us to seek for what is indispensable to our corporal life, but He objects to our giving ourselves up to those inordinate anxieties which will lead to our ruin!"

Now there may be four different kinds of disorder in this anxiety about temporal matters. The *first* would be to look upon them as our final end, and to serve God in order to obtain the food and clothing we require, which our Saviour forbids when He says, "Lay not up to yourselves treasures on earth." The *second* exists in those who disquiet themselves about temporal affairs, despairing of the divine help; to such our Lord says, "For your Father knoweth that ye have need of all these things." The *third* is a vain presumption which fills a man with the foolish confidence that he can procure by his own industry that which is necessary to him, without the aid of God; whom the Divine Master reproves in the following words: "And which of you by taking thought can add to his stature one cubit?" The *fourth* is that unreasonable eagerness which leads us to be troubled about things altogether indifferent to the time being, and relating only to a future of which we are not the disposers, and our Lord condemns this exaggerated foresight in recommending us " not to be solicitous for the morrow."

Poverty, regulated after the principles which we have put forward, has deserved the eulogy and blessing of our Lord in this same *sermon on the mount* of which we have just studied a few sentences. " Blessed are the poor in spirit ! " exclaims Jesus Christ ; that is to say, blessed are those who despise honour, riches and transitory goods, obeying thus the double influence of their own reason and of divine grace ; blessed are they whom common sense and the divine Spirit jointly conduct to the perfect possession of Spiritual goods, by a detachment from exterior goods. This is the first of the eight beatitudes, not that it is the most complete nor the most sublime, but it is the one, which allied with the fear of the Lord, opens to man the path of wisdom and the royal road of perfection, by destroying in him those outward obstacles which shackle his progress in holy charity. Now, perfection is the root of happiness ! and it is thus that religious poverty is both the first of the evangelical counsels and the first among the beatitudes.

We have already seen the power of this virtue in the manifold work of perfection, its superiority over almsgiving, its character of total consecration to the glory of God, its excellence as compared with riches; its efficacy in procuring true happiness, its reasonable limits, and, lastly, the spirit which it should preserve in the acquisition of the necessaries of life. We are now left to consider what is its field of action.

CHAPTER IV.

The Domain of Religious Poverty.

IT is not only of the religious man that voluntary poverty is the queen and the lady, as St. Francis of Assisi expresses it. It is not a merely personal virtue confined to the conscience of each individual. It holds its sway over whole communities, congregations, and regular societies. Then emerging from the enclosure of the cloister, it extends its sceptre over the whole world, having received both the mission and the power to bring it under the yoke of the Gospel, to win it to God, and, finally, to take entire possession of it, according to this promise of our Lord; " Blessed are the poor in spirit, for theirs is the kingdom of heaven."[1] This great extension of the sway of holy poverty claims our attentive consideration.

By the profession of religious poverty man renounces for ever his right to the possession of exterior goods; he abdicates also the power of using them independently, and according to his own free will. It does not, however, follow from this that the Christian should be necessarily and absolutely poor, since the community of which he becomes a member may possess riches and hold property. There is this wide difference between the virtue of poverty and those of chastity and obedience, that these last, in destroying in the

---

[1] Undoubtedly this word of the Divine Master bears directly upon the complete and supernatural happiness which is the reward of voluntary poverty. But, as the "kingdom of heaven" frequently signifies in the Gospel the Holy Catholic Church, we may also understand that our Saviour promises to "the poor of spirit" a particular efficacy in the works of the Apostolate, in the propagation of the faith, and of Christian virtues.

individual the right of enjoying sensual pleasures, and of fully disposing of his powers and acts, are not liable to the renewal, under the *social* form, of that which they have already destroyed. Thus, when each member of a religious order is chaste and obedient, it is impossible that the community should be wanting in chastity and obedience; whereas the right of property being a legal matter, belonging as much to a corporate and moral as to a real person, it may so happen that a congregation possesses abundant riches as a whole, whilst each religious, taken separately, is bound to poverty. It may even happen that men, who were poor and destitute in this world, may pass suddenly to a commodious and wealthy life in religion. But in that case will not this edifice of perfection, which one pretends to raise on the groundwork of poverty, as upon its corner stone, fall into ruin at the first attempt at a superstructure? Is not this a criminal mockery or a vain illusion? Does not the religious abandon with one hand the goods of this world but to lay hold of them with the other? Ought we not, therefore, to exact from communities as complete a poverty as from individuals?

THE RELIGIOUS STATE. 61

It is easy to see that this question of poverty in common is one of the greatest importance. Perfection, which is the essential end of the religious state, must necessarily be protected against those perils which might accrue to it from the wealth of the community. We must therefore determine, in accordance with the principles of ascetic science, the exact proportions of these riches, reconciling them with voluntary poverty in so prudent a manner that the threefold danger of exterior riches, as well as the menaces which our Lord denounced against them, may be effectually averted from those who have made themselves in order to become perfect.

The admirable St. Thomas proves first of all that vain glory and the love of corruptible goods, those two deplorable fruits of the possession of riches, proceed only from superabundance of those goods. For so long as they are insignificant how can they effectually win our affection, or puff us up with pride? Human weakness is indeed an unfathomable abyss, and is often held captive by trifles of little or no value. We have, however, the right to expect that an energetic soul, who has spontaneously engaged itself in a state of perfection, will be able to resist such puny temptations, and that thus a religious society may, without incurring great danger, reserve to itself riches in moderate proportion and with due precaution. And even should these riches be great, yet if faithfully employed in the service of our neighbour, for the good of the Church, and the interests of God, they would lose much of their pernicious character by their being possessed in common. In fact, we are so disposed by nature that we do not entirely bestow our hearts on those created things which are not flattering to our self-love. Experience shows us, that if those goods are directed towards an object which is not our own conceit and self-love, we find them less attractive to our affection, and we proportion our attachment to them accordingly; and thus we do draw from them more profit than vanity. When the ecclesiastical laws relative to regular life are duly observed, they raise a sufficient barrier between the religious and the possessions of the community. They prevent riches seducing the inmates of the cloister with their false sweetness and delusive joys. They maintain the authority of poverty even in the midst of plenty; and they construct, as it were, a deep channel, by which all that is not strictly needed for a simple and mortified life within the cloister may find its way to the outer world, and thus exercise over it a holy and salutary influence.

As to the other dangers of exterior goods, namely, the anxieties of which they are the source, they are inseparable from them; these cares follow them everywhere like a cankerworm, which is ever devouring, and never dies. Whether they be abundant or not, riches bring in their train inevitable uneasiness and cares; and in this case little does it matter whether they be the property of one only or of many; the community possesses wealth as a legal person—a corporate body; but its individual members will, in reality, bear the burden of labouring to acquire them, of the care to preserve them, and the trouble of management. If, therefore, a religious congregation desired, sought after, or possessed great wealth, without justifiable reason, the result would be a deplorable injury to the holy liberty of the soul.

But if they are kept in due proportion with the real wants of life, they will only involve that trifling care which, as we have seen, is permitted by our Divine Master. Were they even considerable and productive of great disquiet, they would still be compatible with the spirit and exercises of religion if they be really common property, and by this very fact consecrated to the glory of God or to the edification of our neighbour. For if it is true, on the one hand, that the anxiety of persons in regard of their personal goods proceeds from self-love, and at the same time increases this egotistic passion, so that one cannot be both rich and religious; it is also true, on the other hand, that the numerous cares attached to the proper management of the wealth of the community are dictated and inspired by charity, and contribute to the growth of this virtue in truly faithful souls. We are further aware that the regular state has for its immediate end the perfection of charity. The administration of the common store may then be used as a means, and constitute a praiseworthy and perfect act, even should the anxieties inherent to this occupation impede deeds of superior worth; as for example the contemplation of the divine mysteries, preaching the Gospel, and instructing children. Yea! even then it will be possible to compensate for the inferiority of these works by the excellence and fervour of our spiritual affections!

From this fundamental doctrine the Angel of the School deduces several consequences. To possess abundant riches in common is an obstacle to perfection; which though real, yet is not insurmountable, nor does it totally exclude the possibility of attaining the principal end of the religious state. Nevertheless one should surround oneself by continual and serious precaution, so as to lessen its gravity and surmount its difficulty. To possess in common such an amount of exterior goods as just suffices for the maintenance of a simple and frugal livelihood, is not an impediment to that degree of perfection which should be the ambition of all religious orders, and which consists in devoting oneself with perfect freedom to the divine service.

As, however, these regular societies propose to themselves, besides this common perfection, and this general end, a definite object determined for them by their founders which they are expected to realize, be it in the active or in the contemplative life, it follows that the poverty proper to one congregation may not be sufficiently rigourous for another, and that the austerity of one might be too commodious and easy for another. Poverty, not being of itself an absolute perfection, will be so much the more perfect as it is best adapted to the particular object of each community. Contemplatives practice it the most severely. The active orders must unite the spirit and the merit of it with their possessions in common, for they would be imperfect and wanting in the elementary rules of Christian prudence if they deprived themselves of the resources necessary for the exercise of hospitality, care of the sick, ransom of prisoners—in a word, for the accomplishment of those works with which they are charged.

Two anxieties thus stand face to face, almost in contradiction to each other in the religious life : the noble solicitude of spiritual things, and the indispensable but humiliating anxiety for temporal goods. These are two contrary tendencies which must however be reconciled and harmonised by a perpetual equilibrium. They are proportionately in mutual opposition to each other. When the first would mount to its highest point, the second must be reduced to its lowest level. Now, if a religious order is instituted principally, not only to contemplate the truth, but also to communicate to the world by teaching and preaching the beneficial lights which by prayer and supernatural study fill the soul, such an institution should have more anxiety to acquire spiritual things than that one which is solely instituted for contemplation.

Hence the former should fix upon that kind of poverty which frees us the most completely from temporal anxieties, because, the only way of arriving at that holy and happy detachment consists, not in procuring and preserving[2] riches long beforehand, but as the want of them presents itself, for the sustenance of the body and of life. Consequently the religious order which unites the contemplative life with more active duties, such as teaching and instructing, will extend its zeal for poverty so far as to abstain from forecasting the needs of a distant future, and from the care

---

[2] St. Thomas here remarks, in answer to vain dreamers, that if religious have the right *to use* exterior things, they have evidently also the right to *store* and *possess* them in common, at least for a certain time.

taken by others to possess lasting goods and to watch over their investments and devise the best means of obtaining the highest possible interest.

Thence our Angelic Doctor in connexion with poverty distinguishes three degrees in this religious state. *Firstly*, the active orders which apply themselves to outward works, and these may possess even abundant riches but always in common.

Secondly, those orders which are chiefly contemplative. To these it is more fitting to have moderate riches, unless they be bound to relieve the necessities of the poor, or to exercise hospitality either of themselves or through others, for then again it is advisable that they should retain more extended possessions.

Thirdly, contemplative orders which are at the same time apostolic, who must lead a life of entire abnegation, free from all temporal cares; they must confine themselves, even in times of need, to acquire and keep that little which is indispensable to them. This last manner of living was exactly that of our Lord. This most perfect institutor and marvel of religious poverty possessed nothing on earth, save the offerings of His disciples and of holy women: He kept them for a very short time, dispersing them day by day, sometimes to the poor, as tribute money, or for food and clothing. Likewise, after His resurrection, the college of the apostles reserved for distribution to the faithful the price of those terrestial goods, of which those perfect Christians had joyfully despoiled themselves.

To exceed the limits fixed by sound and prudent reason would be to fall into a blameworthy extreme. For should one pretend to live in still greater poverty, it would be to pave the way to the ruin of one's soul, and that of the entire community; and contrariwise should one desire superabundant riches, that is to say, greater than is permitted by the immediate object of each religious order, he would soon find himself troubled by a thousand superfluous anxieties, and by sinful cares which could not be justified by the plea of charity. These accursed riches would soon make themselves liked, coveted and worshipped. Their tendency is to beget in the heart a senseless vanity, and produce a scandalous relaxation of regular life. After having possessed them in common, one would gradually learn to become personally attached to them, and then might one re-echo under the desolate arches of the cloister these words, or rather these denunciations of St. Jerome : "There are some who are richer now they are monks than when they were seculars; they possess, under the empire of Jesus Christ, the model of poverty, an abundance which they never possessed under the rich standard of satan. And the Church sighs with grief when she sees in her bosom people covered with gold, of whom the world had made but poor beggars." [3]

Let all religious houses remain poor, even if they possess great wealth! May they always keep up as a sacred fire enkindled by God, even in the midst of their *interior*, this living spirit of *common poverty*, which St. Gregory so strongly admires in the holy abbot Isaac, "who took as much precaution in protecting and watching over his extreme poverty as the miser takes in looking over his perishable treasures." [4]

The possession of riches in common being liable to lead to jealousies, dissension, and quarrels, members of a community must not stoop either to base sensuality, or indulge in

[3] *Letter to Heliodorus.*   [4] *Dialogues*, L. iii.

unjust suspicions against such amongst them as are burdened with the weight of temporal affairs, and who thus remove them from the shoulders of their brethren. A religious should ever remember that he has made profession to lead a poor and detached life, that he has engaged himself to despise these exterior goods, and that he must neither desire nor expect more than the bare food for his maintenance and clothing sufficient to cover his body. They should rejoice at living thus free from all secular cares, and so being able unceasingly to consecrate themselves without anxiety to the acquirement of spiritual goods. Again, the ministers who are thus charged with the keeping and dispensation of the resources of the religious family, should bear in mind that they are only humble servants in great danger of losing their perfection, and of being themselves guilty of injustice should they not show themselves careful and disinterested in their stewardship. Deprived of that calm and tranquillity enjoyed by the others, they must constrain themselves to exhibit in their works a stronger and ever increasing charity. They should comfort themselves in their inevitable distractions with the thought that in taking care of the interests of their brethren, of the poor and of the Church, they can themselves advance very rapidly in this high virtue of divine love which the religious life considers as its supreme end. And then these riches so often pernicious, this contemptible nothingness wherein man seeks his happiness and finds but death, become themselves, in the hands of holy poverty, a powerful lever to raise the world from its humiliation, and to draw it closer to that God who was born in a forsaken crib and who was buried in a borrowed sepulchre.

Yes, these poor in spirit, who appear to be as nothing and incapable of aught in this world, have, however, received from Jesus Christ the grace to conquer the great and powerful ones of the world, and the right to drag them as a trophy in their train. Religious poverty is a state which is essentially apostolical, and the divine Redeemer, wishing to triumph over the arrogance of a proud world and all its united powers, began by making Himself one of the most humble and most destitute of men. The Son of man had not whereon to lay his head. When it became urgent that He should pay the tribute, neither He nor the prince of His Church possessed the coin requisite for it, and in order to avoid scandal, Peter repaired to the sea shore to fetch that miraculous fish which furnished the tax for the King of Heaven and His earthly Vicar. And as His disciples still expected from Him riches and temporal greatness, St. Jerome deduces from His words the following interpretation : " Why do you desire to follow Me for the goods and rewards of this world ; I who am so poor that I have not even a little dwelling, nor do I possess a roof under which I may take shelter."[5] And this marvellous poverty was in perfect accordance with His life, in the same way as in a more or less vigorous degree, it is in accordance with the religious life of His most faithful imitators.

"*Firstly*," says the learned St. Thomas, "our Lord came to preach the gospel in the country, and in the towns by the riverside, and even in the midst of the deserts. Now a preacher of the Divine Word, if he would give himself altogether to his sacred ministry, should be independent of worldly cares. He should employ all his time, all his attention

[5] St. Matt. x. 9.

and all his powers in the study of the truth, in seeking out souls, and in scattering broadcast heavenly seed! He ought to be so effectively disengaged from worldly interests as never to allow their influence to bind his tongue, or enchain the Word of God on his lip, or even to weaken the energy of its accents. This independence and freedom are manifestly incompatible with the possession of riches, which occupy the mind, seduce the heart, and enervate courage. Thus our Divine Master, not content with giving us the example of voluntary poverty, said to His Apostles in sending them to announce the coming of His kingdom: "Do not possess gold, nor silver, nor money in your purses;"[6] and the Apostle recalled this counsel when speaking later to the Church at Jerusalem, he said: "It is not reason that we should leave the Word of God and serve tables."[7]

Here the religious life shows itself to us under a new aspect. What is, indeed, a religious if not a man voluntarily poor, without a dwelling wherein he can rule as master, without riches of which he can dispose, or which he can use according to his pleasure, and without

[6] St. Matt. x. 9.   [7] Acts. vi. 2.

earthly ambition, for he has placed between himself and the earth the impassable abyss of the claims of God? He is thus placed in the condition to which the Eternal Wisdom vouchsafed to reduce Himself, when, after having spoken to the world by the mouth of patriarchs and prophets, He brought us, in His own person, the glad tidings of our redemption. He is placed in the position which the same adorable Wisdom willed that His apostles should occupy. He is, then, prepared and destined for the Apostolate, as the hand of God disposes nothing without a motive. He has made the stem for the flower and fruit; so He makes the religious poor in order to form of him an Apostle. And where could He find more abnegation, more freedom, and more aptitude for His holy ministry?

Every religious is, then, in a certain measure the herald of truth. He announces it unceasingly either by his lips in the Christian pulpit, or by conduct and example like the Saint of Assisi, whose preaching often consisted in wandering silently and in prayer through the streets of the city.

At times the ministry of the prophets in the old Testament consisted in simple symbolical actions, which were unaccompanied by any word or commentary. Can we not therefore suppose that the mere existence and passage of a religious through this world can be a sermon as intelligible, and a language as eloquent as theirs?

But for this it is necessary that no coarse breath of ambition, cupidity, or avarice should tarnish the image of Jesus Christ in His disciples. It is essentially necessary that in these Apostles, who are to be exhibited as spectacles to the view of the whole world both to angels and to men, the features proper to "divines teachers" of souls should appear in their fullest brilliancy and natural purity, and that nothing should hinder them from exhaling the full fragrance of Him, who is called the Flower of the Fields and the Lily of the Valley. Poverty of spirit will work this miracle, for is not the transformation of our mind, our body, and our whole being into the perfect likeness of Jesus Christ a wonderful miracle!

Secondly, our Lord has associated Himself with a companion in order to keep up that great law of opposition, which maintains between good and evil a perpetual antagonism;

grace and rebellious nature, virtue and sin, life and death—a perpetual conflict. In vain does our proud intellect wonder and be scandalized at it. In vain does it reproach the Apostles with the folly of the cross, and our holy doctors with that which it calls a play upon words and taste for contrasts. It is no question here of human rhetoric! It is the struggle of those contrasts which God has established for ever in this world; and of that fight in which He Himself was the first engaged, of that wondrous duel[8] mentioned in the sacred liturgy, which is but Christianity itself. Thus it is that Jesus submitted to death of the body in order to give us spiritual life. Thus, too, did He embrace a poor and miserable life in order to procure for us the inestimable riches of the soul. "You know," says St. Paul, "the grace of our Lord Jesus Christ, that being rich, He became poor, for your sakes; that through His poverty you might be rich."[9] And whilst He has counselled religious to become poor in order to attain more easily and surely a high degree of perfection, He has endowed their poverty with

---

[8] See the Victimæ Paschali, sequence for Easter.
[9] II. Cor. viii. 9.

the supernaturally infinite value and sanctifying power of His own. That is the reason they should practise it with the same spirit of charity and zeal for mankind and the salvation of souls. Our age is devoured by an incredible fever to amass material riches, and their increase unceasingly occasions an impoverishment of the intellect, and the most terrible misery of the heart. Where are we, therefore, to find an expiation for these crimes, a counterbalance to these excesses, and light for this darkness? In holy religious poverty. It will restore that harmony between body and mind which is so sadly broken, and will compensate by her austerities for the abuse of corruptible goods. It will open the eyes of men, blinded as they are by gold-dust. As time goes on, and the number of those spiritual merchants, as they are styled by our Lord, who seek exclusively the peerless pearls of perfection, increases amongst us, we shall witness also the growing number of those who use their temporal treasures in a Christian manner.

Thirdly, Jesus lived in poverty lest His enemies should attribute His infinite zeal for the sacred ministry to a vulgar desire of earthly gain, to a thirst after power and honours, or to the yearning for glory and popularity. "And even at the present day," said St. Jerome, "if His disciples were possessed of riches, and lived in abundance, they would seem to announce the Kingdom of Heaven, not for the salvation of souls, but for the sake of filthy lucre."[10] The history of the Redeemer and of His Church, proves, beyond a doubt, that it is impossible to avert the Pharisicial scandal of the wicked. It is impossible to escape the envy and hatred of those innumerable multitudes whom we see in our own time idle and avaricious of their neighbour's goods, always ready to curse the sacred hands which dress their wounds, and which generously distribute to them bread earned by the most noble toil. But religious poverty has not yet lost all its power. Let it carefully repudiate all appearance of the love of riches; let men thoroughly know to what projects of charity it destines the alms received from the faithful, and then when it presents itself clothed in its mean and coarse garment, to speak to the people of that merciful God become poor for them, and Whom they have blasphemed, its voice will be heard as the

[10] *Commentary on St. Matthew*, ch. 10.

voice of a sincere friend, and will be immediately welcomed as an echo from heaven.

Fourthly, and *lastly,* our Lord reduced Himself to the lowest extremity of indigence, that His Divine power should shine forth with all the more splendour, as He was the more destitute of all those means which contribute to the good success of human undertakings. "He chose," said a bishop at the Council of Ephesus, "all that was poor and worthy of contempt; all that was low and hidden from the eyes of the world, in order that it might recognise more easily that it was the God-head Itself which transformed the world. It was for that reason that He took to Himself a poor mother, and a still poorer country. Therefore it was that from His birth He was without gold or silver. His crib is a sufficient proof of this."[11] Besides, in order to humble His enemies, not assuredly as much as they deserved, but as far as it was possible to do so without causing their entire annihilation, God attacked them with His weakest, and, as it were, with the most derisive weapons. To their cunningly devised intrigues He op-

---

[11] *Discourse of Theodorus of Ancyra upon the Birth of our Lord.*

poses the ingenious simplicity of children; to their arrogant power, the weakness of strangers. Their strength and their fury He resists by the sorrowful complaints of the crucified One; to their luxury, the poverty of a beggar. His Church is stamped with the same seal of supernatural strength, or, to express it better, of Almighty power. Poverty, above all, is one of the most fruitful means for the propagation of the faith, as it is also for the preservation and development of Christian life. Come, then, to us, and multiply yourselves in every part, oh ye blessed offshoots of the old religious families. Restore amongst us that mantle of voluntary poverty which was the royal robe of Jesus Christ, the Son of God and Redeemer of the world. Ah! when the fringe of this despised apparel, so much insulted by impiety, so much tattered by the thorns of the way, will come to cure some one of those great evils which go by the names of a family, college, city, or nation, then, once more, will the nations acknowledge and glorify the power and mercy of the Lord. But let man, and the strength of man, be more and more effaced from your heart, in order that the poverty of Jesus Christ may be revealed in all its splendour. With St. Francis of Assisi, reject, in the presence of God and of His Church, all that you hold of this world; and thus stripped of everything, offer your hands, your feet and your heart to the sword of light and of fire, which should impress on them the wounds together with the whole might of a crucified God.

Religious poverty may, then, be justly styled a social, as well as an apostolical virtue.

Communities should guard it with scrupulous care, and in as great a degree as is prescribed to them by that special mission with which they are charged. They should also consider and esteem it as possessing a most powerful means of influence over the world; as an incessant and mighty preaching; as a continuation of the work of Jesus Christ. Having seen the Christian stripped of his riches and all his exterior goods by the holy virtue of poverty, we will now contemplate him separated, so to speak, from his own person by religious chastity, which penetrates, like a two-edged sword into the deepest and most hidden recesses of the body and the soul.

CHAPTER V.

Religious Chastity.

However beneficial holy and religious poverty may be, it is not altogether without a certain degree of danger to the soul. It has imperfections against which we must combat; it has limits which we are not permitted to exceed.

Here we find a more sublime virtue, a second means of spiritual progress, which, without being, any more than the others, of absolute perfection in itself, can never become prejudicial to the end from which it draws its value. It can therefore be employed without limit, and be exercised to an ever increasing degree. Religious chastity is so much the more perfect as it is the more complete; so much the more praiseworthy as it oversteps more courageously the boundaries within which our nature, aided by even ordinary grace, appears compelled to confine itself. It has the power of raising man to the dignity of angels, the honour of having given to the

Church the doctor of Aquino, with his eagle and all-penetrating light.[1] It may claim the right of not having to justify itself before pure and sincere minds, and, in fact, to it belongs

[1] Who is there that does not admire and understand that marvellous union of knowledge and virginity in St. Thomas. Human nature elevated above itself by the perfect purity of the mind and senses; the soul thus prepared to receive the extraordinary grace of great simplicity of thought, an astonishing depth of views; a dazzling brilliancy of doctrine, reason attaining almost the direct intuition of angelic minds: this it is what God shows us in our holy Doctor! His body was so perfectly subject to his soul, that it helped him most faithfully in his contemplations and study, instead of being any obstacle. He was the most learned Doctor of the Schools, because he was a virgin, as St. John was the most sublime of the Evangelists on account of his virginity. This explains why our Saviour has confided to his special patronage all young students. We discover virtues natural or supernatural as we lead a chaster life. The Angelic Doctor proves this firstly by his example; and further, his protection and his cord or blessed girdle are of very valuable assistance to souls who desire to preserve the purity of their state. In treating of religious chastity we must exhort persons devoted to prayer and contemplation to aggregate themselves to this *angelic militia of St. Thomas*, who, like to the patriarch Job, girded up his loins to converse with God. (Job xxxviii. 3; xl. 2.)

the privilege of being the more loved and esteemed, as it is the more humble, more silent, and more hidden.

"Oh, holy and immaculate Virginity," says the Holy Liturgy, "I know not with what praises shall I extol thee? for Him whom the heavens cannot contain, thou hast borne for us in thy womb." Now, this Virginity of the most glorious Mother of God is reflected and spread, ever brilliant and spiritually fruitful, throughout the whole Church, and particularly in the religious orders. Who, then, shall praise it worthily if not you, O! Virgin Doctor, O! true Angel of the Schools? No one has spoken of it with so much depth, precision and respect. You enlighten the mind with so soft a light, that the eye is not thereby affected. You exhibit the grandeur and make us realise the divine charm of innocence, while preserving for it the joy and the merit of its humility. O! do thou here mould my thoughts and words upon thine own.

The Apostle wrote thus to the Corinthians: "Let us cleanse ourselves from all defilement of the flesh and of the spirit, perfecting sanctification in the fear of God."[2] Thus does

[2] II. Cor. vii. 1.

Christian perfection exact as a condition and as a means for its advancement, that purity should enlighten the soul, and even purify the body by dissipating those coarse shadows which blind the eye of the intellect, and by destroying those earthly affections, which wrench in a false direction the uprightness of our hearts. And if the Holy Ghost invites us to rise still higher than the ordinary faithful, to be seated still closer to Him at this delicious banquet of prayer and celestial love to which He bids His friends, He requires from us that our wedding garment be cleaner and whiter. St. Paul teaches that this supreme degree of innocence is precisely original chastity: "And the unmarried woman and the virgin thinketh on the things of the Lord; that she may be holy both in body and in spirit."[3] She is absolutely free to give herself to God. The senses and imagination do not divert her from prayer, nor separate her from the love of Jesus Christ. Continually united to God who is infinitely holy, she receives from Him both spiritual and corporal sanctity, increasing in splendour from day to day. And thus virginity fully realizes and inviolably preserves

---

[3] I. Cor. vii. 34.

in man, that double purity which his perfection requires.

This is why our Lord has decided that perfect chastity is indispensable to those Christians who would embrace a state of perfection. "And there are eunuchs, who were made so by men; and there are eunuchs, who have made themselves eunuchs for the kingdom of heaven. He that can take, let him take *it*. All men take not this word, but they to whom it is given."[4] Such a one is indeed a perfect man, generous towards God even unto the most painful sacrifices, and far superior to the weakness and delights of the generality of mankind. And when the Redeemer called St. John the Evangelist to this apostolic life which ever remains as the most excellent model for religious orders, "He did not desire," says our Doctor, "that he should be fettered by an earthly betrothal, giving him in exchange the incomparable joys of spiritual nuptials. But as He would not deprive anyone of either the hope or possibility of attaining perfection, He accepted amongst His disciples those even whom He had found engaged in the cares of marriage, and parti-

[4] St. Matt. xix. 11, 12.

cularly St. Peter whom He appointed the head of His Apostles and of His Church. But, at the same time, on account of that divine jealousy in which He glories in Holy Writ, He exacts the exclusive possession of their heart. He said to them: 'Follow me,' not only in person, but also with all your affection; and they too were enabled to follow the meek and merciful Lamb who sports among the lilies, and to sing in His praise the new canticle which is reserved to the choir of virgins."

The holy patriarchs of the Old Testament had neither the happiness nor the honour of religious chastity. "Ah!" said the illustrious Bishop of Hippo, "if they had had the choice of practising it, they would have observed it with the most ardent zeal, but they had to content themselves with loving and desiring it."[5] They had the merit of it, and they are rewarded for it in heaven; but their foreheads are not crowned with this radiant aureola which belongs solely to virgins. And, that they might unite the high perfection to which God wished to raise them with the duties of their state and cares of their family,

[5] *On the Benefits of Christian Marriage*, ch. xxi.

it was necessary they should have an exceptional abundance of grace and an extraordinary strength in virtue. Without this, Abraham, who was the Father of the Faithful, could never have been so perfect in the sight of the Lord. That age is now past. A carnal people are no longer multiplied by a corporeal birth; but a spiritual race increases by regeneration in the water of Baptism and in the Holy Ghost. Men, now-a-day, may not pretend to unite the cares of the secular life with the absolute perfection of the Christian calling. Except in rare instances, God no longer bestows that grace which maintained the patriarchs of old on the summit of the spiritual world whilst by their condition they were riveted to the enjoyments and goods of this material world. No one is justified by their example in imagining that he can be "*perfect*," unless he observe religious chastity, even, as St. Thomas ingeniously observes, it would be absurd for an unarmed man alone to attack the enemy's battalions under pretext that Samson with the jawbone of an ass destroyed a multitude of Philistines.

But do not content yourself with supposing that the times are merely changed, and that for one kind of life God has substituted another of equal dignity and merit. Times have become better, and vocations more perfect, since the Word was made flesh and dwelt amongst us. "I am not more worthy than Abraham," wrote St. Augustine, "but the chastity of celibacy which I observe is preferable to the chastity of the married state."[6] The perfection attained by a person is not a sufficient argument to demonstrate the perfection of the state he has embraced, for it may happen that such a one makes use of a lesser good with a purer and higher intention, whilst another will exhibit only moderate piety in the employment of a far superior good. What a satisfaction it must be for religious to know that their condition is more excellent than that of Abraham and Moses, and with what diligent care should they not guard that virtue which places them in easier communication with divine and spiritual things, consumes more and more the carnal propensities by which they are drawn to evil, assures to the soul a nobler independence and a more express likeness to God, and puts them on a species of equality with the angels.

[6] *On the Benefits of Christian Marriage*, ch. xxi.

The constant teaching of St. Thomas's disciples then is, that the virtue of chastity spiritualizes human nature in divers degrees. Firstly, there is that chastity which is necessary to all who would attain salvation; its object is to protect the essential rights of the mind, and to act as a safeguard of its dignity against the disorders of carnal pleasures; for our passions like to a furious torrent, continually hurry forward towards the soul their unclean waters, by which they seek to overwhelm and submerge it, and exercise over the entire man an undisputed empire. Should they succeed, these daughters of lust (to make use of the expressive language of the Schools) will soon devour as a vile quarry those virtues and holy dispositions man had received from God. Man's intellect will be darkened and his prudence replaced by a senseless precipitation; instead of reflecting upon his duties he will act without consideration, and if at times he still recognises the word of his Sovereign Master, he will be wanting in constancy wherewith to observe it, and his self-love will cause him to trample under foot the most sacred laws. The voluptuous man will have a hatred of God because God has forbidden evil; he will cling to this world with a kind of despairing grasp; and the world to come will be no longer for him but an object of disgust and abhorrence. In a word, the soul would become an accursed and hideous spectacle if carnal pleasures were not regulated by chastity, and made subservient to the law of reason.

This first degree of continence does not, however, wholly spiritualize us, it only maintains an exact equilibrium between the mind and senses, which latter still preserve an independence always dangerous and disquieting, owing to the possibility of its abuse and the many other troubles to which it exposes us.

Thence, holy purity will not feel satisfied with resisting dangers only, and in strictly obeying the divine commands; it will learn the counsels of our Lord, and submit the body to a more rigorous government. For, beholding the flesh in perpetual warfare with the soul, ever wearying it, prompting it to evil, and creating continual hindrance to the operations of the mind and will, it resolves to hold it in subjection, and allow it only that nourishment, repose, and recreation which are necessary to enable it to be a useful instrument of the spiritual powers. As to other pleasures, or a greater independence, it will vigorously resolve to deprive it's body of them. It will refuse it not merely criminal enjoyments, but even the married state, thereby assuring to the soul a greater liberty and a greater preponderance. This second degree of chastity is that of faithful widows, and of those who, for a time, desire nothing but the experience of the pure delight of the spirit.[7]

But this innocence is not yet sufficient for the religious; he aims at being both completely and eternally spiritualized. He desires to be definitely released from all sensual bonds;

[7] This theory of St. Thomas clearly is an intelligible refutation of those who see in religious chastity only a blind hatred of this world, or an absurd and whimsical condemnation of all earthly joys. Religious and Catholic priests do not deny like senseless beings, or condemn as fanatic Manicheans the legitimate pleasures of the senses; but for more noble interests and more real joys they deprive themselves of some ordinary gratifications. It is therefore on their part a proof of the highest good sense. The end they propose to themselves endows their continence with a real value, which ignorance alone can misunderstand. Is it not an elementary axiom that the goodness of the *end* communicates itself to the *means* (which may be indifferent) which are used for the attainment of that end?

and on that account he raises himself, with God's grace, to the highest degree of Christian chastity, to perpetual continence, to the most holy state of virginity. Virginity does not propose, like temperance, to wrestle merely with immoderate and vehement passions, it rejects even those permitted by reason. It does not confine itself to sustaining the soul against temptation, or to fortifying it against the excess of sensual desires. It thoroughly extirpates them—thus rendering them incapable of attacking or agitating the heart. It inexorably denies to the body all such joys as might furnish it with arms against the spirit; so that, being thus disarmed, and stripped of all its power, it has no longer sufficient strength to wrestle with success against conscience and faith.

Virginity thus carries the war against the appetites of the flesh into that very ground conceded to them by the law of heaven, where it not only encloses them, but destroys them that it may have nothing more to fear from them. It does not simply embank the course of the torrent so that it can no longer ravage the domain of virtue, it dries it up and exhausts it; and whereas ordinary chastity exercises its action only on the soul and the intellectual faculties, virginity reigns wondrously over the very body and its sensitive capacities. These find themselves subjugated and conquered—without action, without enjoyment, they are as dead, crushed under the virginal foot of purity. In vain do they strive to bite its heel; the hand of God has paralysed their venomous teeth. Their poison cannot injure the soul who watches, who prays, and who fixes its eyes upon heaven.

In order to destroy all hope of their re-establishing their extinct dominion, Virginity gives itself a sort of perpetuity by consecrating itself to Jesus Christ by a perpetual vow.[8] It thereby unites itself with the virtue of religion, and henceforth these two immortal sisters glorify and praise the Lord in the entire man. The flesh may perhaps have lost that brilliant purity it received with the white garment of baptism; it may have been the miserable slave of mortal sin, or even have committed sacrilege. However, be this as it may, let no one despair of regaining his

[8] St. Thomas expressly explains that it is by this *vow* that virginity begins to be a *virtue*, otherwise it would be but a pious resolution or good purpose.

rank in the heavenly train of the Divine Lamb. For Virginity resides above all in the soul; it can be retrieved by penance and sanctifying grace, and then, like to a king whose crimes have deprived him of his diadem, and whom repentance has restored to his kingdom wiser and stronger than before, it will crush and annihilate the enemy who seduced and dethroned it. The fallen soul will re-enter once more into possession of that generous and high-minded virtue which admits of no partial sacrifice or half measures. Of this majestic virtue one of the most famous divines of the University of Paris, then so devoted to St. Thomas, has spoken in these glorious terms, which will most profitably close these comments: "The Angel of the School," says Bossuet, "teaches me a beautiful and solid doctrine. We see that amongst moral virtues there are, if I may thus express it, some of lesser vigour, which range within certain limits, but there are also generous virtues which are never satisfied until they have reached the highest point. The courageous man, for instance, is emboldened to face dangers connected with important enterprises, but he who is magnanimous goes still further, for he finds no enterprise daring enough, nor any danger sufficiently great for the exercise of all his virtue. The liberal man makes use of his goods and knows how to dispense them honourably according to the dictates of reason; but there is a certain liberality still more extended, and more generous, which in appearance even borders on profusion, and this is what we call magnificence. The great St. Thomas teaches us that this beautiful and admirable virtue, which pagan philosophy has never known, namely Christian Virginity, is in respect to temperance what magnificence is to ordinary liberality. Temperance moderates bodily pleasures, virginity despises them. Temperance, in partaking of them, puts itself indeed above them; but virginity, being stronger and mightier, disdains even to look at them. Temperance bears her chains with steadfast courage; virginity breaks them with a fearless hand. Temperance contents itself with liberty; virginity requires an entire empire and absolute dominion,—or rather may we say, temperance governs the body, and virginity separates itself from it and rises even to heaven almost entirely freed from the yoke of the flesh; so that though it is still in a

I

mortal body, it fails not to take it's place among the blessed spirits, because it, like them, feeds only on spiritual delights." [9]

Such is religious continence. With ordinary chastity it must first respect the right which God so justly possesses over our bodies: "Know you not that your bodies are the temple of the Holy Ghost, who is in you, whom you have from God, and you are not your own? For you are bought at a great price. Glorify, therefore, and bear God in your bodies." [10] Do not profane His dwelling by disorder or licentiousness. And St. Augustine adds, "You have begun to be His temple, let not your lusts make it fall to ruin." [11]

Secondly, the chastity of the cloister has to keep celibacy with its austerity so sweet and so venerable; for the use of sensual pleasures, especially if frequent, strongly increases those temptations so harassing to the Christian soul, and serves to strengthen that perverse inclination which draws us towards corporal goods, by estranging us from God Who is the su-

[9] *Sermon for a Religious Profession upon Virginity*.
[10] I. Cor. vi. 19, 20.
[11] *Book of the Ten Mystic Cords*, ch. 10. [Pseudo-Augustine.]

preme and infinite Good. "Alas!" does the Doctor of Hippo sorrowfully exclaim, "I know of nothing more sadly efficacious for the undoing of a manly soul, living on the very height and stronghold of perfection, than the enjoyments of lust and luxury."[12] They enervate the heart and render it effeminate, and even "take it away" according to the expressive words of Scripture.[13] It was not in the midst of terrestial joys that the Holy Ghost touched and enlightened the souls of the prophets, and how could He have done so when even the spirit of man, so to speak, is kept out and shamefully banished from God's grace by them! Moreover, although it be really honourable, and sanctified by the grace of a sacrament, the marriage state is overwhelmed with temporal anxieties and exterior works. We have already learned this from the mouth of the great St. Paul: "He that has a wife is solicitous for the things of this world." He is obliged to seek temporal goods for the sake of his family and of civil society, and this is an impediment to the acquisition of spiritual wealth. He enjoys human plea-

---

[12] *Soliloquies*, Book I, ch. 10. [Pseudo-Augustine.]
[13] Osee iv. 11.

sures, but the divine enjoyments of the spiritual world are rare and difficult for him. His existence is principally active; he can exercise many acts of charity, but he cannot enjoy the far more preferable happiness of the contemplative life. This is, *thirdly*, the reason why Religious should retire into the isolation of perpetual virginity, preserving their hearts ever free from all human affection, and like, as a poet of the middle ages most forcibly compares it, to a thurible which is closed towards earth and open towards heaven.[14] Entire chastity is a means divinely

[14] We evidently are speaking throughout of the chastity properly so called, which is the object of the second vow of religion, and not of the *mystic* or *spiritual chastity* that orators appear so often to confound with the first, as if it were a special obligation of the regular state. St. Thomas has defined it in these terms: "The word chastity may be taken in a metaphorical or figurative sense relating to the union of a soul with an object wherein it finds some pleasure. If indeed the soul of man delights in its union with the only Being to whom it should truly unite itself, namely, God, and if on the contrary it abstain from seeking its pleasure by uniting itself inordinately and sinfully to creatures, it possesses spiritual chastity. (II. Cor. xi. 2.) But if, disobeying the order of God, it attaches itself to any unlawful object, it commits the crime of

instituted for the attainment of perfection, and virginity is the supreme state of purity and spiritual liberty, and consequently of religion. This is the summary of the doctrine taken by us from the Angel of the School; and if we cannot contemplate it living and realized in our own person, at any rate the study of the privileges of holy virginity will throw a clearer light and a more intense brilliancy upon the deep mystery of the religious life and vocation.

spiritual fornication. (Jeremiah iii. 1.) In this sense chastity is a general virtue; for all the special virtues produce the effect of preventing the soul from seeking its happiness in forbidden things. Consequently this same spiritual chastity consists, above all, in charity and the other theological virtues by which the soul of man is principally united to God."

CHAPTER VI.

The Privileges of Virginity.

JESUS CHRIST is the supreme type of Christian perfection. His divine nature is the sole principle of life and truth, of perfection and beauty; consequently all that is not conformable with His eternal ideas, is of necessity, false, hideous, and bad.

Having been the Divine Maker of ages, and the Creator of the world, he took flesh and dwelt amongst us, full of glory, grace, and truth. He is the first-born of our race, a second Adam, far superior to the first of olden days, whom He fashioned with His adorable hands, and whom He has come to reform to His own image, Perfect Man in the flower of his age, and in the full possession of all His powers. He is the living law of those whom He deigns to call His brethren; He is the inflexible standard of their merits, and one day He will be their unrelenting Judge.

The supernatural virtues which He bestows on us, are as so many invisible artists who mould us upon His features, so as to imprint upon us His own likeness! They are there kneeling before Him, they contemplate Him by the brilliancy of the rays which emanate from His divine countenance, and each, while kneading the humble clay of which we are formed, studies to reproduce some one or other of the perfections of this inimitable ideal. To religious chastity He especially exhibits Himself in all His unity, power, incorruptibility, and beauty. And it is to it in preference to all other virtues, that He has granted the privilege of stamping these glorious characteristics on our souls.

What am I?—A being living its own life, animated by one only soul, pursuing without faltering or forgetfulness one sole end, and in fine, belonging to itself. Truly that it is which He has wished to make of one. The indivisible spirit which He has given me, penetrates even to the most minute fibres of my body, fills them with its vital energy, quickens me with its own life in so intimate a manner, that I am an individual being, a separate substance and a single person. But consider man such as he has made himself, or rather unmade himself by his own hands, and you will find in him nothing but contradiction, struggles, conflict, and perpetual warfare. He wishes to be good, yet he does evil. He desires to serve God, yet he worships the devil. He is drawn towards heaven, and he prefers to grovel in the mire. Does he ever know himself what he wills, or what he does not will? Why do these opposite laws reign within him, and how is it that the resolutions made to day, are the direct negation of the purposes of yesterday? He grows weary of following the same road, and he therefore loses himself in an inextricable labyrinth; he no more belongs to himself, but to worldly goods, to public opinion, to hatred, to ambition, and to a hundred other tyrants, and sometimes, alas, even to the powers of darkness. Is he still one being, or is he not rather a mass of ruins, an absurd collection of elements mutually repelling each other?

But the triumph of this fatal division is nowhere so complete, or so manifest, as in the carnal man. His sensuality destroys all ties of subordination between body and soul.

It gives license to the senses, and allows them such absolute dominion, that the intellect becomes completely disabled from gaining the light necessary for the guidance of the will. This latter in its turn rebels against all that is truly good, first through ignorance and weakness, and finally through real malice. And when, either by a remaining spark of vitality, or by the merciful impulse of divine grace, the poor soul would fain resume the reins of its fallen power, it discovers that it has altogether disorganized those of its faculties, which are naturally united to the body, so that separate from the spiritual powers, they make common cause with the infatuated senses. Man is divided, and is no longer *one*.

And this profound division which rends life into several parts, and which deprives it of that strength and peace pertaining to unity, is to be found in the very state of Christian marriage.

"But he that is with a wife is solicitous for the things of the world, how he may please his wife: and he is divided."[1] He may certainly be highly just, and greatly

[1] I. Cor. vii. 33.

advanced in sanctity, but he cannot offer to God the entire sacrifice of all his possessions, of all his actions, and of all his feelings. He cannot honour our Lord exclusively and entirely, indeed he ought not to do so, since being bound by the sacred duties of the family, he is obliged to fulfil the laws thereof. He therefore belongs only partially to himself. His liberty is diminished. The beautiful and precious independence he could otherwise have employed in perfectly glorifying his Divine Master, is in a measure exchanged for ties which are less noble, and more onerous than those of the religious life. In a word he is divided, and is no longer *one*. And because, according to one of the fundamental elements of science, unity is always in proportion to the whole in such wise, that if the former is injured or lessened, the latter is wounded and weakened by the same means: so the man who is divided by sensual pleasures and wearied by family cares, necessarily loses so much in manliness, real intelligence, vitality, and power.

Religious virginity repairs this disaster, it preserves, or at any-rate re-establishes in him complete unity, and consequently the sum of perfection of being. It suppresses these most active causes, criminal or otherwise, which, so to speak, tear man to pieces. It recalls him to, and concentrates him upon himself. It does not permit him to give himself to any other but to God, or to waste apart from Him, his purest affections and vital strength. It makes him "*continent,*" which according to our Holy Doctor, signifies a man who contains himself for fear that evil passions, or even exterior pleasures, otherwise conformable with the laws of God, should alienate him from the more sublime possessions of the spirit! a man who confining himself to labours of the mind and of the will, by which our nature is mainly distinguished from all inferior beings, shows himself such as he essentially is, a *man.*

Thus holy virginity does not confine itself to the maintenance of this imperfect unity, which though indispensable to salvation, does not preclude the Christian from dividing himself between God and his family, in giving to the latter some portion of his affections and life. Virginity excludes everything which might be a source of dissolution, diversion or discord, between the several powers with which we are endowed.[2] It therefore rids us from those earthly ties which are founded on the union of flesh and blood, and thereby incorporates us more closely with that heavenly family, which is formed by the union of spirit alone. Further, the existence of virgins upon the earth becomes, by the grace of God, a blessing which is incommunicable to others, and solely dedicated to God, even as is the existence of the Angels in heaven, absolutely incommunicable and independent of any family, since each one of the blessed spirits is in itself a distinct and complete species. An Angelic unity, the sublime likeness to the infinite unity of God, such is then the first result, the chief privilege of religious chastity, and in order to describe still more clearly this perfect unity, to set forth to the mind still more plainly, that it consists not merely in a life of exterior solitude in retiring into the desert, or even into the cloister, but in the deliverance from

---

[2] The disorder caused amongst the powers of the soul by lust being so similar to the *luxation* of the members of the body, St. Thomas, therein following the example of St. Isidore of Seville, derived from it the name of *luxury*.

every sensual tie liable to create division, the religious, says St. Thomas, is called a *monk*, from a Greek word signifying he who is *alone*, he who is *one*.

However, that unity existing within me, necessarily implies that I am in union with God, and if this union could be utterly destroyed, the unity of my nature would be definitively shattered. I should then no longer have any cohesion or harmony; in a word, I should cease to exist. For God is the principle, the preserver and the end of all my perfections, and more particularly of my unity: when it increases, it is that God's influence over me has become stronger and more intimate, that he dwells more closely in me, and I in Him. Whence we may see that the admirable unity produced by virginity, is the manifest proof of a close union with God.

The unanimous tradition of the holy Fathers and theologians, considers this close alliance as a mystical marriage of virginal souls with the virginal lamb. The violation of the vow of religious continence would be a most horrible spiritual adultery, a most frightful dissolution of the soul. But the faithful spouse enjoys an excellent unity; all her thoughts, all her affections, all her actions, refer more or less directly to her divine Spouse, who is both her Creator and her last end. She therefore obeys with the greatest exactness the spirit of the monastic state, which is the adoration and the worship of God. She realizes most fully that perfection for which this state was instituted, and which is the perfect love of the Supreme Good. Finally she practises mortification and regular penance for the protection of this pure treasure, and she thus once more appears to us as the very personification of the virtue of religion.

Instead of an earthly family and its transitory happiness, the virgin spouse receives from her Divine Lord an invisible family and heavenly joys. The prayers, penances, and good works of a religious are supernaturally fruitful to the salvation of men; God Himself giving to virgins, says the Angel of the School, the power of transmitting to souls their own spiritual gifts, as if by a species of propagation equally spiritual. But these deep reflexions must be reserved for another time.

The enemy which religious chastity has to overcome, because it is the cause of discord and ruin, must further be conquered, inasmuch as it is a woful cause of weakness and of inaction. Whilst under the empire of this demon of lust, man is kept in a state of miserable infancy. The soul is stunted in its growth. The heart fails to gain steadfastness; it is incapable of those strong joys and enterprises known only to real manhood. Where, then, is the real Christian to be found? Where is, then, the one who attains the age and perfect manhood of Jesus Christ? Among the chaste; but especially among virgins; for ordinary chastity is not altogether free from those "puerile sins," as the great Greek philosopher styles the sins of the flesh.[3] And in speaking thus, says St. Thomas, he does not mean to tell us that these crimes are excusable like children's faults; his language implies not an excuse, but severe condemnation. Indeed, is it not unworthy of a reasonable man to seek after these inordinate and consequently, ignominious pleasures? Does he not thereby show himself to be without wisdom of mind and firmness of will?

[3] *Morals* of Aristotle, Book III.

Does he not also prove himself to be as blind as the brute animal led by its instincts alone, or as the child, in whom the light of reason shines but partially and unsteadily. The slave of sensuality is again like a child, because in yielding to his evil inclinations, he strengthens their power and multiplies their number, just as the child abandoned to the caprices of its self-will, becomes daily more and more stubborn. "By obeying the impulses of our bad desires," says St. Augustine, "we create in ourselves a blameable habit, which, if not resisted, becomes a necessity."[4] So far from rising out of this filthy slough, the profligate wallows still deeper in it. He cannot be satiated, he is consumed by an ever-devouring thirst. He becomes consequently more like an animal and less of a man. This is so true, that to effect a cure in him, one is compelled to make use of those remedies which are employed with children: viz., the curb of correction and the smart of chastisement. This is why, as our most learned Master observes, the virtue opposed to the vice of lust is called *chastity*, because it has to chastise the vicious man after the manner of an

[4] *Confessions*, Book VIII. ch. 5.

unruly child who obeys parental authority only under the smart of the rod.

Further, the second privilege of religious continence is, that it sets free our poor human nature from those wretched swaddling-bands wherein pleasure holds it weak and dishonoured. Virginity disperses those dark clouds, whose shadows overcast the light of reason and of faith. It effectually prevents the growth of perverse habits. It also checks their stubborn perseverance in their impious ways by renouncing everything that could possibly serve again as an occasion to them. In fine, it treats the body not only as a dangerous guest, but as a victim destined for the sacrifice; and arming itself so to speak with fire and sword, it immolates it in spirit and in truth to the adorable Majesty of the Most High. Ordinary continence would have left the body in close contact with those pleasures which we have seen to be so perilous to reason; it would have abandoned it to the legitimate but enervating influence of the riches and joys of an earthly family; it would simply have restrained its excesses without entirely subduing it, and thus it could not have drawn it out of the perpetual childhood which is undeniably incompatible with high perfection. Holy virginity, then, perfects this sketch. After first ensuring to the Christian entire unity, it now endows him with all his strength and manly energy.

What a fit subject for admiration both for heaven and earth is this soldier of religious chastity! He is engaged in a most arduous struggle against his own flesh, which gives birth to temptations far more terrible than all the uprisings of anger, grief, fear, or of any of the other passions, since, according to St. Thomas, nothing except the fear of such dangers as directly menace our life, can be more formidable than the attacks of sensuality. Virginity is unceasingly battling against inclinations, the most frequent, the most natural, the most vehement, and the most powerful of all others against an enemy who entrenches itself at a distance, sheltered from the action of the intellect and will, for it cannot be attacked save in those very powers which are the most closely connected with the animal world. It can with difficulty be followed without peril of defilement, and it can scarcely be attacked without the danger of allowing it some advantage. Yet this fearful adversary, which made St.

Augustine tremble even on the day of his conversion, this raging lion, which you might deem invincible, is chained up by the heroic hand of chaste and meek virginity. And exhibiting to the astonished world the noble and pleasing legion of children, boys, young men and penitents, who have been superior to all its seductions and have overcome themselves, it repeats to every Christian generation: "Can you not do what these have done? Or rather, it is not by their own strength, but by the power of God, that they have triumphed." Here, indeed, we have one of the most manifest evidences of the operation of God's Almighty power amongst us; and when we see every day new heroes responding to the appeal of religious chastity, we may still say that the human race is not yet lost; and that there is on the shores of this ocean of impurity, ever rising and raging, still one grain of sand which will arrest the course of its foaming billows.

When the strong man armed guards the threshold of his house, says our Lord, all that he possesses is in safety; and this word is more applicable to virginity than to any other religious virtue. This vigilant, bright, and mighty sentinel establishes great peace throughout the whole person. As a honeycomb was found in the jaws of a lion, and as, according to the expression of Samson, from strength came forth sweetness, so too, the ineffable joys of prayer are the fruit of the victory gained by the soul over the senses. Absolute continence is the virtue of the contemplative. " And the unmarried woman and the virgin thinketh on the things of the Lord."[5] The temptations which remain still to be overcome by them, are far less difficult to conquer than those of ordinary chastity, for with this latter, occasions are more numerous and more dangerous, the flesh weaker, the spirit less prompt in its resistance, the imagination and senses more easily excited, and the will is less habituated to the sacrifice. " But when the soul," says St. Augustine, " is held in suspense by the love of spiritual goods, and remains fixed in them, the violence of evil desires is singularly weakened, and after having been checked little by little, it ends by being almost entirely extinguished. It was far greater when we let them take their course than at present, when we keep them in rein ; true, it is not as

[5] I. Cor. vii. 34.

yet wholly destroyed, but it is unquestionably diminished."⁶

The religious also possesses in his constant and religious union with God, a very powerful aid against the passions of the flesh. Our Saviour, whilst He remained on earth, curbed by the power of His divinity the uprisings of sensuality in His beloved Apostles, and this is why, whilst the Pharisees and the disciples of St. John the Baptist fasted so rigourously, His chosen ones did not fast at all, because His presence rendered them purer, says Venerable Bede, than if they had practised the most severe abstinence.⁷ Now, may it not be said that the intimate disciples of the Lord, who dwell in His Temple, who so frequently partake of the Holy Eucharist, who live only for Him, and are more closely allied to Him

⁶ *On Music*, Book VI. ch. 11.

⁷ *Commentary on St. Matthew*, ch. 9. It must not be inferred from this doctrine that the resistance made to passion is less meritorious in virgins than in the faithful. If it is true, that the violence of temptation increases the merit of him who repulses it, it also holds good that real merit is acquired in diminishing by the practice of virtue, the use of the Sacraments, and by prayer the impetuosity and dangers of the enemy's attacks.

than any man in the world, in some measure share in apostolic privileges. Tradition and daily experience of the cloister leave us no room for doubt.

It is true that after days of blessed truce, the warfare recommences and throws the soul into inevitable turmoil; but this is but for a moment, and is lessened by the fact of one's not yielding to temptation, as also by the abstinence and other corporal exercises suited to religious life. On the other hand, the anxieties of the state of ordinary chastity are continual and increasing, since the inclination towards sensual enjoyment augments by the very fact that we are not forbidden their use. In a word, even lawful indulgence is a far greater hindrance to contemplation than would be caused by the vigorous resistance to all sensual desires. Here, at any rate, if the soul is disturbed, it is not overwhelmed by the flesh; insomuch that virginity may claim as exclusively its own, the glory of giving to the Christian, first, strength, and secondly, calm in strength.

However blinded he may be by the darkness of the present world, man cannot altogether ignore how far the immaterial and incorruptible essence of God, of the angelic spirits and the soul, surpass in dignity those things which are material and corruptible. Perverted as he is by guilt, he cannot prevent his heart from feeling sometimes a pure attraction for spiritual goods, and a profound disgust for earthly pleasures. This is because man has, notwithstanding all his wickedness, an innate and unconquerable horror of corruption. What a fearful sight, indeed, is that of a being in decay and becoming putrified, turning into rottenness, the last remnants of which dissolve into stinking and filthy mire! In the material order, our eyes could not support such a sight, and would turn away from it with disgust. Alas! why has not our soul an equal aversion to moral corruption, which is a thousand times more hideous? Yet the name of "corrupted creature" still remains one of the most ignominious with which human language can brand the sinner; if graven, on a forehead of brass, it would cause it even to blush. And to whom does this shameful name belong if not to the unchaste. The creature which thus corrupts itself proves that it belongs to the lower order of creation, that it is made of clay and dirt. The mind can not be made to undergo this degradation, save when it falls below itself by imitating the weakness of the flesh.

The being which thus degrades itself proves that it possesses within its breast a principle of division, a leaven of dissolution and rebellion; and this principle, this leaven, is nought but matter, or some sin which imitates its sorry properties.

This corrupt being proves, moreover, that it surrenders itself to the triumphant force of matter, and confesses that it has not sufficient strength to stop the progress of decay and ruin.

Now, the flesh is never so unbridled, nor does it ever rage with such feverish ardour as in the man given up to sensual enjoyments. Nowhere else is the disunion of our soul so complete. Nowhere is the soul so degraded, debased, crushed, or materialized by the tyranny of the flesh. In no case, is the Christian so far removed from the incorruptibility of Jesus Christ. Even as sacramental grace penetrates from the soul into all the members into which it infuses supernatural qualities, as a preparation and pledge of a glorious immortality; so, likewise, passions leave in the mind and even in the flesh fatal predispositions to other bad desires, to other crimes, and finally to the torments of hell. "His bones shall be filled with the vices of his youth, and they shall sleep with him in the dust."[8] And this corruption is inseparable from pleasures of the senses, even when they are authorized by reason, and regulated by ordinary chastity, which though it frees the conscience from sin, fails to preserve that splendour and charm of perfect spirituality, which is the distinct privilege of virginity. It is to virginity alone that we can apply with all truth the prophetic words of the Psalmist: "Thou wilt not leave my soul in hell; nor wilt thou suffer thy holy one to see corruption."[9]

Virginity, says our profound Doctor, seems to derive its name from the freshness and greenness of plants; for, this is the sign of a vitality in the vegetable world which has not suffered from an excess of heat; so virginity is the state of one who is not stricken by the flame of concupiscence, and who has known, as St. Isidore of Seville expresses it, how to preserve from the corruption of vice the bloom and the innocence of

[8] Job xx. 11.   [9] Ps. xv. 10.

his first youth.[10] "Virginity," says the great theologian, St. Augustine, "is the consecration, the dedication, and the preservation of the integrity of the flesh. It is the portion of the Angels; it is in the corruptible flesh, the love and the possession of an eternal incorruption."[11] And St. Ambrose: "It is an integrity nothing in the world has ever tarnished or wounded."[12] We have seen that it spiritualizes the body as perfectly as is possible in this present life, and that it extinguishes, little by little, that central source of sin, which is the inclination of the senses to the pleasures forbidden by reason. It prevents, moreover, the flame of impurity from drying up the soft dew which the grace of Baptism and of other sacraments has shed in our person. It prevents passion from introducing disorder between the body and soul, or between the divers faculties of the soul itself. It abolishes each day more and more that law of the flesh which is in conflict with the law of the spirit. In a word, it destroys the reign

---

[10] *Etymologies,* Book II.; the word *Virgin.*

[11] *On Holy Virginity,* ch. 8 and 13.

[12] *On Virgins,* Book I.

of sensuality, and stifles the germs of division in man. It consequently suppresses corruption itself in its two-fold cause, and by restoring to the soul its original incorruptibility, it communicates that privilege to the corruptible body. Death will deal respectfully with this virginal body, and if it does not exempt it from the dissolution of the tomb, as it did the body of Jesus the King of virgins, that of Mary Virgin of all virgins, and of others besides, it does not at least deprive it of that precious spirituality which will bloom as the lily on the day of resurrection.

Corruption is the principle of ugliness; virginity the source of beauty. It is vain for passion to deck itself with false splendour, or to adorn itself with frivolous ornaments. It is the most frightful of all other vices, because its movements are less under the control of the will, its enjoyments more fully absorb reason, and, finally, the irresistible disorder which accompanies it, is the sign of original sin, the punishment of our first and universal rebellion against God. It is of this ugliness that it is written: "Man when he was in honour did not understand; he hath been compared to the senseless beasts, and made like to them."[13] The body, likewise, is always its slave, even in the holy and Christian state of marriage. "It is an undeniable fact that sensual pleasures are the most hideous and the most slavish," says St. Thomas, "because they are common both to man and to the brutes." Oh! holy religious virginity, be thou for ever blessed for having given to us so many chaste and brilliant generations stamped with the seal of real beauty. Thanks to thee, the honour, the glory, and the splendour of the angels are realized in our race; without thee we should have been condemned to grovel in the dark paths of a dense animal world. Thou art the crown of the Church and of the whole of creation. We owe to thee our purest gracefulness, our mildest light, our most heavenly perfumes.

Blessed St. Dionysius, the Areopagite, says, that true beauty consists in a well measured proportion of suitable elements;[14] and according to the great Doctor of Seville, St. Isidore, honour is the freedom of a soul from which is banished all that is shameful.[15] Although

---

[13] Psalm xlviii. 21.
[14] *On Divine Names*, ch. 4.
[15] *Etymologies*, Book X.; the word *Shame*.

other virtues may procure us more excellent goods,[16] religious chastity has over them the advantage of maintaining in us the most exact, and at the same time most difficult proportion, between mind and matter, between reason and the senses, between the will and natural concupiscence. It is, therefore, in us the supreme principle of beauty. And as it is constantly intent on preserving us from the greatest infamies which can degrade us, it is also for us the best title of honour.

If we define still more clearly this notion of beauty by limiting it to things of the moral order, we shall discover, *firstly*, that spiritual beauty consists in the order established by the mind, in the performance of a great variety of human acts which always require some effort of virtue, and that an ancient has most justly observed, " beauty is that which is conformable to the excellence of man, to that excellence which distinguishes him from the rest of living creatures."[17] Spiritual ugliness

---

[16] Religious chastity is in fact a virtue *subordinate* to religion and charity, which serve as its end.

[17] Cicero on *Duties*, Book I.

is, consequently, the want of order in our life, the default of conformity between our works and that which is most exalted and most noble within us. But if there is a point where the power and wisdom of reason are revealed in their entirety, if there is an enterprise where the perfection and the superiority proper to us are manifested in all their brilliancy, it is without a shadow of doubt when our soul renounces the most seducing and most lively pleasures of the flesh, in order to attach itself the more freely to the invisible goods of the spirit. Man appears then even greater than his nature, and worthy to be likened to the angels; he then reaches the highest expression of beauty which his sojourn on this earth permits Divine grace to realize in him.

Secondly, spiritual beauty can be no more conceived of by us than physical beauty, unless by an agreeable light, which as a delicate splendour shines upon elements harmoniously disposed by reason. "God," as the pseudo Areopagite further observes, "is the sovereign beauty, inasmuch as He is the source of harmony and splendour in all creatures;"[18] and St. Thomas thence concludes

[18] *Divine Names*, ch. 4.

that moral or intelligible beauty consists in the works of man being enlightened and directed by the spiritual light of reason. If, then, we attribute beauty and splendour to ordinary chastity, should we not with still greater reason, declare, that religious virginity possesses the treasure of marvellous beauty? Where is the body more illuminated, more transfigured, more spiritualized by the intellect and the will? Where is the light of the soul more dazzling and more triumphant? Where does thought so absolutely govern feeling? Where does contemplation so completely replace the enjoyments of the body? "Who can imagine," asks St. Ambrose, " a grander beauty than that of virginity, which is loved by the King, approved by the Judge, bound to the Lord, and consecrated to God?"[19] And St. Cyprian wrote long before: "We now turn our discourse to virgins, the care of whose souls is the dearer to us, as their glory is the more sublime. They are the flower of the Church's field, the charm and ornament of spiritual grace, the most illustrious portion of the flock of Christ; the joy of our heart, a gladsome condition of life, a perfect work of

[19] *On Virgins*, Book I.

honour and praise, an image of God corresponding perfectly with the sanctity of Christ."[20] Lastly, this interior beauty which is reflected so often exteriorly by the nobleness and purity of the countenance, receives from heaven a last and ineffable perfection by the halo which will glitter in the souls and on the foreheads of virgins. Even as the sacred table, whereon were placed the show-bread offered to the God of Israel in His mysterious tabernacle, was first adorned by a crown of gold and over the same another little golden crown,[21] So, say the disciples of St. Thomas, besides the diadem awarded to the elect, God gives a aureola, a special glory and joy to those Christians who have distinguished themselves in this world by their more brilliant victories, and by their more entire conformity with Jesus Christ the Conqueror. And what an admirable triumph is that which virgins win over their own flesh! What likeness have they not to the Divine Lamb whom they follow whithersoever He goeth, because they imitate Him, says St. Augustine, not only in the integrity of the soul, but also in the integ-

---

[20] *On Virginity*, Book I.
[21] Exod. xxv. 25.

rity of the flesh![22] And whilst martyrs and doctors have also their halos, virgins receive a brilliancy proportioned to the length, constancy and dangers of their warfare, which often proves more perilous than the torment of the prætorium or the conflict of the amphitheatre. They sing a new canticle, that is to say, unknown to nature, dictated by the grace only of Jesus Christ. The Word puts on their lips a lovely and sweet harmony, which rehearses to the whole of heaven the beauty of their life and the union and peace which they have known how to preserve in their spiritualized nature. Blessed are they who shall see this pageant, blessed the ears that shall hear these songs, but still more blessed are they who shall be called to take part in them, in order to glorify for ever the Son of the immaculate Virgin.

If religious perfection reproduces in man the unity, strength, incorruptibility and the beauty of our Lord Jesus Christ, it is principally from virginity that it derives its means, and that it reaps its merit. Poverty had prepared our transfiguration by the retrenchment of exterior goods, virginity continues it by

[22] *On Holy Virginity*, ch. 27.

immolation of the body. Obedience will consummate it by the sacrifice of the will itself, so that there will remain nothing of man which is not purified, consecrated and fashioned to the likeness of the second and true Adam.

CHAPTER VII.

Religious Obedience.

The visible world is to us as a mirror in which we can contemplate the invisible world, reflected therein. The order of material creation is the symbolical imitation of the harmony established by God in the spiritual sphere, for the plan of Providence is, perfect unity, concord and beauty.

Matter, mind and grace form a harmonious whole, wherein the same divine idea is developed, and every part is closely connected and rendered subordinate one to another, according as it reproduces more or less perfectly, the likeness of its sole model, which is the infinite essence of God.

Now, nothing is isolated or detached in the material order of nature. All is combined and all is allied. The inferior forces are at the service of those powers which God has destined to fulfil a more exalted mission, and they receive in return from the former the impulse required by them for the performance of their respective functions. Thus physical motion descends from the first and immoveable Author of the world to the smallest grain of sand borne away by the tempest. In the moral order, minds are equally associated amongst themselves and arranged in similar gradations. The Angel receives his light from the Archangel and communicates it to man. And, in the natural order, the will of the son is directed by the will of the father, the mind of the disciple is led forward in its progress by the mind of his master, the subject is moved by the order of his sovereign. So too the primordial impulse given by the Word Himself is transmitted, step by step, to the darkest mind and the weakest heart.

From the moment that our Lord destines

us to a special end, and the more particularly to this most noble and elevated end of religious perfection, He necessarily places us in a hierarchical current by which we receive the assistance indispensable to the success of our undertaking. Not that He deprives Himself of the right of communicating His actual graces directly to us, but He gives them to us upon the very just condition of our remaining in our own sphere, or of restoring us to it should we have unhappily abandoned it.

The spiritual impulse which determines us to any act of the soul, is imprinted upon it by a law or precept of a superior will, and we receive it by obedience. It is therefore certain that the religious aspiring to perfection should be obedient. To refuse this direction, or to pretend to independence, is to tear oneself away from the path marked out by God's Providence, to withdraw from the supreme authority of God, and is a violation of both the divine and natural law, whilst it senselessly deprives us of the only means suited to the attainment of our proposed end. But the Divine Will is the necessary, eternal and supreme rule of all our actions, and if it pleases It to establish between Itself and us an intermediate will, in nearer connexion than ourselves with that heaven where resides the source of all legitimate power, that medium although created and finite like yourself will, however, become your rule, secondary, indeed, but still obligatory. "He that resisteth the power, resisteth the ordinance of God," says St. Paul;[1] "and to obey it, is an act of great justice."[2] It is also an act of real love for oneself. For, says the admirable St. Thomas, the virtue of an inferior, whoever he may be, consists in being submissive to his superior. The perfection of the air is to be lightened by the sun which is its King; the perfection of the body is to be quickened by the soul, which is the formal principle of its movements; the perfection of the sensitive powers is in

---

[1] Rom. xiii. 2.

[2] There is no question here of common justice based upon the equality of rights and duties, but of a justice so much the more necessary as we are nothing in the sight of God. Obedience, so far as it is a virtue apart, is the constant inclination to perform the commands and so to submit to the right of a superior. It here supposes that the *act commanded is necessary;* but at the same time that man is *independent* and *willing* to perform it. There can be no obedience where there is no free will.

their perfect obedience to the intellect, which is their guide; the perfection of the whole man consists in his being the faithful subject of God Who is his Creator and last end. But if this dependence be in any way violated, if the ties of obedience be loosened between the master and his servant, the latter recedes from his position, is in dis-accord with the spirit of his state, and deviates from the path of perfection. And, while he wishes to shake off his state of inferiority and become independent and free, he is no more than a miserable rebel, who has fallen into error, falsehood, and disorder far below that former condition which so humbled his pride, and which should on the contrary have gladdened his spirit. Such being the case, with what sweet confidence should not religious submit to the laws, commands and directions of their rules and superiors? These divers manifestations of the Will of God are for them an inexhaustible source of perfection and happiness. In obeying them they accustom themselves to the practice of an infinity of pious works; they acquire virtue; they dispose themselves to ascend higher and higher by the immediate action of the Holy Ghost, they preserve and increase His gifts, and after having borne, perhaps with anguish, the sacred yoke of obedience, they find in it at last an enjoyment such as the independence of the world can never give to its votaries.

Religious obedience rests on still more precious and precise reasons. The regular life being the school of the privileged disciples of our Lord Jesus Christ, their perfection will be so much the greater, as the imitation of this Divine Master shall be the more complete. "If thou wilt be perfect," says Jesus Christ Himself, "come *follow me*."[3] Now, of all His virtues not one of them is more highly extolled by the Prophets, Evangelists, or Apostles, than His absolute, unhesitating and unfaltering obedience. "For that which is pleasing to My Father, that do I always."[4] "He humbled Himself, becoming obedient unto death, even to the death of the cross."[5] And such is and has been in every age the distinctive and glorious mark of the perfect Christian, as well as an efficacious instrument of his progression in spiritual life.

As the religious state is an apprenticeship, a system of supernatural education, a series of

[3] Matt. xix. 21.   [4] John viii. 29.
[5] Phillip ii. 8.

exercises destined to give us all the development of which we are capable with the aid of grace, it is certain that we should observe that fundamental law of every school, which obliges the disciple to follow the advice of a discreet person, to act conformably with his method, to meditate upon and to remember his lessons. Thus only can he derive fruit from his instructions, and thus only can we attain learning and virtue. Religious are, consequently, bound by the law both of God and of reason to submit to the authority of a guide and chief in all such matters as lead them to perfection. Has not the holy Pope, St. Gregory, said: "Obedience is the only virtue which implants the other virtues in our souls, and which maintains them after having implanted them."[6] Doubtless it is no easy matter to eradicate from our hearts the deep roots of the natural love we have of our independence and unshakled direction of our lives. Can one, exclaims the worldling, forego the sweets, and, as he fancies, the merit of a life free from every restraint, and in which nothing compels us to spend ourselves for God? Nonsense! Is it not preferable to offer daily

[6] *Morals*, Book XXXV.

to heaven a spontaneous homage, than to immolate oneself by a single impulse of unreflecting or blind enthusiasm? But it is in this precisely that man manifests all his power and dignity. Left, as the Scriptures express it, in the hands of his own counsel, he makes the most noble use of this privilege by determining to obey the commands of a superior will. "By submitting humbly to the voice of another, he rises above himself in his own heart."[7] Far from being constrained or enslaved he shows himself perfectly free, since he often performs acts of virtue which are unpleasing to him, either on account of their intrinsic difficulty or of their oppositions to his natural passions and tendencies, or by the intervention of some external enemy. Superior to all these obstacles, stronger than himself, he soars aloft like the mountain eagle in defiance of the despicable trammels by which they seek to arrest his flight. And because religious obedience derives its strength from the thought of God, whom it acknowledges in its superiors, every act, however insignificant, possesses the highest value. It is for God, for His love, and for His glory

[7] St. Gregory the Great, *ibid.*

that these are performed, they bear the twofold character of charity and religion; they are as so many sacrifices in which the victim is all that man holds most precious, namely, his own will, which for the sake of God, he submits to that of another, and although these actions performed at the command of a superior have not the merit of being gratuitous or spontaneous, yet, they receive from the obedient will, a perfection which superabundantly compensates for it. Does not man therefore show more humility and greater energy in obeying, than in following the bent of his own inclinations?

Were this important theory of the Angelic Doctor properly understood, it would deliver many religious persons from the incessant temptation which torments them, of performing works of supererogation, to the neglect of their rules and of the wishes of their superiors. Should one have to forego, out of obedience, many mortifications, prayers and pious occupations, he ought to be comforted for their loss by the merit of obedience, as well as by the merit of the works which it sets us to do. According to Cassian, the ancient fathers, whose *Conferences* he published, used to say that the worst kind of monks were the Sarabaïtes, because, though they spent more time both by night and day in prayer and work than any of those who lived in monasteries, they undertook to provide for their own wants, were independent of the yoke of the elders, and were allowed to live according to their own good pleasure and inclination.

In truth, though inferior to the theological virtues, particularly to charity, and subordinate to the virtue of religion, from which it derives the motive of its acts,[8] obedience is the most perfect of all moral virtues—more excellent than either religious poverty or chastity. Amongst these virtues, says the Angel of the School, the chief is that which despises the greatest earthly advantages, in order to attach

---

[8] The motive of obedience to God is the respect with which His excellence inspires us: now it is by devotion, the principal act of religious virtue, that we render to this Sovereign Master the respect due to Him. In obedience to superiors, next to this first and chief motive, we are also impelled by a feeling of piety, or as the School expresses it, of *observance, i.e.,* reverence. Faith enlightens us supernaturally as to all these motives, and hope and charity impel us to carry them into effect.

itself to God. Now, there are three kinds of created goods which man may abandon in order to follow the Lord. Firstly, exterior goods, the most contemptible of all; secondly, corporal things, which hold the middle rank; and lastly, those of the soul, which are the most estimable. And amongst these, the most precious is the will, insomuch as it places man in possession of all other goods. This is why, according to the natural order of things, the virtue of obedience (which despises self-will, in order that it may the better serve God) is more praiseworthy than all other virtues which renounce for His sake only such things as are secondary. St. Gregory is of the same opinion when he says: "Obedience is justly considered better than sacrifice, as the sword of obedience destroys self-will."[9] The practice of the other virtues is, in fact, only meritorious in the sight of God, when they are performed in accordance with His divine will, for it would be useless to suffer martyrdom, or to distribute the whole of one's wealth to the poor, unless we desired, at the same time, to act conformably with the divine laws or counsels, in other words, we

[9] *Morals*, Book XXXV.

should in that supposition be acting without charity, for charity itself is impossible without obedience. "He who saith that he knoweth Him, and keepeth not His commandments, is a liar, and the truth is not in him; but he that keepeth His word, in him in very deed the charity of God is perfected."[10] For it is friendship or charity which makes two minds to be of one accord, both in what they love and in what they hate.

Need we add, that obedience, like holy poverty, has also its limits. The reason of this is, that self-will is not universally and essentially opposed to the religious state, like sensual gratifications, every act of which the virtue of virginity inexorably excludes. One makes profession of an unbounded chastity, but not of an absolute obedience. There are, firstly, things forbidden by the law of God, which a superior cannot prescribe without injustice, since his will, being then no longer subordinate to the Divine Will, can no longer serve as a medium between him and his subject: this is equally applicable to a superior who places himself in opposition to a prelate, of a more exalted hierarchical rank

[10] John ii. 4.

than his own, and who is consequently placed nearer to the sovereign Master. There are also things absolutely indifferent to the essence and laws of the religious state, as, for instance, says St. Thomas, to pluck up from the earth a blade of grass: they do not belong to any virtue, they do not bear either upon the love of God nor that of one's neighbour, and are only sinful when they are forbidden, and they cannot be forbidden, because they are neither helps nor hindrances to perfection. They are therefore without the pale of obedience, and the superior has no authority to enforce them. Neither has he any over such things as are purely interior, as the inward movements of our will, or over the life of his subjects, whom he cannot oblige to excessive austerities or insupportable labours. Religious, concludes our Doctor, bind themselves to obedience, according to the regular life to which they are subject by their prelates, and are therefore bound only to that obedience which bears upon the religious life, and this obedience suffices for salvation. If they choose to obey also in things indifferent to their state, this will be the fulness of perfection, provided that in so doing they do not act contrary to the law of God or to the rule which they profess to follow; for such obedience would be illicit. Thence we distinguish a threefold obedience. The *first*, *sufficient* for salvation, being obedience in all matters of obligation, the other *perfect*, because it obeys in all things, even though they be permitted, the third *indiscreet*, because by it we obey, even in that which is sinful.

Notwithstanding its limits, religious obedience, as compared with that of seculars towards either their ecclesiastical or secular superiors, is as the universal is to the individual, or as the whole is to the integral parts of which it is composed. Living in the midst of the world, man retains the habitual control of his actions, sacrificing only that little to God which He claims, either by His commandments, or by the just laws of the powers He has established. But in the cloister, man abandons himself absolutely to an authority which deliberates and decides instead of the religious, which gives the impulse which he must simply follow, determines the end he must obey without discussion, puts in his hand the instrument of his perfection, which he should employ with gratitude and cheerfulness. This is the holocaust in place of the mere sacrifice, the absolute renouncement of all earthly goods, even of those most dear to man, which will enable him to devote himself with a greater feeling of religion, and with greater tranquillity and energy, to the contemplation and love of the eternal goods.

Let no one imagine that the virtue of obedience is not of equal necessity to experienced religious, who have been long exercised in the practices of regular life, and have attained the height of wisdom and spiritual perfection. It is more particularly essential that these last should prove themselves the most faithful, humble, prompt and exact in the observance of every iota of the rules and every command of the superior. These, especially, must anticipate the rule, and be submissive, even to the tacit desires of their superiors, as soon as they are sufficiently intimated to them. In fact, it is not enough to have made great progress, and to be esteemed very holy and perfect. We must persevere in this exalted position, and preserve the fruits of our victories; and this is only possible by the employment of the same means as served for progress in and acquisition of virtue. Should these means be neglected, and obedience despised, the mind will be at once disquieted, the heart distracted and divided by a thousand interests and personal anxieties; and by withdrawing self-will from the altar of sacrifice, where it was but so recently and so generously immolated, we no longer offer the best part of our religious life to God, but to an idol. Besides, if anyone has really acquired perfection, how can we suppose that he will feel the yoke of obedience to be a burden? After having so long fulfilled its duties, will not the habit have become a second nature to him; and will not this habit incline him joyously, frequently, even naturally to abandon himself, without any reserve, to the power that guides him? The true proof of religious sanctity, the sure token of perfection, is the perfection of obedience to all superiors, even should their age or defects render them apparently unworthy of their charge.

The superior is like a sacred vessel, wherein God has placed for us all His desires and graces. It signifies little whether it be of gold or of clay, the majesty of the King of kings overshadows it. Our admirable Doctor also compares the superior to Mount Sinai, when the Lord declared thereon His laws to Moses, and commanded that anyone approaching it, within the prescribed limits, should perish;[11] or again, to the Ark of the Covenant, wherein were deposited the tables of the Law, which could not be rashly touched without the punishment of instant death.[12] Thus, regular prelates bear in themselves the treasure of the Divine law; and if it be sometimes permitted to reprove them with meekness and respect, it is never allowable to lay hands on their authority and reputation, by any movement of anger, contempt or malice. As an instance of a wholly opposite extreme, a religious might be found so naturally attached to the person of the superior, or lastly, so pleased and satisfied with that which he is ordered to do, as to lose the merit of obedience, by following his own inclinations rather than an authority coming from God. Religious should be on their guard against such pernicious dispositions, and great care must be taken to consider in the superior, not only his personal qualities, but his authority—not nature, but grace.

This whole doctrine clearly shows that

[11] Exod. xix. 13.   [12] 2 Kings vi. 7.

strict religious obedience should be shown more especially to the Sovereign Pontiff and to Bishops.[13] The Catholic Episcopacy, who have but one only chief, as the Doctor expresses it, is the highest state of perfection that Jesus Christ has established in His Church; and conformably with the law of transmission, by which the supernatural impulse descends through the medium of hierarchical degrees, the Episcopacy is also the instrument by which grace is shed upon the faithful in general, and particularly on monastic orders; Bishops lead the people to perfection, and people can never advance in that heavenly path, except by submitting to the authority of their princes, their fathers and pastors. "The religious state," says the Pseudo-Dionysius, "is subject to the hallowing powers of the Pontiffs, and is instructed by their divine illuminations;"[14] and this mainly holds good, continues the Angel of the School, of the Supreme Pontiff—the Bishop above all other bishops—of that master who teaches by his infallible judgment and decision. Thus,

---

[13] It is clear that this does not in any way affect the true doctrine on the exemption of regulars.

[14] *Ecclesiastical Hierarchy*, ch. 2.

all regulars, both superiors and inferiors, are bound to obey our Holy Father the Pope, not only in those things common to all the faithful, but also in such as bear more immediately upon religious discipline. And this necessity of obeying the Bishop of Rome is so great, that although he can dispense religious from the submission promised by them to their prelates, he cannot exempt them from that obedience which they owe to St. Peter and his successor, in those matters which concern the perfection of regular life.

As the inferior angels receive from the more exalted choirs knowledge and special missions, so too, in the Church militant, the true doctrine, and the good impulses of our Lord are communicated to us by him who has the charge of feeding the sheep and lambs; yea, by him who has the power to confirm his brethren. He distributes wholesome food, he inspires the breath of true interior life, and is the doctor of genuine piety as well as of orthodox faith. He determines the legitimate import of the vows and rules of religion, as he does that of the Gospel. Rome is the guiding star for those who seek Jesus Christ. Rome is the quickening spirit; finally, in

Rome resides the only true sanctity, since our Lord has bestowed sanctity upon His Church, even as He has given her unity, catholicity and apostolicity;—all this He has pledged to that Church built upon Peter, which word signifies a rock. So that the perfection of souls and the rectitude of minds must spring from the soil which was cultivated by the mighty and immortal hand of Peter.

Obedience is of essential necessity to the government of the world, and particularly to that providential government by which God leads man on to perfection. It is the ordinary channel of grace, the characteristic mark of the true disciples of Jesus Christ, the key to spiritual science, the triumph of perfection over an imperfect nature, and the victory of liberty over those fetters which are vulgarly mistaken for independence. It is also a most excellent act of religion; and although it has bounds which we may not exceed, still it is the noblest of the three virtues of the regular state. Practised with an upright and supernatural intention, it opens to us the very heart of the Church, and allows us to draw from thence treasures of knowledge and strength.

CHAPTER VIII.
Religious Vows.

WHEN there is a question of realizing the work of religious perfection, God and the soul join together and mutually aid each other in the struggle. Firstly, God sheds upon the path which man must pursue, the bright radiance of the three counsels of poverty, chastity, and obedience, and the mind expanding under the influence of this threefold truth, takes it in and meditates thereon. Then the will is moved thereby under the impression of grace, it determines to act conformably with the designs of this good and bounteous Providence, and thus do the evangelical counsels lead to the practices of the three virtues of the regular state. It is indeed from Our Lord that the soul will receive those supernatural virtues which are henceforth to animate it, and to urge it to so many acts conducive to its advancement;[1] but on its own side, actuated by a holy greed for spiritual goods, it aspires to be poor, chaste,

---

[1] In fact it is not the virtues of themselves, but the actions which proceed from them that lead man to perfection : inactive virtue would avail him little.

and obedient. It is ever labouring to become so, and to continue so. It is not God who imposes on the soul these eternal chains, but it is the soul who solicits and lovingly binds itself with them. It is not God who takes possession of man against his own will, rather it is man who consecrates himself voluntarily, by imprinting on his whole being the inviolable seal of religion; it is he who by the poverty, virginity, and obedience, which he heretofore may have practised as common virtues, takes upon himself that poverty, virginity and obedience, which are both *religious* and *perpetual*.

This co-operation, by which the Christian associates himself with the divine impulse in order to mould himself upon the model of the evangelical counsels, and thus to acquire religious virtues and perfection mainly consists in *the profession of three religious vows*[2] in

---

[2] The word *profession* signifies, firstly the exterior and authentic manifestation of a resolution one has taken, and now fulfils, of embracing a *state*, say for instance the religious state. By an extension of the meaning, the *state* itself sometimes bears this name, which we always use in its primitive sense. A *vow* is composed of three necessary elements: deliberation of the mind, determination of the will, and that which is

a public, formal, and authentic declaration, the nature and effects of which we must study. For this purpose it will be now necessary to go back over several points already explained; but who could begrudge the repetition, yea even a hundred times, of those grand principles, which the Angelic Doctor inscribes at the head of nearly every page of his works? A science is never so complete as when a few simple and evident truths illuminate all its ramifications.

The Holy Doctors point out to us in the old Testament, noble types or figures of the catholic religious. These are the Nazarenes, to whom the great apostle disdained not to ally himself on two occasions[3] borrowing both their rites and customs. Their names signify those who were set apart from the profane vulgar,

most essential of all, a promise made to God by the reason, under the impulse of the will. We shall see elsewhere the important result of this promise. Although many orders add to the vows of poverty, chastity, and obedience, some vow peculiar to themselves, for instance one of absolute devotion to the Holy See in the matter of missions, we speak here only of the three vows essential to every order, and which serve as a centre and type of the others.

[3] Acts xviii. 18; xxi. 26.

so were made *pure;* or, taking another interpretation, those who were the *flower* of the nation. They abstained from wine and intoxicating drinks, they maintained a dignified bearing, and they were forbidden to come in contact with the dead. They were holy and consecrated to God, and their sanctification was effected by a series of symbolical sacrifices.[4] And though their separation was but temporary, and their sanctity but exterior and legal, they obtained neither these advantages nor this perfection, except by an oblation of themselves to God; they were accordingly consecrated by a *vow* in order to be Nazarenes. How much more excellent is the condition of our religious, true Nazarenes indeed, the immediate and chosen disciples of Him who suffered Himself to be called the son of a carpenter of Nazareth. They are withdrawn from the midst of the crowd, they lead lives which are both austere and pure, uncorrupted by the contamination of vice and untarnished by death. They are united to God, not only by legal sacrifices, but by the holocaust of their own persons. The sanctity to which they aspire is that of the soul; the perfection

[4] Numbers vi. 1—21.

which they would acquire is like the beauty of the King's daughter, so much the more real as it abides in the heart. It is that the power of the vow has, so to speak, seized and transported them out of this world; this spiritual sword has destroyed in them the life of earth, to substitute for it the life of angels.

The intervention of these sacred agents, the vows, is especially important at the outset of the religious life, because at this time what is needed is not merely to produce a temporary sanctification, or to implant a mere habit in the soul, but to fix oneself in a special kind of life, and to enter upon a permanent state.

We have to give to those virtues, upon which this state rests, the solidity indispensable to the foundation of a great edifice, in such a way, that they be no longer mere virtues, but states of life, the state of poverty, the state of chastity, and the state of obedience.

Let us clearly note this difference between a *virtue* and a *state*. Even as every man who knows how to bear arms, or to defend himself occasionally from the attacks of an enemy is not necessarily a soldier; nor because he is acquainted with the rules of agriculture and of domestic economy, is he a farmer; so too a man is not necessarily living in a state of perfection, because he is perfect; nor is he a religious because he practises the religious virtues of poverty and obedience. There is still wanting to him that which forms the social condition, that which determines his rank and duties.

There are two things which principally contribute to this end, says St. Thomas. First, that man be *bound* by a new obligation, or *loosed* from one by which he was formerly restrained, in fact that there be a change in his freedom. Thus he who serves a master is not for that reason in a state of slavery, since men, who are wholly free, may continually render service to others; but to make him a slave it is essential that he should be obliged to serve, and bound by that invisible bond which is called the debt of justice. Again, a slave does not pass into the state of freedom the moment he ceases to serve his master, since a slave may rebel against his master or run away; but to become a free man, he must be loosed from his bond, and on this condition only, does he become a free man.

Religious vows tend directly to bring about this result. They impose on the Christian a new obligation, and altogether discharge him from servitude. They bind him to the exercise of perfection, and to the search after it; they make him a subject, a servant, the happy slave of the divine service; they put on him the livery of Jesus poor, of Jesus chaste, of Jesus crucified by obedience. Previously, this man might watch over his temporal interests; now his mind must be fixed on heaven; once his own master, he now belongs to himself no more. He may have already courageously fought under the banner of the divine counsels, but he was after all but a volunteer, free to abandon this spiritual camp of perfection at his pleasure; but now, under pain of treason, he must live, fight, and die under the shadow of his standard. Consider again what new liberty—what a gladsome release—the yoke of his new captivity engenders. These vows have burst the heavy chains, and broken a humiliating yoke which his virtues had scarce availed to lighten. The professed religious is a man perfect in liberty, disembarrassed of the goods of this world, to which he once gave a share of his thoughts and of his heart; he has declared himself independent of secular affections, even of those which are pure and legitimate, so as no longer to love other than God or in God. He has freed himself from himself, from his own will and its caprices, and with still greater reason from those most alluring and frequent occasions productive of sin. Oh how brilliant and sweet art thou, blessed morn, that hearest the voice which pronounces these three vows, that witnessest this admirable profession of captivity and liberty, and seest this Christian stepping with celestial happiness over the threshold of a new state.

The second condition required for the constitution of a particular state in human society is first of all a public and solemn act. Before the sight of God, whose all-seeing Eye searches our reins and hearts, interior virtues, the good and evil hidden in the recesses of our soul, sufficiently separate us one from the other; but to distinguish us before men, to establish a special mode of life in the exterior and visible world, needs equally apparent and exterior signs. In the civil order the installation of a judge, governor, or prince, is accompanied by splendour which is significant of the authority entrusted to them, and of the obedience and reverence henceforth due to them from the people. In the Church the ordination of a deacon or priest, the consecration of a bishop, or the enthronement of a Sovereign Pontiff, solemnly attests that the authority of Jesus Christ Himself is transmitted to His ministers, and from this transmission, thus manifested by authentic signs, results a new state.

Such, too, is the office of religious vows. They are pronounced in the presence of the Church, at the foot of its holy altars, and during its sacred mysteries. The religious has quitted his father's house for the retirement of the cloister, and is stripped of his secular garb to be clothed in a mantle symbolical of poverty; he has exchanged the manners and customs of the world for the austere practice of his rule, and now he loudly proclaims that he consecrates himself to the perpetual service of God. The liturgical prayers of the Church correspond with this threefold engagement. "Mystical invocations," says the Pseudo-Arëopagite,[5] "are granted him by the Church for his sanctification;" and finally his profession is authenti-

---

[5] Chap. vi. *Ecclesiastical Hierarchy.*

cally drawn up to be perpetually preserved in the monastic archives. Thus religious virtues become stable and permanent and the regular state is established, and thus is accomplished one of the principal laws laid down by our Lord for the school of His chosen disciples.

This Divine Master and Supreme Doctor of perfection will not suffer in His guard of honour any man who abandons Him for the sake of vulgar interests, or who basely retraces his steps. "No man, putting his hand to the plough and looking back, is fit for the Kingdom of God."[6]

Jesus requires faithful souls who, far from imitating those to whom His company is burthensome, will ask with St. Peter, "Lord, to whom shall we go?"[7] "He requires resolute and constant followers like," as St. Augustine says, "to this same Peter and his brother Andrew, who did not move their barks to the shore for the purpose of returning to them; but who followed Jesus and remained under the light yoke of His words."[8] Now this stability, this necessity, so to call it, of being perfect is given to us by religious vows, pro-

[6] Luke ix. 62.   [7] John vi. 69.
[8] *Agreement of the Evangelists*, Book II, Chap. 17.

curing for us in the present life some resemblance to our Heavenly Father, who is immutable in His perfection, and to the elect who enjoy the eternal rest and happiness of heaven. There is no need, oh World, for thee to be so exasperated or affrighted at the thought of these irrevocable promises made to God at a time even when youth but begins to blossom! There is in them nothing mournful, and nothing formidable, they are but the novitiate of heaven, and the first breaking of the dawn of the beatific vision. There we shall be holy and happy without the possibility of being otherwise; here already the religious is relieved from the burden of riches, purified from the contagion of pleasures, and freed from the dangers of independence, without being overwhelmed, stained, or led astray. What, then, is more true than those words of the Bishop of Hippo? "Do not repent of having pronounced vows; but rather rejoice because things which would have been permitted you to your detriment are now forbidden you. O blessed necessity, which obliges us to be more holy." [9] The effect of the three

[9] *Letter the XLIV. to Armentaria and Paulina.* St. Thomas makes the useful observation that the

religious vows is not only to impart to religious virtues that permanency and solemnity which makes of them a true state; they have also a similar efficiency with regard to our acts, which are so transient and so soon forgotten. For this is the exclusive privilege of God, that His actions, or rather, His one adorable act is eternal, even as is His nature. We never could say that God *has* acted; His act is always present without beginning,

obligation resulting from vows does not subject us to any violence or constraint, and consequently diminishes neither the freedom nor the merit of our works, neither does it detract from that true liberty which consists not in the capability of sinning, but in the power of attaining, under the influence of reason and faith, the end which we propose to ourselves. This necessity, however, has not that advantage which comes either from a good and confirmed habit, or still more specially from the complete perfection of the elect, of increasing in us an inclination towards good, and of thus adding to our merits. It consists simply in this, that religious can neither preserve grace nor be saved unless they do the works to which they engaged themselves by vows; these acts then become necessary by their connexion with the end which they had in view, which was to honour God by a complete worship; and as the excellence of the end is reflected on the means, it follows that the necessity created by the vows gives a special religious merit to actions thus rendered obligatory.

although its effects seem to begin in time; they will not end, but continue to exist even when the creature upon whom it is now exercised shall have been for centuries buried in the dust. With us, on the contrary, our activity seems to be exhausted almost as soon as it is exercised, and our actions disappear the very moment that we give them birth. But the result of this religious profession is to fix them and render them immortal. By vows, says the great Doctor of Aquino, the will is strengthened and made immoveable in good, not only for one particular action, or for a determined time: but in a general manner for all future time, and for an infinity of good works. If the intention alone, preceding any one of our actions, extends its influence over the whole of our undertakings, and gives to them a moral and meritorious character, even should we in acting lose sight of the intention which first determined us. For example, it is not necessary that a man performing a pilgrimage in the honour of God should be incessantly occupied with this thought at every step that he takes. It is obvious that the efficacy of a vow will extend over the whole of his life. This sacred promise also shows that a man is not satisfied with wishing, but that he has endeavoured to strengthen himself against the inconstancy and instability of human nature by thus depriving himself of the possibility of not being virtuous. Again, when distractions, weariness, or sufferings hinder the mind or heart from tending courageously towards those works commanded by the rule; when attention to its duties, or the application to its exercises are so slight that the body alone appears to act without the participation of the soul, the vows will still instigate us to such actions, although they be to all appearance empty and dead, and will impart to them a truly supernatural worth.

This teaching is as full of mercy as it is profound. It certainly does not go so far as to countenance effeminacy or encourage spiritual lethargy, since it supposes that our actions thus vivified by preceding vows are not performed with such wilful distractions as to be culpable. But it reassures us against the almost inevitable invasion of routine, against the decline of our first piety, and against the cooling of our first fervour. Religious profession, with its certainty, its lights, its enthusiasm and transports of love, with its absolute renouncement and unbounded generosity perpetually subsists, not only in remembrance,[10] but by a real and powerful influence, in the midst of all the discouragements and spiritual dryness which the future usually reserves to souls eager for perfection. Neither custom which diminishes the attractiveness of monastic employments, nor the temptations which would appear to wrest from the heart its fidelity to the God of its youth, nor the distractions inherent to the active life, destroy religious vows. Life is still sustained by this three-fold vital principle, its actions are still heated by this fire of charity and merit. It may not be felt; but it exists, and this is one reason amongst many others, why one should prepare oneself with all possible care for regular profession, and accomplish it with heartfelt and earnest dispositions. The more abundant the source, and the further the waters spread, so much the more will their fertilizing influence be felt.

After this, we shall not be surprised to hear St. Thomas affirm that joy is the result of the vows. There is certainly one necessity which

---

[10] For the consolation procured by this remembrance see chap. ii. *The Evangelical Counsels.*

is grievous; it is that which those suffer who are constrained by violence, and in opposition to their own free choice. But the necessity resulting from religious profession is altogether in accordance with a well-disposed will; it confirms the Christian in his good resolutions, and gives him the liberty and help he requires for the attainment of perfection, and thus it gives him the purest joy that can fall to our lot in this world—the joy of feeling sufficiently strong to become perfect, and so to acquire the supreme joys of heaven.

It may happen that after he has pronounced his vows the religious will be called upon to perform duties which, considered in themselves, would sadden and displease his will. But if so, he should bear in mind how conducive these acts are to the attainment of his noble end, and a happiness so much the greater, as it is less human, will continue to reign in his heart.

Now, even as the evangelical counsels of poverty, chastity and obedience are the most important of all others practised in the cloister, so also the three religious vows are the chief columns which support the edifice of perfection. It is upon these, that the other monastic observances depend. Round them are grouped the constitutions, so that the vows may be styled the essence of the religious state. If there are in different communities different rules relative to the manner of procuring food for the maintenance of the body, if in one we find that manual labour is prescribed, in another humble and Christian mendicity, in others again other methods; all are brought to bear upon the vow of poverty, the true spirit of which must be observed in seeking after such things as are necessary for life. If there are rules prescribing corporal mortification, such as vigils, fasting and the discipline, they are in close relation with the vow of continence, the observance of which must be insured. If there are laws regarding spiritual reading, prayer, visiting the sick, the instruction of children, the care of the poor and of prisoners, they are closely allied to the vow of obedience, having the same end, namely, the increase of charity towards God and our neighbour. Finally, the determination of the habit worn by religious is a mark of the obligation imposed by the vow, and it is for this reason that the habit is blessed and definitely put on the novice the day of profession.

There is, however, one great thing which does not come within the pale of the vows, and which moreover is not accessory to them. It is perfection itself. The religious does not take the vow of perfection, because this is precisely the end that he aims at, and the end cannot be transformed into the means. Neither does he take a vow of charity, humility, patience, devotion, or of any other interior virtue, because these virtues, joined to charity, whose daughters they are, formally constitute religious and Christian perfection. Besides being common to all the faithful, they could not serve to characterize the regular state, or to distinguish it from any other. Beyond the vows and virtues, and the works which they prescribe, and over and above the exercises and practices commanded either by the rule or by superiors, we must ever bear in mind the interior life which is their object, and still more our Lord and model Jesus Christ, Son of the Living God, Who is Himself the way by which we reach truth, and the truth which alone gives eternal life.

The Evangelical counsels have like heavenly dew favoured the bloom of the religious virtues, but these mystic flowers would have been wanting in vigour and duration, if the vows had not bestowed on them somewhat of the stability of God. Of a mere resolution, they have formed an inviolable custom, and of this habit a distinct ecclesiastical state, and of a transitory act, they have created an ever-flowing fountain of life and spiritual joy. Finally, they have reunited, as in a single sheaf, all the undertakings and works of the regular state, in order to obtain more efficaciously that perfection of which they are the instruments. They have also, as we shall presently show, completed the holocaust and consecration of man to God.

CHAPTER IX.

The Holocaust and Consecration.

THAT the religious profession is at once both a holocaust and a consecration, is a well-known fact, and one that has been frequently set forth in this book; but it also proves to be a truth so profound, and so full of spiritual advantages, that it is right that we should seek a further development of it from the Angelic Doctor. God being the absolute Master of our nature, which He has first created and then redeemed; whose existence He preserves, and in whose actions He assists; which He has invited to enjoy His own happiness, and which He invests in heaven with His glory, He has an unquestionable right to exact from all men, and more particularly from all Christians, that they should do homage to Him and make Him an offering of their whole being. Now it is by faith, hope, charity and religion, it is by all the virtues, be they either of the theological, intellectual or moral order, that we render this homage, and that we present to Him this oblation. It is by believing in His word and desiring Him as our last end, by loving Him because he is the Supreme Good, by adoring His infinite majesty, by being obedient to all His commandments, and fashioning ourselves after the likeness of the Divine model exemplified to us in His son Jesus Christ, that we give Him the most manifest proof of our consecration to Him, and of our belonging to Him, not only by a necessity founded upon

His essence and our existence, but also by the spontaneous offering of our own free will.

This offering, however great it may be, even should it extend to the imitation of our Lord in His poverty, virginity and obedience, is not sufficient to satisfy the ardour and generosity of some souls. For it in no way affects the creature itself, it annihilates none of its powers nor any of its works, which continue to exist whole and entire before the Most High and Most Holy God, to whom we cannot compare ourselves without at once acknowledging that it is *He* alone who *is*, and that nothingness has imprinted an indelible mark upon that little which we are; in a word, it is as yet but an offering, and not sufficient for souls who are eager for perfection.

Something still greater is wanted by them, something more universal and more radical: they must make a sacrifice. This latter penetrates into the very depths of their being; it takes possession of them; it reaches them in that which is innermost; it carries the sword or the torch into their inmost soul, and, as far as may be, destroys and annihilates them, in order to prove and acknowledge that God possesses over His creatures an infinite right of life and death. This is precisely the function of religious vows. They change the state of man. They break his former bonds. They destroy his worldly life, and make him live for God alone. They wrest from him the threefold enjoyment of earthly goods, of family ties, of personal independence and wealth; they bind him by the threefold obligations of being poor, chaste and obedient. Is not this a real and solemn sacrifice?

This sacrifice is the more perfect, from the fact that it is not a body without reason or affection which is thus smitten by vows. The mind itself is the principal victim, according to the Psalmist, "A sacrifice to God is an afflicted spirit."[1] For the soul wishing to acknowledge and adore God as the Sovereign principle from whom it holds all the advantages this material creation affords, sacrifices firstly, by the vow of *poverty*, that exterior wealth and those honours which are the distinctive mark of the whole world. Then, in order to acknowledge and adore this same God, as the Creator of the body, to whom it is naturally united, it sacrifices by the vow of

[1] Ps. l. 19.

continence the power of enjoying those sensual pleasures which are the most lively and intense, and consequently the best fitted to represent all bodily powers and goods. Finally, in order to acknowledge and adore our Lord as the sole source from which it derives its existence, its perfections, and spiritual wealth, it sacrifices by the vow of obedience that free will which is its best title to glory, and which constitutes all that it is, and all that it possesses. Thus, religious vows are a sacrifice which is both absolute and spiritual, and by which man offers himself to the majesty of his Almighty *Creator*.

They are also, says the incomparable St. Thomas, the sacrifice offered to the Infinite Goodness of our last end. In pronouncing them, the soul says to the Lord, "I hope from Thee, oh true and unbounded Good; I expect from Thee, oh divine abyss of happiness, all the joy and glory which Thou hast promised me, and hast already bestowed on Thine elect. In order to merit this robe of glory, this wondrous crown reserved for me, I sacrifice to Thee all the riches and pomps of this world, I make myself *poor*. To rise again with a glorious, incorruptible and immortal body, I make to Thee a sacrifice of all sensual pleasures, I will be a *virgin*. To contemplate Thee one day with a mind enlightened by Thy splendour, to possess Thee with a heart inundated by Thy heavenly delights, I now sacrifice to Thee my soul, my liberty, my independence and its joys, and will be henceforth *obedient*.

" Thou alone, oh my God, art my beginning and my Creator: I acknowledge it by sacrificing to Thee my whole being, with all its possessions.

" Thou alone, oh my God, art my happiness and my last end: I proclaim it, and I give myself to Thee by sacrificing all my goods and pleasures."

And it is to God alone that man may thus speak and render this definitive offering. It is therefore a supreme act of adoration, it is a true spiritual sacrifice, since it is inspired by the soul, and both the soul and the body are the victim thereof; it is an exterior and solemn sacrifice, since it is accomplished in the presence of the Church, who regulates its forms and vouchsafes thereto its blessings; it is a sacrifice similar to that of the cross, since the victim offers itself spontaneously to God, even as our Saviour Jesus Christ was immolated upon Calvary, and as He continues to immolate himself voluntarily on our altar—yea, even at the very moment when the religious comes before it, laden with his offerings and vows; for it is to testify loudly to the resemblance borne by religious to Jesus, Priest and Victim, that the profession is made during the holy sacrifice of the mass.

The great Pope, St. Gregory, does not confine himself to the idea that religious vows are a sacrifice; he sees in them something still more sublime, a true holocaust. "When a Christian," he says, "consecrates to God all that he possesses out of himself, as well as all that lives in him, and all that pleases his natural inclinations, it is a holocaust."[2] Even as the sacrifice exceeds the mere offering, because it changes, in God's honour, either the condition or the qualities of the substance which is offered, and by this change clearly proclaims the infinite and immutable perfection of the Lord; so in like manner the holocaust excels all

---

[2] *XX. Homily on Ezechiel.* The word *holocaust* signifies that the victim is entirely burnt by the sacred fire.

ordinary sacrifices, because not only does it modify the state of the victim, but it immolates it wholly and for ever, and delivers its whole substance to the flames, reserving nothing for the use of men! Although the ordinary practice of poverty, virginal chastity and obedience before religious profession or in the midst of the world, or in the noviciate of a regular order, supposes that a great number of virtuous acts are each day offered to God as so many sacrifices of sweet savour; it is nevertheless certain that without vows, these acts cannot possess neither the merits nor efficacy of the holocaust. The virtue of religion does not as yet animate them with its breath.[3] Besides man still remains in possession of all that he holds most dear and most near, namely, his being, his powers, his liberty, and consequently the possibility of returning to earthly goods, of tasting sensual pleasures, and of being once more his own

---

[3] The virtue of religion can neither direct the other virtues, nor transform their acts into acts of religion or of spiritual sacrifice, unless a formal express act of the will, a vow or a consecration first put it into possession of this authority. We shall shortly see how this investiture is made.

director. The victim is not yet pierced to the heart. The flame has not yet entirely consumed it. But hardly have these vows been uttered than a great holocaust is accomplished; the sacred fire of religion suddenly and for ever burns our whole nature and all its possessions, all its acts, passions, faculties, and its entire life. The vow of poverty destroys exterior riches; that of chastity changes, so to speak, the body into a new substance, which is rather spiritual than material; that of obedience immolates self-will and all the faculties over which it presides. And thus man's threefold possession dissolves before God, as the smoke of those perfumes formerly burned on the altar of incense.

The power of self-action falls under this mystic sword. The religious loses the right of appropriating his works to his own use, and of seeking in them his own interest. He does not offer such or other specific action; he sacrifices the whole, and interdicts himself the performance of every single one which would be in contradiction to the will of the superior. His activity is then bound to the divine service; and the energy which he possesses—this deep source from which spring all his desires and deeds—becomes like to that fountain mentioned in Scripture, which is sealed with God's own seal.

However untamed the passions may be, they do not escape this universal sacrifice. The vow of chastity at once and for ever destroys all such things as conduce to the gratification of the flesh, or which favour sensuality; and, on the other hand, such as tend towards the love of exterior goods are eradicated by the vow of poverty. Pride, anger and hatred are crushed by that most generous and, above all, most humble vow of obedience. And as the man who is poor, humble and mortified, and living a life of privation and self-denial is absolutely incapable of obtaining the false esteem and unreasonable respect that worldlings, who look but to appearances, usually bestow upon the favourites of fortune, thus is the religious freed from the passions of vain glory, ambition, hypocrisy, jealousy, domineering, and from many others which the love of the world engenders.[4]

---

[4] St. Thomas observes, with regard to this, that a religious does not renounce the reasonable honour due, not only to God, but to the just and elect, on account

This holocaust extends its influence even over the future. Not only the present moment, but the next day and every instant which succeeds it, to the day of our death; every pulsation of the heart, every aspiration of the soul, every movement of the body, every working of the brain, and every purpose of the will are at the same moment collected together upon the altar and consumed by the same fire. Even before they exist, they are already laid hold of in their sources, and their origin—that is to say, in our faculties—and are subjected to that perpetual obligation, which is the consequence of religious progression. He who promises, says St. Thomas, gives at once, in a certain manner, that which he binds himself to give later, even as the effect appears to be produced as soon as its cause begins to exist, since the effect is contained in the capability of the cause. Religious vows, then, embrace the whole life, and cast it into the sacred furnace of divine love. On the morning of his regular profession, a youthful soul beholds, as in an immense and

of their natural and supernatural virtues; consequently, the greater the efforts he makes to attain perfection in these virtues, the greater the honour he merits.

accurate picture, a vision of his whole life. He considers it, and beholds it free, happy, honoured and prosperous in the midst of the world. But he also perceives it is menaced by a thousand temptations, and overwhelmed by disquietudes which will maintain it at a fatal distance from God, and perhaps deprive it of the ineffable virtue of charity. He therefore throws himself at once at the feet of our Lord, exclaiming, " My beloved is to me, and I to him."[5]

Either there is no such thing as a holocaust, or it is to be found here!

Since, then, religious profession has a real right to this title of spiritual holocaust, it is proper that souls called to make so great a sacrifice of themselves should fully understand its symbolical signification, and be thus able to fulfil with perfect dispositions the twofold function of priest and victim.

Now the Angel of the School recognises in the holocausts of the Old Law the figurative expression of three grand truths.

The *first* is that the majesty of the Lord is infinite, and that it is worthy of respect; yea, as deep as the unfathomable abyss of the

[5] Cant. ii. 16.

ocean, as vast as the broad expanse of the firmament. This is why the holocaust was completely destroyed without anyone daring to withdraw the smallest portion. In like manner, the religious should bear in mind that in devoting himself entirely to the divine service, he is as yet but an unprofitable servant, whose true motto is those verses of our Doctor:

> " Strive thy best to praise Him well ;
> Yet doth He all praise excel ;
> None can ever reach His due." [6]

And would you reserve to yourself any part of your being, when every perfection you possess, though gathered into one, were not homage equal to a single ray of His glory?

The *second* truth taught us by the holocaust is that, since, the goodness of God has no bounds, it ought to excite within us an affection as pure and ardent as a flame. Are you to be as an icicle towards Him? In your religious profession will you not imitate those victims whose whole substance dissolved into vapour so as to ascend to heaven? Will you refuse to make a return for the eternal fires of that charity, which has given you the Son of God to be your Brother, your Saviour, and

---

[6] *Lauda Sion*, 2nd Stanza.

your food, by making the offering of yourself? Finally, as we further study the sacred rites of the holocaust, they remind us of this *third* truth, which is that the religious in pronouncing his vows, pledges himself definitively to a state of perfection, wherein he will perfectly observe not only the Divine law, but even the evangelical counsels. The holocaust only admitted as victims, those animals which were clean and whole, and if, notwithstanding their little worth, doves and turtle doves were permitted as offerings, it was that the height of their flight symbolized the sublimity of souls bound by vow to the noblest virtues.[7] In the other sacrifices the priest or the people partook of the victim, in order to show that man as well as God had an interest in the rite. Sometimes it was a sinner who came to the Temple to seek forgiveness of his sins, sometimes it was a grateful heart who made a thanks offering to the Lord for his goodness, or it might perchance be a beggar or one in sorrow who implored His favours. But in the holocaust it was forbidden to touch aught of the victim; the divine Majesty absorbed everything to

---

[7] For the rites of the Mosaic holocaust see *Leviticus* ch. i. and xxii.

Itself the splendour of Its glory effaced, even the very shadow of man, and man lost sight of himself in order to be wholly taken up with the worship of his Creator and last end; attaining thus the supreme degree of charity and religion. And to remind us that the perfection of the present life, however high and complete it may be, is not our final end, but only a means of arriving at the eternal and immutable perfection of heaven, every day upon the altar of holocaust the Israelites offered a lamb, in testimony and as a figure says St. Thomas, of the perpetuity of Divine bliss.[8] Such too is the import of religious profession. It is more excellent than the *expiatory* sacrifice of the penitent, or the *peace offering* of those who advance in the right path; it is truly the *holocaust* of the perfect,[9] and the certain pledge of that great and ineffable holocaust, by which the elect give themselves wholly to God, and God to them, in the heavenly kingdom.

There is, however, this difference between religious vows and the ancient holocausts,

[8] Exodus xxix. 38; Numbers xxviii. 3.

[9] Compare the first and second chapters of this book with this explanation of a holocaust.

that as these latter exhausted the substance of their victim, it became necessary that they should be unceasingly multiplied and renewed, whilst the religious profession is a permanent sacrifice of the victim, which remains in its state of immolation, always bound to the sacred stones of the altar, perpetually consumed by the fire of divine love, and this for a duration of a lifetime, or to express it better, it is a long mystical death under the appearances of bodily life. From this we must conclude that the religious is a being absolutely *consecrated*, a truly *holy* object, and the profanation of which would be sacrilegious.

The consecration of a person supposes three conditions very necessary to be known, in order to live according to the spirit of regular life. The first is *purity*, which effaces the sins and stains of the soul, and leaves it resplendent with the likeness of its Creator and Saviour. This is so clear, that the human language readily finds words to explain this necessity. Indeed the Greeks designate that which is *holy*, by an expression which in itself marks separation from the earth, and which consequently signifies *purity*.[10] The Latin word *sanctity* recalls the same idea, being derived from the word *blood*, because in the old dispensation one was *purified* by the blood of victims.[11] For if we would be consecrated to God, it is indispensable to begin by being *pure*, by detaching oneself from earthly things, and by washing our robes in the blood of the Lamb, who was slain for the sins of the world. The impure soul has certainly fallen into the mire of corruptible things, for it is thereby that she has soiled herself, as everything that is superior lowers and stains itself by the contact with inferior objects, as silver, says the sublime Doctor is debased by its being alloyed with lead. Now if you are bound down to the material world, how can you pretend to unite yourself to that which is spiritual, or higher still, to Him who is above all things visible and invisible? The impure soul is delivered over to creatures, it is sold to sin. How then can this miserable slave of the devil at the same time wholly belong to

[10] It is the word *agios (holy)* which is used in the Roman liturgy on Good Friday.

[11] *Etymologies:* the word *Holy*.

God? Let it rise from this earthly mire, let it implore freedom in virtue of the Blood of its Redeemer, in a word, it must be purified!

But where can this purification, so necessary to every consecration, be more perfectly found than in a true religious profession? When a man is detached from exterior goods, from the pleasures of sense, and from his own will, can he still be said to belong to the earth? Is he not rather the heavenly man of whom Jesus Christ is the perfect type? Has the blood of this Divine Master left anywhere else a deeper and more universal proof of its efficacy?

The second condition exacted from him who consecrates himself to God is an immovable *constancy* in the divine service. For his consecration is an adhesion and, so to speak, an application of his soul to God, as his first principle and last end. Now, what is there more stable than these two divine claims on our love and worship? Can they be ever extinguished or weakened? No, this is impossible; and for that reason it is necessary that a consecration founded upon these eternal principles should be, even as they are, immutable, permanent, and eternal. We are not sufficiently consecrated by a pious, but transitory, movement of the heart, nor by a simple wish of being faithful to the Sovereign Master. The name alone of *sanctification* or of consecration reveals the idea of *sanction*, of the definitive confirmation that the legislator gives to his laws.

Man's fidelity to the practices of the divine worship is especially complete and perfect in the monastic state, in the abnegation of every faculty, in this renouncement of all the independence which he enjoyed, and lastly in these vows, which impart to us a special likeness of the power and stability of God. For who can repeat with greater truth than the religious these words of the Apostle: " I am sure that neither death, nor life, shall separate me from the charity of Jesus Christ."[12] Purity of soul, and its perpetual attachment to the Lord would not be a formal consecration if it had not for its end the *adoration* and *praise* of this great God; if man did not become in a certain sense a priest and victim of the Most High, offering in his own person that holocaust demanded by the excellence both infinite and incomprehensible of Him

[12] Rom. viii. 38, 39.

who has drawn us out of nothing in order to lead us to an unbounded and never ending bliss.

And this third condition is admirably fulfilled by the religious profession. In fact, the three vows which take entire possession of man, in all his deeds and faculties, in his passions and in his pleasures, in his future as well as in the present, are, in themselves, acts of religion ; and all that they regard, and all that they prescribe, they necessarily transform into a religious object. Firstly, they are religious acts because, says St. Thomas, they are promises made to God, and if we make any promises to God it is a sign that we acknowledge Him to be worthy of them, that we wish to honour Him, in fine, because we feel ourselves inspired by the virtue of religion. And if you have thus promised in a spirit of religion to be henceforth poor, chaste, and obedient, the practice of these virtues will become in their turn religious acts, since you not only accomplish them exactly, but you perform them for God, to whom you have consecrated them, out of respect to His Adorable Majesty, for fear of offending Him, or of lessening the honour due to Him; in a word, by the order and under the same inspiration of the virtue of religion. All these acts will therefore be truly acts of *religion;* you yourself will be a *religious;* you will live in *religion.* And as it often happens that one single sin contains the malice of many different faults, thus each of your works of poverty, chastity and obedience, will be doubly meritorious, for besides their natural and intrinsic goodness they will really be religious acts, sacrifices of praise, and spiritual holocausts. It might be truly averred that a nobler and more generous blood is infused into your veins; that a superior spirit dwells within you, invigorating with a purer and more vigorous breath all that proceeds from your energy, and renovating all your virtues, all your enterprises, and all that you are, under the sole empire of *religion.*

In truth, there is no consecration so profound or so entire as that of religious on the day of their profession, because there is none so purifying, so constant, or so religious. The consecration of bishops and priests is more exalted, as being a sacrament; it is more noble, as conferring a more sublime dignity and an ineffaceable character, yea, it is more powerful, because it imparts to a mere creature some of the powers of God. But it is not so complete as the monastic consecration, because it does not include a man's entire separation from himself and from the world; it is not so entire because it does not absolutely consume the liberty, the independence, and the spontaneousness of his nature; it is a great sacrifice and a great sacrament, but not a true holocaust. The violation of the vows is then a very grievous sin against the virtue of religion—the crime of sacrilege. Man, consecrated to God and to His service, becomes something divine, just as everything else which being intended for, and directed towards a good and praiseworthy end, becomes equally praiseworthy and good. He owes himself, therefore, a religious respect which redounds even to God. And if he should ever dishonour by mortal sin the virtues of poverty, obedience and virginity of which he has made profession, he would commit an outrage against the divine honour, he would be guilty of sacrilege. "The purple which is become the king's robe," says St. John of Damascus, "is revered and honoured, and should anyone be found rash enough to tear it, he should be punished with death." [13] And you, O religious! you are not only the most beautiful ornaments of the Church, of that Queen whom the prophet saw in her mantle of gold bordered with a variety of rich colours, with glittering jewels and precious stones. You are not only one of the most brilliant diamonds with which the diadem of our Lord is studded. You are the choice fruits of the Church's holiness; you are the personification of the apostolic virtues of the Redeemer, just as the ecclesiastical hierarchy is the complete representation of His authority. What rashness, what crime and impiety would it not then be in you to violate your vows. The infidelity of consecrated persons is more awful than the sacrilege committed against holy places, eucharistic vessels, or holy pictures and relics. Your soul, who would shudder at the mere thought of a desecrated temple, a dishonoured ciborium, a broken crucifix, or of a saint's body cast into the flames! would it then consent to far more horrible crimes, or to more infamous violations?

Having acknowledged in the religious profession both a perfect holocaust and an entire

[13] *On the Orthodox Faith*, Book IV. ch. 3.

consecration, we may easily estimate its value and accurately appreciate its results. In the first place, three obvious reasons demonstrate the superiority of a life sanctified and governed by vows, over one of ordinary virtue.

First, says St. Thomas, " a vow made to the Lord is an act of adoration inspired by the virtue of religion which reigns supreme amongst the moral virtues. Now, the nobler the virtue, the more excellent and praiseworthy are its works. Consequently, the act of an inferior virtue will be more valuable and more meritorious when called forth by a superior virtue it becomes the act and fruit of the latter. It is thus that an act of faith or of hope is more perfect when it is produced under the influence of charity. Hence the works of the other moral virtues, like fasting which is an act of abstinence, or of continence which is an act of chastity, acquire greater value and merit when they form the matter of a vow. For from that moment, they are consecrated to the divine service, and are true spiritual sacrifices to the glory of God." The great St. Augustine also says that " Virginity derives not its nobility and worth from itself, but rather because it is an offering to the Lord inspired and preserved by prudence and piety of the soul." [14]

In the *second* place, he who has vowed the performance of a good work, and who afterwards executes it, submits himself more fully to God than he who performs what he has not promised; because the former gives, not only his act, but also his power of acting, being reduced by his vow to the impossibility of doing otherwise; in proof of which St. Anselm furnishes us with an ingenious illustration by saying, "That he who gives a tree laden with fruit assuredly gives more than he who gives the fruit alone." [15] Does not the mere promise of a gift, or of assistance, already deserve our gratitude?

A *third* effect of vows, and one which we have noticed before, is so to strengthen the will as to render it immoveable in that which is good, not only for a particular act or for the precise time in which it is performed, but for all the actions which may present themselves in the future. An action emanating from a will thus confirmed in justice is the height of perfection, even as the sin of

---

[14] *On Holy Virginity*, ch. 8.
[15] *On the Similitudes*, ch. 84.

impenitence is the most heinous of all other sins, so much so, indeed, as to be called a sin against the Holy Ghost, and to be considered as an assured sign of reprobation. If then it should happen that a religious in drawing comparison between his life and that of Christians in the world, should be seized with a holy fear lest he be less zealous, less pious, or less fervent than many of them, he may still find a legitimate reassurance in the thought that his actions, though they be apparently less virtuous and brilliant, derive notwithstanding greater value and more real devotion than theirs from the virtue of religion, which is their chief source, and which has so high a place amongst the moral virtues. He may be consoled by the certainty that he has eternally consecrated to the Lord the root of his actions, in such a way that they all bear the threefold character of a profound religion, ardent generosity and an eternal attachment to that which is good.

If religious give themselves wholly to God, this good Master knows well how to reward them with His unbounded munificence. "Vow ye, and pay to the Lord your God," exclaims the Royal Psalmist, "all ye that are round about the Lord bring presents."[16] From which the Angel of the School remarks, how much promises made to God, differ from those made to man; to the latter we promise something that is profitable to him, and the very assurance we give of our favourable dispositions in his regard is equally beneficial to him, either to encourage, or strengthen him, to second his plans, or to prepare for him a happy future. But, on the contrary, that which we promise to God is not for His benefit, but for our own. "He is," says the Doctor of Hippo, "a Creditor full of goodness, and who needs nothing. He does not desire to be enriched by anything we return to Him, but rather thereby to enrich ourselves. He adds all we give to Him to that we already possess."[17] My promise is of no use to Him for He already knows my intentions and motives in virtue of His infinite and infallible knowledge of all things.

Thus my promise works to my own sole advantage by strengthening my will and imposing on me the happy necessity of doing good. We may therefore reasonably suppose

[16] Psalms lxxv. 12.
[17] LXIV *Letter to Armentaria and Paulina.*

that on its entrance into religion, by making profession of the vows, the Christian soul obtains the remission of all its sins. For if, according to the prophet Daniel, almsgiving expiates faults—" Redeem those thy sins with alms, and thy iniquities with works of mercy to the poor," [18]—with much greater reason can we say that the absolute consecration of oneself to the divine service, makes an atonement for a life hitherto spent in tepidity or even in forgetfulness of God. Again, we learn from the ancient laws of the Church,[19] that this solemn holocaust surpasses every other kind of reparation, even that of public penance; and we read in the *Lives of the Holy Fathers*, that by embracing the monastic state, they received grace equivalent to that of baptism.[20] Not that religious profession, considered in itself, possesses a sacramental virtue, operating by its own intrinsic and independent efficacy, or that it can, like Baptism and Penance blot out the stain of sin; but if it be sincere, it is a most excellent act of perfect charity, which unites us very closely to God

---

[18] · Dan. iv. 24.
[19] *Decree of Gratian*, Cause xxxiii. q. 2.
[20] Liv. vi. v. 9.

by an especial outpouring of His sanctifying grace, and by an abundant remission of those temporal punishments which remain due to sin after its guilt has been forgiven. The learned St. Thomas places it upon an equality with pilgrimages to the Holy Land, and he adds: even if the religious profession had not such expiatory value, and that in devoting oneself to a regular life one was not immediately absolved from one's whole debt to the divine justice, vows would not fail to be preferable to a journey to the Holy Land, because they are more favourable to the advancement of virtue; and this progress in perfection unquestionably exceeds the advantage of being freed from those temporal punishments to which the sinner is liable.

In your solitary and peaceful exercises of the cloister, at the foot of that altar where your years are consumed as a perpetual sacrifice, in the care of children, of the poor, and the sick, you will find more spiritual advantage than in pious and toilsome journeys to the banks of the Jordan, or to the summit of Mount Carmel. Here your charity, freed from those impediments which in the world check its development, may increase with greater vigour, and thus more surely lighten the burthen which your faults have heaped upon you. Do not envy, nor sigh after the long journeys made by a St. Paul or a St. Melania; you have in the interior of your monastry, the crib of Bethlehem, the portals of Sion, the house of Bethania, and the heights of Thabor, the cross of Calvary, and the tomb of the Lord.

Before dismissing this noble subject of religious profession, let us not omit to observe that the vow of obedience is its chief feature. It may claim this pre-eminence for these three reasons. First, the man who thus undertakes to obey, offers to God all that is most intimately connected with himself, and that is most noble and most essential to his being, for his will is assuredly preferable to his flesh, which he sacrifices by the vow of chastity, or to the riches and honours of this world, which he renounces by the vow of poverty. Again that which is done by obedience, is more agreeable to God than that which is performed by ones own will, as is shown by these words of St. Jerome to the monk Rusticus: "above all, that which I would have you learn, is not to abandon yourself to your own free will," and shortly afterwards he adds: "do not do as you wish, eat that which is appointed for you, possess nothing but that which you receive, neither have other clothing but that which is given to you."[21] This is why fasting is not pleasing to God when it proceeds merely from caprice, or the whim of man. "Why have we fasted," one may ask, "and Thou hast not regarded. Have we humbled our souls, and Thou hast not taken notice?" and the Lord answers, "behold in the day of your fast your own will is found, and you exact of all your debtors."[22]

Secondly the vow of obedience is the most sublime, because it includes all the others, without being in its turn contained in them; continence and poverty although they be the object of special promises are also comprised in its laws, but obedience is not confined to them, it imposes more numerous duties, it extends much further in the domain of perfections.

Thirdly, obedience directly prescribes those acts which most efficaciously and most rapidly lead the soul to the main end of religious

---

[21] IV *Letter to Rusticus.*
[22] Is. lviii. 3.

life. Let us suppose for example that you already practise the virtues of virginity and voluntary poverty, we may even suppose that you are bound to them by a vow, but if you have not obedience you are not yet a religious, you are not in a state of perfection; "No one I am sure," says St. Augustine, "would dare to prefer virginity to the monastic life."[23] Now to live this celestial life it is not sufficient to be chaste and detached from riches and honours. It requires this entire submission of the soul, which is the supreme homage of the creature to his Creator, in other words the most exalted act of religious virtue, and the characteristic mark of the religious. It is necessary to have this definite self-abnegation, which St. Gregory styles "a perfect holocaust," giving it the preference over all other sacrifices,[24] and hence over the vows of chastity and poverty. Obedience is then of the utmost necessity to enable us to break through the strongest fetters, and to overcome the most formidable obstacles that man can encounter in the path of perfection, which are the spirit of independence, self-will and self-

---

[23] On *Holy Virginity*, ch. 8.
[24] See the chapter on *Obedience*.

love. In a word it requires the complete adhesion of the intelligence and of the heart to Jesus Christ, and to those of his representatives who hold authority over us. Having said to our Lord "*we have left everything,*" St. Peter adds that which constitutes perfection, "*and have followed Thee,*" [25] as if he would say: "O! infinite and everlasting perfection, O! Supreme Teacher of the good and beautiful, O! word full of grace and wisdom, we enter into Thy blessed school, we come to listen to Thy teaching. Thy words shall be our light, and Thy counsels our laws. Our feeble intellects would fail to lead us to perfection, but we are certain to attain it by Thy direction. Chaste and poor we are free, but yet inert and motionless; it is obedience that will give us a definitive impulse towards good. Divine love is the end of our state, but it is not virginity, it is not voluntary indigence which prompts its acts or kindles within us this sacred fire; it is obedience. It is obedience which makes us perform so many acts of religion and works of charity towards God, and deeds of zeal and mercy towards our neighbour; and if on the one hand it is a

[25] St. Jerome, *Commentary on St. Matt.*, ch. 19.

sharp sword penetrating into the very marrow of the victim of immolation, it is on the other hand a most ardent fire inflaming our lips and hearts with apostolic zeal and Christian charity. The two first vows should be considered as being rather negative and passive, confining themselves to the work of liberating and purifying us. The nature of the third is principally active, for while it sunders our tenderest and strongest ties, it attracts us to the service of the Lord, enrols us in His company of Saints, and makes us run after the sweetness of His perfumes."

Thus a religious is priest and victim, participating in a wondrous manner in this twofold character of our Lord, and offering a spiritual sacrifice to the honour of his Creator and last end; and this is no ordinary sacrifice, but a universal and perpetual holocaust, and one which is the perfect symbol of finished sanctity. The religious is thus a person consecrated for ever to the divine service, and who cannot disgrace his high dignity without committing a sacrilege. But if on the contrary he carefully fulfils all his duties, his life will henceforth be like a clear stream which, springing from his religious profession, and more especially from the vow of obedience, as from a second baptism, will bear onward to the ocean of eternal bliss inexhaustible waters of supernatural grace and merit.

CHAPTER X.

Sin in the Religious Life.

ALAS! even in cloistered life, in that state of consecration and sacrifice, in that School of our Lord's privileged disciples, hideous sin may find entrance, and sometimes reigns even on the altar of holocaust itself. It comes like the devil, the persecutor of Job, Satan who, having travelled over the earth, crept in among the angels assembled in the presence of the Lord. It comes as a sworn enemy, and so to speak, a direct negation of the religious *state*, since this vocation professes to be a continual and vigorous effort towards perfection, while sin is nought else but deliberate, voluntary and manifest imperfection. The religious has solemnly vowed that he will belong to no other but God, and that he will give himself wholly to the divine worship; but the religious in sinning submits to the dominion of exterior things, to the yoke of the senses and to the tyranny of his self-will, thus disowning and dishonouring his God. The religious has devoted himself to follow after Eternal Wisdom in order to become perfect, and the religious in sinning has stripped himself of his justice and merits, and become a shameful ruin and a horrid corpse. Sin is then the direct contradiction of the evangelical counsels, of the virtues and vows of religion.

It must indeed be admitted that these sacred vows are the occasion of the most grievous sins that can be committed in the monastic state, namely, the crimes of irreligion and sacrilege. But they no more deserve the odium thereof, than the law can be condemned as the cause of the rebellion and transgressions which the evil one excites against it. True, as our admirable Doctor says, no one should expose himself to danger; thus when my danger is the direct result of my actions, I am as truly culpable as if I crossed a river upon a rotten bridge; but, on the contrary, when the peril wherein I find myself results from my own inconstancy in not making good use of the means which I had formerly adopted, these means do not on that account cease to be good. For instance, it is dangerous to fall off a horse, yet no one can deny that a horse is serviceable in bringing us to the end of our journey. To deny this distinction would be to reduce oneself to the necessity of doing no good at all, for what is best may, under certain accidental circumstances, become dangerous. "He that observeth the wind shall not sow, and he that considereth the clouds shall never reap."[1] Now the spiritual dangers of religious life are not to be attributed to the vows, but rather to the fault of him who by changing his mind transgresses those vows. St. Augustine was therefore right in saying: "Do not repent of having consecrated yourselves to God, but rather rejoice in it."[2] The religious state is the safest road to the summits of the rough and steep mountain of perfection. Angels guide and sustain your steps; it is, indeed, for you the royal road to heaven. But if you

---

[1] Eccles. xi. 4.
[2] XLIV *Letter to Armentaria and Paulina.*

voluntarily forsake it, you will be plunged into the outer darkness, and will fall to the bottom of the abyss. Do not then, though under pressure of the most cruel temptations, regret the profession which you made in the fullness of your intellect and liberty, but rather labour the more diligently to subject your impatient nature to so salutary a yoke. It is easy to understand that faults committed in the religious state are frequently marked with a special heinousness, which should inspire us with a most lively horror. And it may truly be said, that this again is especially providential; for since the hideousness of sin is at the same time a preservative against the allurements of satan and a motive for repentance, its efficacy under this two-fold aspect will be the greater as it is the more horrible and disgusting.

This hideousness is never so apparent as in the violation of religious vows, which is a real sacrilege, and which to the malice of an act already prohibited by a natural or positive law, as for instance the sin of theft or impurity, adds a formal outrage against the honour of the Most High. We must not, however, exaggerate this solid doctrine by considering every sin committed by religious as so many sacrileges. It is true that he has consecrated himself to God, and from that time forth all his faults are in a certain manner opposed to the sanctity wherewith he is penetrated. But this consecration, universal though it be, has not equally affected all his powers and all his virtues. This consecration is the result of the vows, and these vows do not extend their influence over every action of life. The religious has not taken a vow of charity, nor of zeal, nor of patience. Therefore the religious consecration is not formal, save in such points as are determined by his vows. The man has been consecrated to God, but not each one of the parts which compose him; even as in his whole being he is endowed with intellect, even though every separate portion of him is not intelligent. Thus his sin is not really and distinctly a sacrilege, unless it be in direct opposition to the perfection required by the vows of poverty, chastity and obedience. Beyond this, as it injures an imperfect consecration, and one improperly so styled, it is rather a nominal sacrilege, than a true one.[3]

[3] This sort of imperfect sacrilege is styled in theological language, a *material* sacrilege, and, so to speak,

Even when he is in rebellion, not against his vows, but only against a commandment common to the whole Church, still a religious may be far more guilty than the ordinary faithful, if he sins by contempt of the law, that is to say, as our Angelic Doctor explains it, if the cause of his disobedience be neither frailty, ignorance, nor passion, but the pride of his self-will which refuses to submit to a command or rule. Such would be a mark of an extraordinary ingratitude to our Lord. For our Lord has laden this soul with many signal benefits, which He has not granted to the immense crowd of seculars, and has given it a more perfect knowledge of the truth, a more frequent participation of the sacraments of faith, greater actual graces and more efficacious exterior assistance. He has admitted

accidental, in opposition to *formal* and *positive* sacrilege. Considering it in the first sense, many Fathers have said that idle and frivolous words are sacrilegious or blasphemous in the mouth of a priest. On the other hand, St. Thomas teaches, that vows *solemnized* by the consecration or blessing of the Church, impose, in the sight of God, a much greater obligation, thus their transgression is more grievous than that of a vow devoid of this supernatural consecration.

it among His well-beloved servants, who are especially devoted to His glory; and in return for all this He receives nothing but distaste for His service and contempt for His Holy Word! Assuredly the guilt of this sinful soul is of no ordinary kind; it has attained a rare degree of blackness and malice!

If the contempt of God, according to the testimony of St. Paul, exposes all Christians, without exception, to the heaviest and most terrible punishments, "how much more do you think he deserveth worse punishments who hath trodden under foot the Son of God, and hath esteemed the blood of the Testament unclean, by which he was sanctified, and hath offered an affront to the Spirit of Grace."[4] Religious have greater reason than other men to fear the divine vengeance, should they fall into that abyss of obduracy where the sinner possesses knowledge but to despise it. Oh, may they never be thus insensible to this sorrowful and pitiful complaint of our Lord: "What is the meaning that my beloved hath wrought much wickedness in My house: My heart is broken within Me, for the prophet and the priest are defiled, and in My house I have found their

[4] Hebrews x. 29.

wickedness saith The Lord."[5] This contempt of the divine law is certainly very rare amongst the faithful, although they may sometimes unfortunately consent to mortal sin; and it is rarer still in the religious life, where the multiplicity of pious and spiritual exercises serve as efficacious barriers against its intrusion. Let them, however, be watchful; persons consecrated to our Lord's service may yield to faults which at first blind them, and then inspire them with a haughty disgust for obedience and a criminal rebellion against all authority. A religious thus depraved becomes the worst and often most incorrigible of all sinners, and St. Thomas addresses to him these terrible reproofs of Holy Writ: "Thou has broken my yoke, thou hast burst my bonds, and thou saidst: *I will not serve.* For on every high hill, and under every green tree, thou didst prostitute thyself."[6] "Since I have begun to serve God," wrote St. Augustine, "I have remarked that it is difficult to find worthier souls than those sanctified by the monastic life; but at the same time I have experienced that there are none so detestable as those

[5] Jer. xi. 15; xxiii. 9—11.
[6] *Ibid*, ii. 20.

who have been unfaithful to their vocation."[7] Another source of guilt for the religious who yield to sin, is the constant and pernicious scandal to which their evil doings gives rise. Their life is far more noticed, more carefully observed than that of lay persons. Whether from curiosity, or from malevolence, every eye is fixed on their conduct, and their shortcomings are no sooner perceived than they are made public. God has formerly deplored this in saying: "And I have seen the likeness of adulterers, and the way of lying in the prophets of Jerusalem; and they strengthened the hands of the wicked, that no man should return from his evil doings."[8]

But, O! Lord, is the regular life but a new snare prepared for our weakness, and shall these sacred vows, by which it begins, serve but to increase our faults in this life, and the rigour of Thine avenging justice in the next? No, it is not so, and the Angelic Doctor gives us other thoughts which are as full of consolation and peace as they are of wisdom and truth.

If the religious, he says, sins only by in-

---

[7] CXXXVII *Letter to the people of Hippo.*
[8] Jeremiah xxiii. 14.

firmity or by ignorance, without contempt of the law, without infraction of his vows, and, lastly, without scandal, the sin he commits is less than if he were a Christian living in the world. First, let us suppose his fault to be simply venial; it will, as it were, be absorbed by the numerous good works which he daily performs,[9] in such wise, that the tenour of his

[9] In order to place this point in the clearest light, let us make a summary of the teaching of St. Thomas upon the remission of venial sin. Firstly, neither the Sacrament of Penance, nor perfect contrition is required to get them pardoned. Secondly, the virtues of Charity or Penance, though equivalent to an *habitual aversion* from sin, are not *alone* sufficient, apart from their acts. Thirdly, yet it suffices that there be an *actual* displeasure, or even merely *virtual*, that is to say, an act of Penance *explicit* or *implicit*: thus, for instance, were the soul borne towards God, or divine things, with such affection that every venial sin which would prevent its following this good inclination displeased it, and occasioned sorrow for its commission, it would immediately be pardoned, even though there were no actual thought of this sin. Fourthly, every act, therefore, of charity, of contrition and attrition, every infusion or increase of sanctifying grace (sanctifying grace being granted to adults only by means of a motion of their will towards God), can remit all the smaller offences committed against God. Fifthly, hence it follows—*firstly, that holy Eucharist, extreme unction,* and generally, all

life will be very pure and pleasing in the sight of God, notwithstanding the multitude of lesser failings with which our life is, so to speak, wholly interwoven. He should, how- the Sacraments of the New Law, remit these offences because they confer on us grace ; *secondly*, when in reciting the *Confiteor*, or in beating the breast and saying the Our Father (which contains an explicit act of penance, "*forgive us our trespasses,*") the same remission is obtained, because these pious exercises excite within us some feeling of detestation of sin ; *thirdly*, by the Episcopal Benediction (and for a greater reason—the Benediction of the Blessed Sacrament) the sprinkling of Holy Water, all the Sacramentals, prayers recited in a consecrated Church, and other practices of the same kind (as the use of the Rosary or of an Indulgenced picture), work, the remission of lesser sins, by inspiring our soul with reverence for God and holy things. Sixthly, should one, however, be actually attached to any one of these faults (and above all to a mortal sin), it could not be pardoned. Seventhly, this remission directly effects the *fault*, and not the temporal *punishment* due to it ; this last is more or less diminished, and often entirely expiated by the feelings of fervour which these prayers and Sacraments excite, as well as by their expiatory value. The regular state being a tissue of such pious actions, we are now in position to judge the astounding affirmation of St. Thomas : that venial sins committed by religious are, as it were, *absorbed* by the multitude of their good works.

THE RELIGIOUS STATE. 213

ever, never relax his efforts for the diminution of their number, under pretext that their pardon is easily obtained, for he would expose himself to the great danger of perishing, since by neglecting to wrestle against venial sins which are real hindrances to his spiritual progress, he unfortunately proves only too clearly, that he has neither inclination nor ardour to advance in the way of perfection.

On the other hand, even should his sin be mortal, he will recover himself more easily than the ordinary Christian; *firstly*, on account of his habitual good and righteous intentions towards God, for should his supernatural affection, or his complete adhesion be momentarily interrupted, it will speedily be renewed. Upon this text from the Psalms—" When he shall fall, he shall not be bruised "—the learned Origen makes this beautiful and profound commentary: " If the unrighteous man sins, he does not repent, he knows not how to amend his fault; but he who is righteous, knows both how to amend and to atone for it. Such was the case with him who said " *I know not this man*," and who, having been looked at by the Lord, wept bitterly; and he who from the roof of his palace had seen his servant's wife, and had carried her away, could exclaim, "*I have sinned and done evil in Thy sight, O my God!*"[10] *Secondly*, the religious who has fallen into grievous sins, will be assisted by his brethren; their example, their words, their intercession at the Throne of Grace, will aid him powerfully to recover the grace he has lost. "It is better, therefore, that two should be together than one; for they derive great benefit from their union: If one fall he shall be supported by the other. Woe to him that is alone, for when he falleth he hath none to lift him up."[11]

An important question here presents itself. Is it a grievous sin and a great impediment to perfection to disobey the rule of one's order, in any of those things not commanded either by the laws of God or of the Church, and which are moreover not the matter of religious vows? It is not to be doubted that the monastic rules approved by the Church, are but the expression of Her sovereign will, from which emanates all holiness, for it is not from human wisdom that she derives the rectitude and authority

[10] Upon Ps. xxxvi. 24.   [11] Eccles. iv. 9.

to which the religious bows; it is from Divine Wisdom, which manifests itself to us by the light of reason, and above all by Holy writ and apostolical traditions, and by the divine illuminations imparted to holy founders. The rules are themselves regulated by the eternal and immutable law of all good and truth. It is on this that is based their indisputable right to direct you; this is ground of their power, of your confidence. It is from them again, and by the exact analysis made of them by the Angel of the School, that you will learn in what they oblige you, and also the degree of this obligation.

Religious constitutions contain, *first*, fundamental directions concerning the object of the order, and which consequently are not the objects of the vows.[12] Such are for

---

[12] Interior acts of virtue though not the objects of the vows (refer to chapter vii. and viii.) may however, be prescribed by the rule only, or by the rule and some general law together, as is the case with acts of adoration and charity. The rule is then more extensive than the vows, since they indicate and command, *firstly*, that which is the proper end of the vows, and *secondly*, since they include many means conducive to the exact practice of the three religious virtues of Poverty, Chastity, and Obedience.

instance those which prescribe interior acts of virtue, religious sentiments towards God, or love to our neighbour. It is clear that they are the end and the centre of the whole rule, since it proposes to conduct souls to perfection, and perfection consists in the excellence of charity and the other virtues.

If therefore these essential points are also commanded by a general law, whether divine or human, their omission in a matter of importance certainly constitutes mortal sin. But if their obligation proceeds exclusively from the rule, there would be but a venial fault in transgressing them, even in weighty matters, provided always that this transgression proceeds not from contempt, of which we shall speak later on. This decision is founded upon the undeniable principle, that the religious is not bound to be actually perfect, but only to desire perfection to which he must seriously tend.

In the *second* place, the rule contains secondary precepts relative to the exercises and outward means, necessary to attain the perfection of spiritual life. Such are all exterior observances and practices. Now these in their turn are divided into two classes. Some are absolutely indispensable to the monastic state, and the three essential vows of poverty, chastity, and obedience expressly pledge us to their observance; therefore any serious violation of these promises, and every considerable neglect of these three points of the rule is a mortal sin. The other observances bear upon these, and being subordinate to them are less essential, and are binding only under venial sin, unless the disobedience proceeds from contempt or is the object of a formal command, whether expressed in the text of the rule,[13] or given verbally by the superior, since such command could not be disobeyed without the violation of the vow of obedience.

When the will positively and deliberately refuses to submit to the direction of the rule, and when such a contempt of it leads the religious to transgress it, such acts, though trifling in themselves, constitute a grievous

---

[13] Let us observe with St. Thomas, that everything contained in the monastic rule is not set forth as a command; there are some things which are mere counsels, or simple dispositions and statutes, and only oblige those that infringe them to submit to a certain punishment.

offence, for the rule points out to them the means of reaching perfection, and the efforts they should make to attain this end, and if they treat it with contempt, they necessarily refuse to tend to perfection; they consequently rebel against the fundamental principle of their state, and they trample under foot the solemn profession they made on entering the order. But again we must not confound contempt with the impulses of envy, anger, or passions; relapses, even should they be frequent, are not the exclusive effect, nor are they certain signs of contempt, as St. Augustine says, "all sins are not committed by a feeling of proud contempt." [14] However, venial sins often repeated against the rule, prevent religious from profiting by the great assistance they have in that rule of perfecting themselves in charity, and lead them by imperceptible degrees at first to indifference, and finally to contempt, according to this passage in the book of Proverbs, "The wicked man when he is come into the depth of sins, contemneth." [15]

[14] *On Nature and Grace*, ch. 29.
[15] Prov. xviii. 3. According to St. Thomas it is *contempt* of the will which formally constitutes the sin

Thus, in making his profession, the religious embraces a rule, and acknowledges that he is bound by its authority; but he does not make a vow, says the Angelic Doctor, to observe all that it contains, so that if he should neglect certain points, he would necessarily commit either sacrilege or mortal sin. That which he has vowed, is to practise the regular life and to remain in the regular state; and this life and this state consist essentially in the three virtues of poverty, chastity and obedience. Just as the civil law does not punish with death smaller infractions of its ordinances, so, too, every law and constitution of the Church does not bind under mortal sin, so in like manner the rules of religious orders have not all the same force, and do not always impose a serious obligation.

Thus, continues St. Thomas, in some religious orders they have the prudent custom, for the avoidance of perplexities and scruples of *disobedience*. Venial sin is not properly speaking an express disobedience to the Divine authority, and even mortal sin only bears this character when it proceeds from contempt of the law. But every act of formal disobedience being absolutely opposed to charity towards God or superiors, is of its nature a grievous sin.

of conscience, to make profession, not of the rule itself, but *of a life conformable to it*, thus engaging themselves to endeavour strictly to conform to its observances, as being for them a holy model. Whence we see that it is only the contempt of the rule which constitutes a formal violation of this profession. In some orders, and with still greater prudence, they make profession simply of *obedience according to the rule;* from this it very clearly follows, that mortal sin is committed only when resistance is made against an express and positive command, or by real and wilful breach of the vow of obedience. By means of these precautions, the other omissions are but trifling faults, being simply opposed to the secondary ordinances framed for the protection of the vows.[16] But let us not forget,

[16] It must be understood that we speak here neither of sins against the vows nor of scandalous faults. Our Doctor observes that in the Order of Friar-Preachers to which he belonged, transgressions and omissions which are not in violation of the formal precepts of the rule, are not by their nature real faults: but only subject the transgressor to a definite punishment which was sufficient a check usually to insure regularity; they may however become venial or even mortal sin by negligence, passion, or contempt.

that as these ordinances are, so to speak, indispensable for the observance of the highest and most formidable laws, the venial sins which impede their execution denote an alarming tendency of mind, and are unfortunately very closely allied to mortal sin and sacrilege.

The preceding theory may help us to fix the limits within which the religious is obliged to tend towards perfection, and to determine the circumstances where his want of earnestness in this work, his negligence, or his carelessness relative to the advancement of his soul should be considered as serious faults.

Spiritual perfection may be regarded in itself, in its fruits, and in its means. In *itself*, it is nothing more or less, as we have frequently repeated, than the entire fulfilment of the laws of charity. Now, the religious proposing for his end this complete observance of the precepts of divine love, is not obliged to have reached it already. He does not sin directly against his profession in sometimes failing in the performance of the acts of this virtue; but he is strictly bound to desire efficaciously and constantly to be united to the Sovereign Good for whose sake he has withdrawn from the world and stripped himself of corruptible goods. He would, therefore, be very guilty, if he were wanting either in attention, care, or zeal for his sanctification, and if he merely vegetated in the cloister, like the slothful ivy creeping along the walls, or as the withered moss which time has fastened to the arches.

The *fruits* of perfection consist in holy works, inspired by real charity, such as patience in supporting all kinds of injustice without complaining, or as courage to return blessings for the hatred of those who curse us. These works are, in a certain measure, commanded to us all, for our Lord requires of the Christian that his heart should be ready to fulfil them when necessity presents itself. This good disposition or preparation of the soul does not constitute perfection, it is but the essential condition of charity, and it is very evident that in the regular life it is obligatory under pain of grievous sin; hence the *contempt* of the fruits of charity would be a criminal violation of the monastic profession. In another light, these fruits or consequences of charity are real acts of perfection, as is the case when they are produced freely and without necessity by superabundant charity, and the religious is not bound to them any more than to that actual perfection of which we shall speak hereafter. He does not sin in not imitating that resignation, humility and meekness of which we find an example at every page of the lives of the Saints, but he sins grievously if his will refuses to imitate them when duty prescribes these acts as necessary either to his own salvation or to that of his neighbour. Finally, as to the *means* which will aid him to acquire perfection, he is clearly bound to employ some of them, since his conscience unceasingly recalls to him the great and admirable end to which he is devoted, and his reason clearly shows him that without the use of some means he cannot attain the end. But these means are, in this case, so numerous and various, that it would be impossible for one man to embrace them all. He therefore places first the three essential vows of poverty, chastity and obedience; and then, in the second rank, the specific vows of his order, and the positive commands of his rule or of superiors; and in the last place, he attaches himself to the simple counsels which that rule, pious books, or persons may prescribe.

The obligation of tending towards and

working for his perfection reduces itself then practically, for religious, to the duty keeping of the precepts common to all Christians, never violating his vows, and obeying the formal precepts, whether "written" or "verbal," of regular authority. He is certain that, in following this path, he can never fall into grievous faults, but that, on the contrary, he will easily attain to that perfection which divine Providence desires to realize in him. There is no doubt that all the faithful in the world, as well as those in the cloister, ought in a certain measure to do all the good they are capable of, for to all in general the Holy Ghost addresses this exhortation: "Whatsoever thy hand is able to do, do it earnestly."[17] But this universal obligation is not to be taken in its literal sense, nor is it, so to speak, of a rigorous, mathematical application. Even as the general commandment to love God with one's whole heart does not extend to the works of perfection, nor consequently to an absolute exclusion of all other love, but only to a love which prefers God to all created goods, and which excludes all mortal sin, so, too, the duty of inclining all one's powers to

---

[17] Eccl. ix. 10.

perfection simply requires of the religious that he should do all that he is morally able to do, according to his condition and state. And he satisfies this requirement provided he does not despise the better works, the more excellent practices and more perfect observances of those of his order. This contempt would indeed be the work of a soul obdurate in its imperfections, and form an insurmountable barrier to real advancement in sanctity.

We may then conclude that the regular state is happier and more secure than that of seculars. If it were true that each transgression of the rule involved great culpability, the monastic life would be extremely dangerous on account of the multitude of observances which one is bound to practise. But it is not so. Although the violation of vows, the contempt of authority, and giving of scandal may aggravate the heinousness of sin, they are also at the same time effectual preventatives against temptation. And the defects which are not marked by any of these three characteristics are extenuated, and sometimes even absorbed by the incessant good works and spiritual advantages of a community life. Further, the rules and constitutions are far from always obliging under pain of sin, far less of mortal sin; for if religious are compelled to work out their perfection, this law of labour does not tyrannize over them, nor crush them—transform their weaknesses into crimes, nor their negligence into sacrilege. It is as easy as it is precise, it is the yoke of the privileged servants of Jesus Christ; and for this reason it becomes truly sweet to devoted minds, and easy to great and generous souls.

"The life of the world is as a troubled sea," said the Pope St. Gregory, "but the religious life is like unto a peaceful harbour." [18]

CHAPTER XI.

The forms of the Religious Life.

THE study of the religious life has shown us its principles, limits, and essential aims. The counsels by which it is regulated, the virtues

[18] *Morals* on Job; at the beginning.

which serve as its organs, the vows from which it originates, the holocaust of which it is the victim, the rule and authority which presides over its growth; and, above all, the spirit of religion which animates it, even as the soul inspires and sustains life in the body. This delineation will suffice to enable us to understand to what a grace of resemblance with our Lord Jesus Christ, to what heights of perfection, to what a degree of close consecration to the worship of God, religious are divinely and happily predestinated.

But still this description is not yet sufficiently precise; like all general ideas it is still vague and abstruse. It is rather ideal than real. The means for faithfully practising poverty, obedience, and virginity are so numerous. Between the soul which desires perfection and the perfection which it proposes as the final term of its efforts, there are so many intermediate ends amongst which it must necessarily choose an immediate, and a secondary end; in a word, Divine perfection, the adorable model of all created justice and holiness, so infinitely transcends our ideas, and so thoroughly defies our powers of imitation, that it would be impossible for a religious to attain the end of his state had he had no other instruction than those of the evangelical counsels, or no other means save those of the three vows; even as it would be impossible for a child to excel in the arts of music or drawing were his master contented in simply teaching him the definition of sound or of lines.

Our Lord's counsels stand therefore in need of a practical commentary. The monastic virtues require a positive direction, and amongst the innumerable exercises of spiritual life a prudent and exclusive choice is of the highest importance. The immense domain of perfection must be harrowed out; the field wherein the Lord's disciple is henceforth to pray, work, and suffer, must have its limits. It is necessary to individualize this kind of life. In a word, special forms are essential to the religious state. The object of this chapter is to give us a more perfect knowledge of the constitutions and rules peculiar to each order, and to lead us to dwell more fully upon their spirit, tendencies, and benefits.

Of this astonishing variety, which divides the one tree of the religious state into a thousand distinct branches, St. Thomas Aquino gives striking and profound reasons. In the entire creation, in the order of grace as in that of nature, the beings which are moved, governed, and perfected by others are always in greater number than those from whom they receive their impulses, their direction and perfection; and the number of these latter grows less and less as we ascend the scale of being; so that at the summit of each class and category, of which the world is made up, we find one only head, one single influence, one mover, and that lastly, above the material world, mankind, and the angels, there reigns one God, one Principle, one Providence, and one last End.

Thus, whilst the episcopacy of the holy Catholic Church is one, that is to say, not multiplied or divided into different orders, for all bishops have the self-same character; and in the midst of them rises one only spiritual King, their head and their centre: religious, on the contrary, are divided into many families, independent one of another, having a self-contained organization, proper constitutions, a particular mission, and special privileges. This is because the episcopacy is endowed with an *active* perfection, which diffuses itself amongst the Christian people to enlighten and strengthen them; while the perfection of the religious state is rather *passive*, God having made it subordinate to episcopal perfection, as the effect is subordinate to its cause.[1] So too, in the sphere of the world, round a single sun, which sheds on every side its light and warmth, we see numerous planets gravitate, each having a distinct train of brilliant satellites.

This diversity of regular congregations does not however tend to confusion or to disorder in the firmament of holy Church. For there exists amongst them a real distinction, founded either upon the difference of the objects they propose to themselves, or upon the different

---

[1] The greater number of religious orders are, it is true, entrusted with the teaching of the Christian doctrine, administrating the sacraments, and are thus actively employed in the work of sanctification. But it is not in virtue of their actual condition that they do this, or by a power intrinsic to their state. They are naturally in the inferior condition of disciples or subjects. When, therefore, they act as masters and spiritual superiors for the sanctification of the Christian people, they act as *ministers* in the name of prelates of the Church—as *living instruments* in the hand of the Sovereign Pontiff and the Bishops.

means they employ to attain the same identical end. They do not therefore become entangled one with another; neither do they encroach upon each other's territories, the ground that each undertakes to cultivate is distinctly marked out.

It is to maintain this distinction, so necessary to the peace and beauty of the mystic body of Jesus Christ, that the holy Apostolic See, the careful guardian of monastic perfection, as well as of ordinary sanctity, has reserved to itself the definitive approbation of religious orders. It keeps them within their individual vocation, it promotes their advancement in their respective paths, it reminds them, when necessary, of the seal which it has formerly stamped on their foreheads; and when it judges them incapable of maintaining their honour and duties, it has the power to suppress them, and to transfer their inheritance to others. The angelic St. Thomas compares the Church governed by the Sovereign Pontiff to the house built by Solomon, wherein reigned so much order, and which was regulated with so much wisdom, that the Queen of Saba was transported beyond herself in contemplating the servants of the King of

Jerusalem, who were ranked according to their tribe, distinguished by a special livery, and worked together without the least confusion in the performance of their various offices; and this caused her to exclaim; "Blessed are thy men, and blessed are thy servants, who stand before thee always and hear thy wisdom." [2]

His household was the prophetic type of the order which reigns in that great family of which St. Peter is the Pope, that is to say, the Father. Around this pacific King, this true Solomon, the religious are arranged in that perfect harmony of duties and ministries which remind us of the choir of angels. May all those souls engaged in this mystical army scrupulously guard their post in the fight! May none of them yield to that inconstancy or curiosity which induces many among them to leave their ranks to imitate everyone and burden themselves with the rules and practices of others to the neglect of their own observances and paternal traditions. But if the distinction between religious orders is quite sufficient to prevent all possibility of their being confounded with one another, it

[2] III. Kings x. 5—8.

is not, however, so radical as to forcibly separate them, or to justify a spirit of cold indifference or formal antagonism between them. They are all labouring in one common cause, which is the perfection of charity, intimate union with God, and the perfect practice of the virtue of religion. Again, they all tend to this end by the same essential means —by the three-fold holocaust of riches, of the flesh, and of self-will. They have likewise one only and similar destiny, which is the very essence of their being. So that they are not distinguished from each other in this respect. One order does not retain one portion of the victim, and the other another part: they one and all agree in the unreserved sacrifice of self. We find some that say, "We have for our supreme object the glorification of God;" and while others declare that they aim no higher than at the interests of the world and of the age, but they are all united in the same indivisible centre, the same final object, and one common desire and love of the same infinite Good. Their differences are to be found in their secondary aims, in means which are wholly inferior and subordinate to the three religious vows.

They are therefore closely united by their essential principles; they are divided only by their accidental element. The tie of moral relationship, which connects them together, consists in their nature and in their fundamental virtues; the characters which individualize them are but on the surface. Thus, they owe to each other a truly paternal affection, and are all mutually bound to assist one another, walking hand in hand to the same triumph. To lay stress with jealousy upon simple divergences, to exaggerate and transform them into party strife, would be to disown practically that which is theoretically manifest and true. It would be to close the heart to the evidence of reason, and to introduce hatred into the family of the Prince of Peace.

We can now understand of what vital importance it is that we should be accurate in describing the origin of the divers phases of the religious life, so as to protect at the same time the rights of unity, variety and harmony; and so that we may the better understand this origin, we must return to those principles of Catholic theology, which bear upon charity and religion, on man and his supernatural perfection.

The virtue of charity, the progressive development of which is to be secured by the religious life, exhibits itself in two different ways, and in regard to two different objects. Its *first* act relates immediately to God, to this infinite good, who is alone and sovereignly amiable, and from whom flows all possible goodness and amiability. And as the object of our affection continually attracts our will to Him, according to those divine words " Where thy treasure is, there is thy heart also ;"[3] and because the will cannot weary of embracing aud possessing Him, it commands the mind to contemplate Him unceasingly, to bring Him into the soul, there to keep Him for ever.[4] The *second* act of charity, instead of

[3] St. Matt. vi. 21.

[4] The necessity of knowing and meditating upon God in order to love Him, is expressed in the following axiom : *nothing can be the object of love or hatred if it be not previously known.* At the same time this does not mean that charity loves not in God Himself, but only in the knowledge it has of Him. In reality, although we do not *directly* see this infinite Good, we do nevertheless love Him *directly* in Himself.

soaring directly up to God, endeavours to love Him in mankind, whom He has been the first to love, and upon whom He has poured out the chalice of his bounty and of His redeeming blood. But our love cannot be bestowed upon a limited and created perfection in the same manner as upon the creating and infinite Perfection. This latter needs not our riches nor our labour; we cannot exhibit our love for It better than by incontemplating It. The former is ever poor and indigent, and if you truly love it you must work and suffer for its sake.

A religious desiring to attain the perfection of that celestial charity, may choose between the two motions that spring from it. If he should prefer to follow that impulse which tends directly to God, he will be a *contemplative;* but if on the contrary he is animated by that other inspiration which seeks Infinite Goodness in His works and the traces He has left of Himself, he must adopt a life which is mainly active.

The virtue of religion, which may be styled the soul of the monastic life, fulfils a double function in the Church. Sometimes it adores the Majesty of the King of Kings, by withdrawing into the solitude of the cloister. Following the counsel of Jesus Christ it carefully closes its doors against anything whatever which savours of the world, and there in secret prays to our Heavenly Father, who beholds every hidden thing, and who repays in ineffable enjoyments that which is offered to His honour and glory.[5] At other times, it goes forth into the midst of the darkness of the world, and there shines as a brilliant light. It glorifies the Lord publicly. It exalts His greatness, and proclaims His mercy in the face of an astonished world; and men seeing the good works which it does, either by itself or by ministry of the other virtues which it presses into its service are thus drawn to glorify our Father who is in heaven.[6] "To visit the fatherless and widows in their tribulation, and to keep oneself unspotted from this world, is," according to St. James the Apostle, "a religion clear and undefiled before God."[7] We see then that the religious life is divided into two distinct currents, both of which flow from the same source, from the same desire of honouring God, but which run through different countries. One flows gently

[5] St. Matt. vi. 6.   [6] *Ibid* v. 16.   [7] James i. 27.

through the deserts to the foot of the sacred mountains of Lebanon and Sinai, in the shade of those forests which are impenetrable to worldlings: and this is the course of the *contemplative life.* The other sheds its blessed waters over the scene of human toil, ambition and industry, and maintains on its banks a supernatural fertility, a service, the desire of heaven, of God, and Christian virtues, which otherwise would soon perish and decay; and this is the current of the *active life.*

It is neither by our bodies nor by our sensitive powers that we are truly men; for there are other beings that possess these secondary perfections. What distinguishes us, and gives us the eminent dignity with which we are clothed, is our intellectual life with its immaterial knowledge, the source of will and love. And as the Catholic religious ensures to himself the predominance of the spiritual life, by suppressing, in so far as lies in his power, his purely animal life, we may justly claim for him the title of a perfect man, of *man above others.*

Now, spiritual knowledge, which is the sovereign act and highest manifestation of the human life, and particularly of the monastic life, has two terms or objects. It sometimes seeks the truth solely for its intrinsic beauty. The mind rests in it and delights therein, and will taste of nought but the ineffable sweetness derived from the knowledge of God, and of divine things. Time is nothing to it; what more could it desire in heaven or on earth: does it not already possess the Lord, its eternal portion? Such is the *contemplative* religious, the chaste lover of pure truth.

Sometimes also the soul searches after and considers "truth" not on account of the charms which it finds therein, but for the use it can be to the world. To teach truth to others, by its rays to illuminate those paths wherein so many minds go astray and lose themselves, to introduce its reign into every heart, to bring out from its treasury the consolation, strength and assistance which it offers to man, weighed down under the painful burden of labour, in a word to apply it to the practical life; such is the part of an *active* religious, the indefatigable labourer of truth.

Lastly, Christian sanctity, the acquisition of which is the object of the regular state, consists in the intimate union of the soul with its God. Now, it is impossible to be perfect if we are removed from our Beginning and last End, the Author and Centre of all perfection. And, on the other hand, it is equally impossible to be imperfect when in complete union with God! Does not the perfect happiness of the elect result from the immediate presence of the adorable Trinity, which fills the very depths of their heart and intellect?

Now, this mysterious communication of divine life, which renders us supernaturally perfect, is equally promised to those who love God and to those who love one another for His sake. After recording for us that promise of the Redeemer, "If any one love Me, he will keep My word, and My Father will love him; and We will come to him, and will make Our abode with him,"[8] the same Evangelist further tells us that, "If we love one another, God abideth in us, and His charity is perfected in us. In this we know that we abide in Him, and He in us; because He hath given us of His Spirit."[9] Therefore the religious life possesses two methods equally assured of drawing their nourishment from the di-

[8] John xiv. 23.   [9] I. John iv. 12, 13.

vine life, and so of attaining to a sublime degree of perfection. The first is the concentration of all its efforts and its labour upon the sincere love of God, increasing every day the ardour of this celestial flame, by reading, meditation and prayer, and thus uniting itself directly with God by *contemplation*. The second is to devote oneself to the love and service of one's neighbour, wholly expending oneself for him, multiplying around one works of charity, scattering with generous hands both spiritual and corporal blessings, and being thus united to the Supreme Good by *action*. Here are some of the reasons of the classification of regular congregations into contemplative and active orders. This classification is fundamental and serves as the starting point for all others, because it proceeds not only from the diversity of means employed by religious for the realization of their pious ambition, but from the object which they propose for their end; that is to say, from that charity in which they desire to increase, from that religion which they are anxious to practise in all its perfection, from that human life which they wish to raise to the highest possible degree, and, finally, from that divine union to

W

which they aspire. Of this charity, this religion, this human life, this union, and, consequently, of this religious life, manifesting itself under two forms, contemplatives will have for their share peace and tranquillity in God, the study of the Holy Scriptures and prayer, full liberty of the soul and the foretaste of the joys of heaven, light supernatural and much supernatural beauty. They were typified by the favourite spouse of Jacob, by Rachel, whose name signifies a lamb, and also, according to St. Thomas, the *sight of the principle*, the contemplation of eternal Truth, Rachel, whose beauty and agreeable aspect have been praised by the Holy Ghost, but who was almost barren and died in giving birth to her second son. Contemplative religious are also similar to Mary Magdalen, faithfully seated at the feet of our Lord, listening with delight to His divine word, and receiving from His sacred lips the assurance that she had chosen the better part which should not be taken from her.

As to the active orders, they possess in a special manner the moral virtues, they bear courageously the heats and burden of the day. They resign themselves, according to the exigences of prudence, to the bondage and distractions of this transitory world. They have been represented in the Old Testament by Leah, the first wife of Jacob, whose name signifies *laborious* and *wearied*; by Leah, whose diseased eyes were not intended like those of Rachel for the full light of day. Their vocation is that of Martha, who was occupied and necessarily troubled about many exterior things, so that, as St. Augustine says, "While Mary heard these words: *In the beginning was the Word*, Martha translated them by her deeds into this other phrase: "*And the Word was made flesh.*" [10] An admirable remark which is perfectly applicable to our divers communities, some of whom contemplate in the sacred tranquillity of the cloister the Divine Word and the immutable truths of which He is the Principle, whilst others prefer to serve in the midst of the world the Word Who was made flesh and dwelt amongst us. The former more especially remind us of eternity and its grandeur—the latter of the mystery of the Incarnation and its blessings. The life of

---

[10] *The Words of Our Lord*, Discourse XXVII.

contemplation resembles more nearly the divinity of Jesus, the active His humanity. [11]

We just now compared the religious life to a large river, which having diverged into two

[11] This reflexion of St. Augustine, which is quoted by St. Thomas, does not favour in any way the error of false mystics, who think the contemplation of the human sanctity of our Lord a mark of imperfection. We must not separate that which God has substantially joined. Jesus Christ, true God and true man, is the sovereign type, the indivisible model, and the object of both the contemplative and active life. But this is not the place to treat of the magnificent subject of contemplation. If it be God's holy Will, we will fathom this doctrine in another commentary upon the Ascetic Theology of the Angel of the School. The simple allusion we have made to the figurative characters of Leah and Rachel, Mary and Martha, suffices to demonstrate what abundance of light and piety the Scriptures, studied from a symbolical point of view, may shed on souls. Jansenism and the excessive critical tendencies of certain modern theologians, have dried up in France this source to which our religious formerly came, after the example of St. Gregory the Great, St. Augustine and St. Bernard, to draw so many and deep and graceful inspirations. But we know that grave and eloquent works are now being prepared for the adaptation of Holy Writ to the requirements of souls. May God bless the seed thus cast upon the earth by the hand of a friend of him who wrote these pages ! (See *Ruth*, by M. l'Abbé TARDIF DE MOIDREY. Brussels : 1871.)

currents, unites again, emptying itself into the same ocean of divine love. In an historical point of view it would perhaps be more useful to consider it as an everlasting vine, whose one trunk, watered by the Redeemer's blood has produced two enormous branches. For eighteen centuries these boughs have sought to stretch themselves over the surface of the globe, and there is no climate however sterile it may be, where they have not at some time or other extended their growth and spread their foliage. First of all, one of them advanced into the solitudes of the East, until the West and the New World had opened to it their wildernesses; it has avoided the concourse of men, highways and great cities, and it is in the deserts that its virginal fruit has ripened. The other more animated by the spirit of the Christian apostolate, was during the same time spreading over Roman cities, barbarian fortresses and feudal manors. It gradually penetrated, as it were, through the interstices of the walls, even into the very heart of paganism and barbarity; it produced its fruits of chastity, strength and charity; and the ancient nations, transformed by its divine influence, prepared to carry it on the vessels of Colombus and Gama, even to the uttermost boundaries of the earth. But on the sands of Egypt, no less than on the triumphal roads of Rome, it is ever the same vine-stock which spreads itself out, encircling in its two arms the whole universe, and reproducing everywhere in its mystical offshoots the perfect image of Christ crucified, and of Jesus crushed under the wine-press of His passion!

The two branches of this sacred vine, I mean the two principal forms of religious life, have frequently united themselves and mingled their sap in order to produce boughs contemplative and active in one. These are the *mixed* orders. They are most useful to the Church for the preaching of the Gospel, and are consequently very numerous in every era of spiritual conquest. Their economy may be summed up in the indisputable principle that all well directed exterior works are an excellent preparation for the contemplative life, and that, on the other hand, contemplation is the true source of the energy and virtues necessary to the active life. It is therefore possible to reconcile interior practices with outward works, perfect prayer with a vigorous apostolate, the study of divine things with the care of souls. Whether the active element be stronger than the contemplative, whether the latter predominate, or whether they be well balanced, the general rules which we have explained when treating of the simple form of the religious life are easily applicable to this state, which is produced by the combination of the two first.

In every age the hand of God has unceasingly engrafted on the essential branches of religious life secondary branches, which impart to the original sap (from which they derive their vitality), add new properties, fresh strength and a special efficacy. In classifying them, our Angelic Master no longer considers the end proposed by religious, but the means they employ in order to attain it, be it by contemplation, action, or by the perfect observance of their vows. And as a distinction founded upon a diversity of means is always less radical and less conspicuous than that which results from a difference of objects or ends, it frequently happens that one order ruled by a single head is divided into several congregations, so that whilst the end remains the same for all, each employ different means.

These means are almost innumerable, and it may be easily understood that whilst the fundamental classification be reduced to three terms, viz., contemplative, active and mixed orders, their subdivisions are indefinitely multiplied. Thus, charity towards our neighbour may find its perfection and continual growth in the care of the sick, the education of children, mercy to the poor, hospitality to pilgrims, foreign missions, preaching in a Christian country, the administration of the sacraments, and a thousand other works of zeal, each containing an incredible variety of excellent acts. Has not the education of children alone excited in divers ways the zeal of Saints Benedict, Ignatius of Loyola, Jerome Emiliani, Vincent de Paul, of the Blessed Pierre Fourier, and the Venerable de la Salle, without counting the numerous pious founders who have, in these later days, sought the same end by parallel roads. Again, all congregations necessarily agree in the rigorous profession of the three vows of poverty, chastity, and obedience, which are the principal means of the religious state. But the observances which dispose and which assist a religious in making proper use of this threefold spiritual lever are extremely numerous. It is necessary in every congregation to mortify the flesh in order to maintain it in humble submission to chastity, which spiritualizes it; but with some, this mortification will consist in abstinence; with others in solitude; with others, again, in the community life, manual labour, or a coarse and poor habit; some will have recourse to assiduous study and recollection; others to austerities and discipline. The end is identical, but the means will be variable and numerous.

Amongst these means of perfection, which serve to characterize the secondary forms of the regular state, we must place in the highest rank the complete solitude of the religious who lives far from the world, and even from his fellow men, habitually buried in the deserts, like Paul and Antony, or at least hidden in the silence and humility of his cell, like Romuald and Bruno. Diametrically opposed to this absolute isolation, and assuredly more beneficial for the greater number of souls, the community life offers us its cloisters, its schools, its libraries, its workrooms, and its famous Churches. And from this two-fold observance proceeds the great division between religious families into *recluses* and *cenobites*.¹²

Voluntary poverty extended to the farthest point which it may be permitted to reach is a sure way to attain to the perfection of charity, and of the other supernatural virtues, and is the specific characteristic of the *mendicant* order; while common property, wisely administered, and dispensed with rigorous discretion, are, in the active orders, needful instruments of a multitude of holy works.¹³ Preaching the Gospel, giving Missions in country places, or amongst infidels, the teaching of sacred and profane sciences, the sanctification of souls, and other spiritual works capable of making us advance rapidly in Christian perfection, are objects which have given rise in every age, and still distinguish many congregations that might be called *teaching* or *apostolical*. Besides these, we find the *laborious* and penitential orders, devoting themselves mainly to corporal exercises, to abstinence,

---

¹² The name hermit signifies one *who inhabits the desert*, which is the most perfect form of the religious state, and he is consequently the *monk* or *recluse par excellence*. The *cenobite* is one *who lives in community*.

¹³ Compare Chapter IV : *The domain of poverty.*

watching, rough clothing, the discipline, manual labour, to the care of sick children, to hospitality, and even to the armed defence of Christianity against its visible enemies.

A constant application to solemn services, the celebration of the sacred mysteries, the practice of the sacred liturgy, has led to the establishment of *regular canons*, who, consequently, must be *clerics*, that is to say, persons set apart to offer to the Lord the praise of a perpetual psalmody, persons educated on that account for the ecclesiastical state, and invested with the necessary faculties such sacred functions require. Religious belonging to orders, simply monastic orders, do not make use of this liturgical method for the attainment of their object; thus they are not bound to enter the clerical state, and may still, though they be monks, remain amongst the laity. Finally, mercifully wishing to accommodate itself to the weakness of many persons who might be terrified by the austerities practised in the great orders, desiring to meet the impossibility which many Christians experience of entirely abandoning the world, and more especially to provide against an infinity of needs, evils, and calamities, to which every day gives birth, and which afflict us more and more, and which the old orders are insufficient to remedy, an ever-bountiful Providence has frequently inspired in modern times the foundation of *third orders*, which are open to every class of the faithful, societies of *regular* clergy, who serve as intermediaries between the secular clergy and monks, also, congregations with *simple and temporary vows*, or even without any *formal* vows. All these are different forms of the religious life, but of a religious life making itself, so to speak, little, and popular, in order to accommodate itself the more easily to the infinite details of human misery, by this means to effect a more efficacious cure of all its ills!

The fundamental principles which the Angel of the School has laid down for the regular state properly so-called, must therefore be applied to all religious societies, in proportion to their degree of connexion with the absolute type of life. Each and every one of them will find therein the light and strength suited to them; and the teaching of St. Thomas on this point while respecting the distinctive properties of each of them, unites them altogether in one self-same and perfect love of their common end, and in one and in the solid practice of the virtues essential to their condition. Is not unity of being with variety of forms the source of strength and beauty, and who knows whether the Spirit of God will not one day exhibit to us a great movement towards union and association amongst all these numerous congregations which cultivate in harmony the field of the Master of the household, and whose self-sacrificing efforts might perhaps gain a new impetus for their zealous work of sanctification, were they more closely combined. It will not be uninteresting to draw comparisons between the various forms of religious life, and to weigh their precise excellence. Souls eager for perfection should know the privileged regions where this precious pearl is hidden, where this admirable treasure is buried. Moreover, the greater number of regular congregations of the present day being composed of contemplative and active elements, it will be useful to be able to ascribe to each of them that degree of esteem and attention which they deserve.

In the first place, it is evident that this comparison cannot be brought to bear upon the last end or essential object of religious orders. All are equal in this regard, since all aim at perfection in charity, the divine worship, and the glory of God. Likewise it cannot refer to the three vows of chastity, obedience, and poverty, for these are indispensable to every kind of truly religious life. Where the comparison begins then, is in the special properties which distinguish one from another—the divers manifestations of this life which divide this mystic tree into separate branches. In order to form to oneself a correct idea of the real value of each community, it is necessary to examine, first, their immediate object, and, secondly, the means which they make use of to attain that object.

The superiority of one order over another does not really so much result from the austerity of its practices, the number of its observances, or the sublimity of its exercises —in a word, from the intrinsic excellence of its means—as from the greatness of the *end* to which they all converge. As the beauty of the King's daughter was from within, so, too, the value of an order appears not on the surface: you must not judge of it by its outward brilliancy. Reason must dive deeper into the matter, and must not allow itself to be influenced by the too often hasty and erroneous opinions formed by the world. Again, it is not only the world that makes this mistake. In making choice of a community wherein they would serve God in the fulness of perfection, do not souls often dwell upon details which are altogether superficial and exterior, rather considering the principles; instead of determining their choice by the end to which they feel themselves attracted by grace?

Means which are of themselves very imposing and worthy of consideration, may be subordinate to an inferior end, and enterprises almost heroic in themselves may lead but to a sorry result. On the other hand, an order which is really sublime from the greatness of the object which it pursues, may attain its end by very modest and insignificant methods. How simple were the practices of the great Eastern ascetics! When those illustrious Roman ladies of whom St. Jerome was the instructor and biographer, visited the Fathers in the desert, what did they see, and what was their surprise! With what astonishment did they not behold aged men humbly and silently seated on the sand weaving baskets! They were astounded at their sanctity, but even more so at their ingenuous and childlike simplicity.

Therefore we should not draw comparison between two religious orders in regard to their exercises and observances, unless we have previously settled that their end is wholly identical.[14] And even then we have to consider whether the more brilliant and more rigorous means are as exactly adapted and proportioned to the end in view as those which are more humble, more hidden, and more easy. If these last insure better success, the order which employs them will probably excite least admiration amongst men, but will be far the most pleasing to the infallible Eye of God. St. Anthony preferred discretion and moderation in all things to vigils, hair-shirts, and rude penances; "for these," he said, "often expose monks to discouragement and relaxation."[15] And St.

---

[14] It is scarcely worth while to observe that we here suppose an equal fervour on both sides; for a relaxed community would be certainly inferior to a community less noble in its end and means, but more zealous and regular in their practice.

[15] *Conferences of the Fathers*, Conf. II. ch. 2.

Thomas observes that a tool is of very little value in itself, and that it acquires its worth only from the work which it helps to perform, and that it is not better in proportion as it is more of a *tool*, but only in the degree that it is best suited to its purpose. For example, it is not by the administration of a variety of medicines that a doctor effects a cure, but by the application of that one remedy best suited to the complaint. Thus, although the nakedness, immobility, cold, and terrible scourging to which several hermits subjected themselves are unquestionably more formidable than abstinence from certain meats and beverages, yet abstinence is more conducive to the preservation of the holy and perpetual chastity of both soul and body. Austerity itself is not an undeniable proof of the superiority of an order. It is necessary to return to the analysis of its end, and to observe whether it proposes as its object a more considerable good, or, at least, a greater number of advantages.

According to this doctrine, the life of contemplative religious is preferable to the active life, and Our Lord has congratulated them in the person of St. Mary Magdalen for having chosen the better and more excellent part. What happiness is more real, more intimate, or more complete than this peaceful, tender, and absolute union of the soul with its God? To possess Him alone, without being condemned to seek Him in creatures; to honour Him directly in Himself, instead of resting in the trace He has left of Himself in His works; to give Him all one's heart without division or distraction; to realize thus, with the most perfect truth, this noble unity, which is the stamp of the *monastic* life;[16] to live, so to speak, only in the spirit, in a bright halo of faith and reason, and consequently to attain to the most perfect beauty possible; to belong no longer in any way to the world, neither by the heart's affection nor even by bodily presence—is not this human life in its most exalted state?—is not this already a heavenly life? For what is the ineffable beatitude of Paradise if not the completion and prolongation for an eternity of this initial

---

[16] Compare ch. vi., *The Privileges of Virginity.* The unity of the religious life, so well begun by the virtue of continence, finds thus its perfection in the practice of contemplation; so the word *monk* applies especially to contemplative religious.

and transitory contemplation here below? We may almost say that the contemplative religious is indeed already, by his state, in a condition similar to that of the elect.

And yet this state may be exalted still higher. To this privilege of divine contemplation may be added another, which I will freely call apostolic. It is that sometimes the contemplative soul is so inundated by light and love, that in its plenitude it overflows and is shed upon the earth, like the odoriferous perfume with which Mary anointed the sacred feet of our Lord. The religious comes forth from his cell overflowing with knowledge, charity, and zeal. He goes forth to his brethren in the world, and teaches and announces to them all that he has seen, all that he has observed with his own eyes, and that which he has touched with his own hands. It is to "these perfect men who return to us after their sublime contemplations"[17] that the Pope St. Gregory applies this verse of the Psalms, "They shall publish the memory of the abundance of Thy sweetness, and shall rejoice in Thy justice." This active life proceeds from the contempla-

---

[17] V. *Homily on Ezechiel*.

tive which it brings out,[18] and spreads abroad, without, however, forsaking it. And orders which are devoted to this angelic ministry—to this transmission of divine truths to the human mind—are certainly superior to congregations purely contemplative. Even as the angelic St. Thomas says, even as it is better to give light than to shine under a bushel, so it is better to communicate that which one has contemplated than only to contemplate it.

Such was the custom of our Lord Jesus Christ upon earth. The Prophets had foretold that He would be seen conversing with men.[19] And although He would sometimes by retiring to the desert give us the example of a purely contemplative life, He nevertheless passed the greater part of His mortal career in the midst of the world, in order to manifest to it His divinity and His miracles; and amongst the poor and infirm that He might seek them out, and bring them to Him, like the shepherd seeking for his lost sheep. He dwelt in the midst of publicans and sinners in order to inspire them all with a

[18] Ps. cxliv. 7. [19] Baruch iii. 38.

salutary and invincible confidence in the mercy of their Redeemer.

But when the active life is not like that of our Lord, the reflection and effusion of superabundant contemplation—when it is wholly engaged in exterior occupations, such as the distribution of alms, or the exercise of hospitality, it then becomes much inferior to that which is exclusively contemplative. No question but that it is religious life, a continual hymn of adoration and praise, an excellent holocaust; but it does not tend so nearly to God. It does not belong to Him so exclusively, withheld from Him and divided as it is necessarily, through the distractions of earthly cares. It is not so admirable as the contemplative life, and if it is more fruitful than its heavenly companion, it is nevertheless obliged to daily borrow from it the food which sustains its activity, the power which animates its members, and the divine dew which prevents its spirit from being parched. It loves not this world, which has no charms for it. What it uses, it uses as if it used it not. It has been chosen from and drawn out of the world by its vocation, and yet it ever remains there, and is enchained by its bodily presence, by its cares and labours. Its freedom is not complete: it is distracted, distressed, and tempted, which causes it to weep and moan. It awaits, with a holy sorrow, its deliverance and change. Like the hireling, it sighs after the evening's repose; and like Martha it looks with an eye of legitimate and supernatural envy on the privileges and joys of Mary. Still the maternal fecundity of Leah gives her a real pre-eminence over Rachel, beautiful, yet almost barren. At a time when the apostolate and works of charity are absolutely indispensable to the Church, and the voice of the supreme Pastor calls all his children to share in the combat, the active life may become preferable to the contemplative. Not that this latter ever ceases to be useful by its merits, its expiations, and its intercessions; but in the time of war, the soldier may be more necessary than the doctor, and there are times of calamity when mercy is more useful than science.

Whatever may be the case during such exceptional periods as we have just considered, in the normal condition of Christianity the *first* rank belongs to those regular orders who are devoted to teaching and preaching; they are most closely allied to the *active* perfection of Bishops, and form a kind of transition between the sanctifying church and the church sanctified. The *second* degree belongs to institutes which are purely contemplative; and the *third* is that of those congregations which devote themselves principally to exterior works. When pious communities are of the same class, we should esteem that one as most noble which has for its object the practice of the highest virtue. Thus amongst the works of an active life, it is more perfect to ransom captives than to exercise hospitality; and in the contemplative, prayer is above reading and study. Finally, if two congregations of the same rank propose to themselves an end which is wholly identical, superiority must be attributed to the one which is most fruitful in its results, or which in connexion with their common end possesses the better system of rules and observances.

It would be easy, but it appears to us superfluous, to extend this comparative examination, and to apply its principles to many other societies who, like the foregoing, are not distinguished by diversity of ends, but merely by the variety of their methods for the attainment of perfection. In this category, St. Thomas confines himself to the comparison of the life of the recluse, with that of the cenobite. Solitude, he says, is not the essence of perfection; like poverty, it is but an instrument. The *Conferences of the Fathers* warn the religious that isolation as well as fasting and other bodily mortifications should be practised in order to obtain purity of the heart.[20] Thus one must not be surprised to find that habitual solitude is not suitable to active and mixed orders—that is, to the immense majority of religious. Indeed, how could they exercise acts of spiritual and corporal mercy living as they would do apart from the world which they are called upon to heal and to save? If you are a member of one of these communities, guard yourself as scrupulously as you would from a dangerous snare from that aversion to outward works, from that antipathy to men, from that suspicious liking for silence and recollection, and from those sad and gloomy humours which assume to themselves so willingly and yet so falsely the appearances of a pious love for retreat. For

[20] Conference i. ch. 7.

you the kingdom of heaven is not wholly within—it is equally without, it is in charity to your neighbour, in the faithful protection of his interests, in soothing his sufferings, and in lightening that burden of moral or physical pain under which he sinks.

Solitude, on the contrary, is the real home of contemplation. "I will lead her into the wilderness," says the Holy Spirit, "and I will speak to her heart;"[21] and if God speaks must not His creatures be silent? What can the eye darkened by the shades and phantoms of this world see of the infinite splendours of eternity? Can the will engrossed with worldly business maintain the mind in the consideration of heavenly things and be fixed on their love alone? Solitude is indeed the state for contemplatives; "but," adds our Doctor, "for such as are already perfect." The anchoret must necessarily find in himself all the resources he requires, and should therefore not stand in need of anything; and if he wants nothing it is because he is perfect. Whether his perfection proceeds from the efficiency of grace alone, as was the case with St. John the Precursor, who was filled with

---

[21] Osee ii. 14.

the Holy Ghost from his mother's womb, and led by the same Spirit into the desert from his earliest infancy; or whether this perfection has been acquired by a long apprenticeship of virtue, in such a way that the soul being sufficiently guided by the divine impression, and having learned to discern with certainty good from evil, the motions of grace from those of nature, heavenly inspirations from the illusions of the devil, may henceforward be contented with affective obedience, having no longer need of a human master whom he must actually obey each day. Under these conditions, solitude presents no dangers, is even preferable to common life, and deserves the praise given to it by the Bishop of Hippo—" Such persons are most holy who, avoiding the presence of men, give access to none, and live in a great habit of prayer."[22] But this life is beset with grievous dangers for imperfect and unexperienced souls, unless Providence deigns to supply their infirmity as It did in the cases of St. Anthony and St. Benedict, who withdrew whilst still very young into the silence of a hermit's life. But who would dare to

---

[22] *On the Works of Monastic Life*, ch. 23.

expect from heaven such miraculous assistance?

Therefore, before embracing this sublime state, but yet none the less to be feared, it is necessary to prepare seriously for it, and there is no method better adapted to this purpose than community life. Here youthful minds are directed, enlightened, and instructed in those things on which they must meditate hereafter; "formed to this solitude of the heart, without which," says St. Gregory, "the solitude of the body is nothing."[23] "I am delighted," wrote St. Jerome, "for that thou profitest by the society of saints, and that thou art not thine own teacher."[24] In their pious company the evil inclinations of the will are corrected, and pernicious affections become extinct; good example and prudent corrections anticipate or retrieve our falls; the invisible but actual contact of souls communicates to all a holy spiritual warmth, and a powerful impulse to good. "Is it then," continues St. Jerome, "that we censure the life of the anchoret? By no means, for often indeed we have praised it. But what we would wish is, that these spiritual warriors

---

[23] *Morals*, Book XXX. [24] *Letter IV. to Rusticus.*

should first be formed in monasteries—as it were in a gymnasium—that they may come forth with sufficient strength to remain unscathed by the hard life of the desert, and be proved for as long a time as may reassure us concerning them for the future."[25] The Greek philosopher whose doctrine St. Thomas completes and characterizes so admirably, has made a remark which is in itself a deep summary of the privileges and perils of solitude. Man is naturally made for society, and if he breaks the ties which unite him to it, it is the effect either of a fatal and cruel degradation which renders human life insupportable to him, or it is a sublime elevation which transports him beyond himself and unites him intimately with heavenly things. "He who lives not in communication with others is either a brute or a god"[26]—that is to say, a divine man.

God made man, our Lord Jesus Christ would Himself show us the path of retreat, and teach us by His own example that even if all religious are neither destined nor fitted to bury themselves definitely in solitude, they

[25] *Letter IV. to Rusticus.*
[26] Aristotle, *Politics,* Book I.

should, nevertheless, know it, and retire into it occasionally to draw from it the faith, understanding, love and courage which are so indispensable to a holy life in their respective communities, and more especially in the world into which they are called by the apostleship and exterior works. The Angelic Doctor alleges three reasons which, while explaining the conduct of our Lord, establish the extreme importance of this temporary retirement for all monastic orders, even of active ones. At times our Divine Master retired into the wilderness to seek *repose* for the soul, and refreshment for the body. "Come apart," said He one day to His disciples, "into a desert place, and rest a little," " because, adds the Evangelist, " there were many coming and going : and they had not so much time as to eat." [27] At other times, it was to *pray* more freely, or to prepare His Apostles for more fruitful ministry: and that is what He did during forty days preceding His public life, "withdrawing to a mountain to pray, He spent the whole night in prayer with God." [28] Finally, He taught us in this manner to despise and shun the favour of man ; and St.

[27] Mark vi. 31. [28] Luke vi. 12.

John Chrysostom, commenting upon the following passage, "And seeing the multitudes Jesus went up into a mountain," says: "By selecting a mountain and a desert place rather than a city or public thoroughfare (to reveal the high morality of Christianity), Jesus shows us that nothing must be done for ostentation sake, but that we should retire from the tumult of the world, particularly when it is a question of dealing with things that are most important to us." [29]

Next to the virtues of charity and religion, next to the vows of obedience, of chastity and poverty,[30] there is nothing more grand or more precious in the regular state than the spirit of contemplation and prayer, than preaching divine truths, than community life, or the state of prudent solitude. This is sufficient to determine any soul sincerely religious to make careful use of these powerful means of perfection to the degree of its vocation, and according to the rules of its order. None of those who belong to this holy state can be exempted either from praying, and

---

[29] On St. Matthew v. 1.

[30] See Chapter ii. *The Evangelical Counsels* and the end of VIII. *Religious Vows*.

announcing by word and example, or at least by meriting and suffering and endurance, the Gospel of the Kingdom of Heaven; from living under the rule of a common authority; or in fine, from having his hours and days of retreat. Let all carry out these observances with an ever-growing zeal and attention, and these vows will soon be admirably kept, Divine worship will flourish, and charity will be perfected.

It is scarcely necessary to observe that the excellence of these practices does not authorise our exclusive devotion to them, to the neglect of the constitutions of the community rules; still less, does it justify anyone in cherishing a secret jealousy against such as apply themselves to any special observance, by which they grow in perfection.

In reality each religious order proposes to itself an individual end on which it concentrates all its efforts, it thus attains and realizes it in a very perfect manner, which ensures to it an indisputable superiority in this particular point over all other orders. One order excels in a work of charity, such as the redemption of captives; another in a different work, and which has its own particular value, as in the instruction of children: and all should strive with ardour and zeal for the better understanding of the end and means which Divine Providence has designed for them, that they may thus derive from them all possible benefit, and that finally they may be guided by the principles set forth by ascetic theology for the divers forms of spiritual life.

Would not the advance of religious souls be more real and rapid if the pious readings, instructions and reflexions which hold so prominent a position in their daily routine were always inspired by an accurate notice of the end proper to each congregation, as well as by the knowledge of such books and doctrines as are the best suited to them? Is not much time and trouble frequently wasted in vague but useless research, when a more positive knowledge might have directed them to a more precise and happier result?

Have there never been at the helm of monastic communities inexperienced or careless pilots, who neither know by which tack to sail, nor at what port to land?

It appears then most useful to consider the teaching of St. Thomas as to the existence of a harmonious variety of form in the religious state, to ascertain the principal as well as the secondary causes of this diversity of rule, and to see the relative importance of the elements of which it is composed. Thus only can we prudently select and successfully follow the true path to which we are called by God. And then will contemplation, the apostleship, divine worship, and works of charity flourish once more in the land, and restore to us the glory and joys of the best ages of the Church.

CHAPTER XII.

Works of the Religious Life.

EVERY being, and more especially every intelligent creature, is destined to glorify God, its author, preserver, and last end. And this glorification necessarily constitutes a work, an operation, the result of finite activity seconded by the Divine assistance. How indeed could one give glory to God, if one remained inactive, or shut up in oneself? Can it be supposed that minds without intellect, or hearts devoid of affection, really honour the Supreme Majesty?

The Angelic Doctor has justly asserted that everything is made for an *end*, to which it instinctively tends, for which it solely exists, from which it derives all its goodness, and in which it finds its perfection and complete happiness.

The religious forms no exception to this universal law. He, too, is created to act, be it either in the invisible and interior life of the contemplative, or in the exterior and visible world. Wherefore his vows, his rule, his exercises? Why this renouncement of earthly goods, of sensual pleasures, and of natural independence? It is because he must act, and he wishes, firstly, to rid himself of every fetter which restrains his powers, to divest himself of every burden which clogs his athletic arm, to bind himself to those new and sublime acts from which nature shrinks, and to train himself to the sacred art of glorifying God by labour.

An inactive religious, who does nothing more than an ordinary Christian, and does not put into action those supernatural faculties with which God has endowed him in virtue of his condition, is but a rough sketch, an unformed being, a body without life, a strange contradiction. He is like, according to the Scriptures, "to clouds without water, which are carried about by winds; trees of the autumn, unfruitful, twice dead, plucked up by the roots; raging waves of the sea, foaming out their own confusion; wandering stars, to whom the storm of darkness is reserved for ever;"[1] because, being without fruit or utility, they cannot enjoy infinite happiness in that God whom they refused to praise whilst on earth.

The regular life, which we have hitherto considered in its principles, powers, and forms, will now appear before us in its acts, that is to say, in its perfection; and as it will be impossible to enumerate all its workings—for, as St. Thomas says, there is scope enough in each and every one of the corporal and spiritual works of mercy to occupy the activity of a special religious order, we will at least set forth an estimate of its principal acts, indicating the spirit with which they should be animated, so as to anticipate in some measure

[1] Jude, 12, 13.

the dangers which at times accompany them.² Wisdom is the work *par excellence* of religious. The study of truth is therefore one of their most sublime and most important works. The silent attention of Mary Magdalen was preferred by our Lord to the anxious cares of Martha. And Martha, amid the bustle of her active life, felt the absolute necessity of turning occasionally to her Divine Master, of questioning Him, and of being thus enlightened and strengthened by His words. "She stood and said: 'Hast thou no care that my sister hath left me to serve? speak to her, therefore, that she help me.'"³ She is recollected; she has studied the thought of the Lord; she has heard the oracle from His adorable lips: and if but for a moment, she enjoyed the happy lot of Mary. Thus for every religious order, to whatsoever class it belongs, meditation and study of wisdom are an indispensable work, and a primary duty. For those who are contemplative, the study of the sacred sciences

---

[2] It must be borne in mind that we examine these works exclusively in a religious point of view, reserving for other treatises the general considerations proper to all states, to the faithful and ecclesiastical as well as to regulars.

[3] Luke x. 40.

and even of polite literature, is doubly necessary. Its first and direct utility is to enlighten the mind, and thus dispose it for an intimate union with the sweet object of its contemplation and love; to direct it in the exalted paths of prayer, and to furnish it with those principles, ideas, comparisons, feelings, and method, which form the human basis of contemplation. Hence the just man is commended by the Holy Ghost for having consecrated his days and nights to the meditation of the law of God; for having searched into the wisdom of the ancients; and applied himself to the study of the prophets.[4] Study also affords another help, indirect it is true, but not less precious than the other to all persons engaged in a contemplative order, because it removes from them the evils attached even to the state of contemplation, that is to say, the error of those who aspire to great and superhuman heights without having previously acquired a profound or exact knowledge, not merely of theology, but even of the Catholic catechism. The Angel of the School furnishes us with an instance of the Abbé Serapion, who, being a simple and ignorant

---

[4] Ps. i. 2; Ecclesiasticus xxxix. 1.

monk, fell into the heresy of the Anthropomorphites, who attributed a human form to God.[5] And since that time, how many souls are there who have been mis-led by false mystics through being deficient in accurate knowledge of the doctrine of the Church. The danger still exists, and regular communities can never be too cautious in guarding against all those frivolous sentiments, superficial and worldly opinions, which find entrance everywhere, and expose many persons to the illusions of the enemy. The essential duty of a religious should be to give himself up to a serious study, as deep as may be, of the truths of Christianity; to an assiduous reading of the writings of the Saints; to a constant study of the treatises of these glorious doctors whose teaching has shone on so many admirable ages; and, finally, a prudent wariness with regard to certain works which, while they flatter the imagination, vitiate the taste and the heart.

The education of childhood is usually so vague and incomplete, in a supernatural point of view, that such as are called to the religious state must necessarily recommence it in the

[5] *Conferences* of Cassian. Conf. x. ch. 31.

cloister, under pain of straying into the endless and inextricable labyrinth of scruples, fears, errors, and sometimes even false doctrine. "There are," remarks St. Gregory the Great, "persons who, from striving to raise themselves to a degree of contemplation of which they are incapable, fall ever into perverse doctrines; and refusing to be the humble disciples of truth, they become masters of error."[6] Why do they not rather follow the example of King Solomon, who "turned his mind to wisdom in order to avoid folly?"[7]

Another advantage possessed by profane arts and sciences is that they give us more precise and accurate ideas of the surrounding world, as well as of the interior and more limited world of our own selves; and as all creatures reflect and bear the traces of the divine perfections, a contemplative religious will derive a positive advantage from their study, and will draw from them a greater aptitude for the meditation of heavenly things. For it is totally false to suppose, as some people seem to do, that by the very fact of a person being simple and uneducated, he thereby becomes entitled to or better dis-

[6] *Morals*, Book VI.   [7] Ecclesiasticus ii. 3.

posed for the reception of a greater abundance of supernatural light. That God does work such miracles is certain, but that these wonders are of frequent occurrence, or that knowledge in itself is injurious to contemplation is absolutely false! Would it not be far more to the point to show the numerous and real perils of ignorance, than to talk at random of the dangers of study? St. Thomas of Aquino endeavours to demonstrate the advantages to spiritual progress of systematic study, but is silent as to the imaginary benefits of ignorance. He does not doubt that sometimes "holy rusticity," as it is called by St. Jerome,[8] is accompanied by useful qualities; but he adds with the same doctor, that this usefulness is purely personal, and if such a life tends sometimes to the edification of the Church, it might also be very pernicious to it, if it knew not how to resist the adversaries of truth. The wisdom of the saints, concludes our Master, is then manifestly preferable to the sanctity of the simple.

Scientific labours sometimes occasion vain glory, puff up the heart, and consequently create dissensions. No one dreams of denying

[8] *Letter to the Monk Paulinus.*

that? But where can you find anything human, which is not subject to occasional abuses? Is it not possible and even very easy to unite knowledge with that true and sincere charity which maintains the soul in the love of God, edifies our neighbour, and destroys even the root of all discord? Do we not find a loud and eloquent reply to this question in those hallowed cloisters where for ten centuries and more, learning and holiness have unceasingly intertwined their flowering branches? It is true that human science would be unfitting for men who have sacrificed and devoted their whole lives to the divine service, if they could not be applied to that which is "according to godliness,"[9] and thus contribute to the increase of religious virtue, but the two can easily work together. Secular and profane science, says the hermit of Bethlehem, is the daughter of Moab, the captive from abroad, whose earthly charms might corrupt the heart. But let her be divested of these worthless attractions, purified from her criminal beauty, let the rays of Christian wisdom transfigure her countenance, and she will become a true Israelite, piously fruitful among the children

[9] Titus i. 1.

of God.[10] Did not Ruth the Moabite choose for her God and her people, the God and people of Noemi? And had she not the honour of reckoning David and Christ Himself amongst her descendants? "We will not," writes St. Augustine, "abandon the poor souls whom the heretics seduce by hypocritically promising them philosophy and mysterious knowledge; and for this reason, we are resolved to trespass upon this profane territory. We should not, however, dare to do so, did we not see that the necessity of refuting the impious has compelled many devoted sons of our holy Mother the Catholic Church to act in like manner.[11]

Study is no less necessary to religious leading an active life, if they would be surely guided in those difficult paths which their vocation obliges them to pursue; but it is especially indispensable to orders established for the preaching of the Gospel and for the sanctification of souls. For as they are destined to become the auxiliaries of the episcopate in those supernatural illuminations of

---

[10] *Letter to the Monk Pammachius.*
[11] *On Music;* on its end.

which we have spoken,[12] they should, like it, embrace "that faithful word which is according to doctrine, that he may be able to exhort others in sound doctrine, and to convince the gainsayers."[13] The day has passed away wherein the Holy Ghost made poor and illiterate fishermen His Apostles, and inspired them with the truths which they were to teach to the whole world, to the sages of Rome and Athens and to the barbarians of the desert! The daily study of the Divine Scriptures, assiduous meditation of theological truths, and practice in the art of persuading and convincing, such are the means to be taken in preparation to a serious apostolate. For this end, it is necessary to possess human eloquence, with its skill and elegance, its happy choice of language, of figures and rhetorical embellishments! And it is, indeed, a truly religious work thus to cultivate our minds to the glory of God.

Moreover, the utility of these intellectual labours extends itself further and wider still, and that for a reason which effects the very essence of the religious state. How useful study proves to every religious who wishes

---

[12] Chapter vii. ; *on religious obedience.*
[13] Titus i. 9.

perfectly to fulfil his sacred obligations! And, reciprocally, what facilities do not his vows afford to enable him to pursue it with profit and in holiness? Study is, first, a very powerful method of detaching us from the goods of this world, and of enabling us to see clearly their vanity, and of inspiring us with a just contempt for them instead of the natural inclination which we have towards them. "And I preferred her before kingdoms and thrones, and esteemed riches nothing in comparison of her," says Solomon.[14] And Jonathan the high priest, and the ancients of the nation, and the priests, and the rest of the people of Israel wrote thus to the Spartan Republic: "We have no need of the alliance or amity of men, having for our comfort the holy books that are in our hands."[15]

Against the temptations of our feeble and lascivious flesh study is a solid and insurmountable barrier, because it diverts the mind from sinful thoughts, dangerous imaginations and base feelings, and fixes it on the love of immaterial and pure truths; and at the same time it mortifies the body as effectually as the practice of fasting, or the

[14] Wisdom vii. 8.   [15] I. Mach. xii. 9.

use of the discipline, because it imposes upon it the pain inseparable from all contemplation. "Watching for riches," saith the son of Sirach, "consumeth the flesh, and the thought thereof driveth away sleep." [16] The great St. Jerome likewise wrote thus to his disciple Rusticus: "Love the knowledge of the Scriptures, and thou wilt not love the vices of the flesh."

Finally, the vow of obedience finds a protection and excellent safeguard in literary labour, not only because sacred or ecclesiastical books contain a multitude of pressing exhortations to humility, respect for law, and submission towards superiors, but also because the frequent consideration of this ocean of truth wherein we are, so to speak, submerged, shows us the more clearly the impotence of our reasoning. And this habit of submitting to the evidence of truth, or to the authority of the wise, disposes the will to bend readily under the yoke of obedience. Moreover, religious life being based upon the threefold renouncement of exterior goods, pleasure, and independence, it makes a noble return to science for the benefit it derives from it. For to have no solicitude for ex-

[16] Ecclesiasticus xxxi. 1.

terior things, to be perfectly spiritualized by virginity, not to feel the tyranny of the petulance and whims of self-will—what happier disposition can we have for study? The religious who would refuse to profit by it to the fullest extent permitted by the spirit and rule of his community, would be truly absurd and cruel to himself. Ignorance is a great imperfection, and one which has been often condemned by God. Blamable and pernicious in others, what would it be in a soul who makes profession of striving after perfection, were it wilful or affected.

Again, study is an eminently religious work. It excites the noblest faculties of the mind and obliterates the vilest; it draws humanity out of the swaddling bands of animal life; it bears us rapidly to the summits of supernatural contemplation; it discovers to us more thoroughly what *we* are, and shows us more clearly what *God* is; it opens out to action new paths, and affords us more powerful instruments and more efficacious means. And yet there are those who would banish it from the cloister! "This," says St. Thomas, "was the crime of Julian the Apostate, who forbade Christians to cultivate letters; it would be depriving souls of their sweetest and most legitimate consolation; and above all other considerations, it would debase religious in the eyes of the world—it would take from their hands that bright sword and terrible lance of divine science, even as the Philistines deprived the Israelites of all their weapons." [17] In fact, it would deprive the Church of one of her chief glories and of her principal strength. Rather than submit to this shame and misfortune, O! religious communities, "learn whilst you are on earth," says St. Jerome, "those things, the knowledge of which will serve you even in heaven."[18] What joy and what greatness to prepare even in this land of darkness for the clear vision of heaven; to fix one's eyes upon these ineffable truths, the contemplation of which will constitute our everlasting happiness; to be able to say to ourselves every day, while studying the scriptures and the writings of the Doctors of the Church, that we have already a glimpse of the magnificence of heaven; and that through the veil of human letters it is the Word who radiates, the same Word whose infinite majesty will one day be

---

[17] I. Kings xiii. 22.
[18] *Letter to the Monk Paulinus.*

impressed on our countenance, transfiguring it so to render it capable of looking face to face at the Eternal One! Behold what an aid study is to hope! Both sacred and profane learning incessantly receive from the fruitful and vivifying sources of monastic science the living water by which it fertilizes the world. This teaching, says the angelic St. Thomas, is an alms which a generous hand distributes to the feebler minds of man —alms which are a thousand times more munificent and useful than those of gold, clothing, or food. It is also a universal sacrifice which the religious makes of himself and of all his faculties—an immolation preferable to that of material wealth, and more agreeable to God than any other kind of adoration or praise, since God loves nothing so much as souls, and in saving them, we glorify Him in one of His most admirable attributes.[19] Indeed, teaching is a spiritual war declared

---

[19] The Apostle St. Paul shows us in what manner the sérvices rendered to our neighbour, for the glory of God, become acts of religion and real ˙sacrifices when he says, " Do not forget to do good and to impart ; for by such *sacrifices* God's favour is obtained " (Heb. xiii. 16).

against heresies, impieties, errors, temptations, and sins; a nobler war than the prowess of Christian chivalry, and more necessary than any Crusade. Can there be any doubt as to the superiority of the religious over all others in this supreme act of charity, religion, and strength? Poor, chaste, and obedient; engaged in a life of perfection, the exercises and sanctity of which exalt him so highly, he is more immaterial, more enlightened, and consequently more closely allied to episcopal perfection. A layman will contribute much to the edification of the Church by the great lesson of good example. A secular priest will rank foremost among those seventy-two disciples whom our Lord appointed as coadjutors to the Apostles, and whom He sent before Him into all the cities and boroughs which He intended to visit. The monk who is invested with Christian priesthood is sovereignly fitted to receive the mission of instructing, preaching, and administering the sacraments. He is a man of prayer and study, he practises not only the precepts, but also the counsels of the Gospel. "He imitates," says St. Thomas, "that which the woman of Samaria did when, having acknowledged the divinity of the

Messiah, she left her pitcher at Jacob's well (which is symbolical of the cares and burdens of this world) to be able to announce more freely to her native place the glad tidings of redemption."[20] And in an age like ours, when naturalism threatens to engulph society, to pluck from it all belief in the providential action of God, and in the constant influence of His grace; to stifle in every heart all feelings of respect and confidence towards the supernatural authority of the Church and Her ministers—who should be better fitted to arrest the floods of the deluge than the true religious? He is removed from the world— free from its enthralments—so thoroughly superior to the things of this age that his very existence almost appears both mysterious and heavenly. He is more completely poor than the secular priest; his austerities, penances, self-denial, and renouncement are more perfect. His dwelling is a school of asceticism and holiness; and to-morrow will not his abode become a centre of supernatural—nay, even of miraculous action? Oh, how easy it is for him to make the grace

[20] John iv. 28. See chapter iv. of this book, *On the Domain of Holy Poverty*.

of Jesus Christ triumphant! If he only wills it, what powerful weapons are his life, his words, his conversation, and his sermons! But for it to be so, the root of the great monastic tree should not quit the ground wherein God has planted it; it should penetrate deeply into it, with a species of obstinate tenacity and holy blindness; it should imbibe exclusively the parent sap, without which every leaf languishes and all the fruit dries up. The noviciate should be a vigorous school of virtue, strongly opposed to that old spirit of falsehood which is so incorrectly styled the modern spirit; the soul should be nourished by those eternal yet ever new principles which alone produce spiritual progress, and which alone can honour God and serve the world.

To the aureola of virginity the religious may then add the aureola of doctors and even of martyrs. He may obtain the threefold happiness of having conquered the furious passions of the flesh, of having overcome the trials and persecutions of the world, and of having vanquished the devil by science and by preaching the cross. And upon the forehead of the conqueror, God will place three crowns, formed of the purest rays which emanate from the virginal and immolated body of the Lamb.

The monastic state conduces directly to this victory and happiness, because it is *par excellence* the valley of lilies, the school of the Word Incarnate, and the arena wherein the soul wrestles to obtain its highest power, its entire freedom, and the complete glorification of the Divine Majesty.

Even those exterior works, which apparently seem most foreign to the regular state, serve to actuate and exhibit its progress in virtue. The religious is no longer of this world; earthly riches are nothing to him; and, according to our Lord's counsel, he must leave the dead to bury their dead. Duty, however, leads him sometimes into this lower world—yea, into the very midst of its corruption. He reappears then in full vigour, animated with a heavenly spirit which he communicates to all around him.

Sometimes, by the order of his superior, he administers the goods of the community, defends its temporal interests, and distributes its revenues. At other times, he is employed in the direction or in the service of the poor, of the helpless, or of the persecuted, in those difficult circumstances of life wherein his assistance may be needed by them. But he must show himself in all his doings the disciple of Christian wisdom, mingling with his care of worldly things, a disinterestedness, moderation, and charity, which will spiritualize, so to speak, the earthly substance which is in his hands. Does he not know that Providence has purposely pre-arranged these occasions, which are so favourable to his progress in the perfection of divine love, and serve to consume in its pure flame the last vestiges of ambition, cupidity, avarice, or curiosity, which might, perhaps, still have existed, although hidden and unperceived in the depth of his soul, and which the touch of earthly things has brought to light, by working up these passions in his heart. If, therefore, I should see him beneath the porticoes of the rich, or even in the palaces of kings, I know that he goes there neither to taste of delights, in search of glory, nor to beg riches of their hands. He reminds me of the prophet Elisheus preaching the people's cause;[21] or he makes me think of the Precursor John the

---

[21] IV. Kings iv. 13.

Baptist reproaching Herod with his crimes.[22] "Bear ye one another's burdens," says St. Paul, "and so you shall fulfil the law of Christ;"[23] and the monk, who is of all men the most free, the most disengaged from those burdens of the soul—from anxieties, anguish, and sin—is consequently the best fitted to relieve those of others; and, in a greater measure than any one else, he will thereby fulfil this precept of our Lord, and that sympathy which he shows us in our troubles is indeed a high act of perfection.

The religious life penetrates the entire man. It sanctifies at once both body and soul; and by its sacred inspiration, the body which virginity has already transported to a supernatural sphere, thus produces new acts, strange in the eyes of men, but excellent in the sight of God. The Holy Scriptures speak of the abominations of carnal corruption, impurity, idolatry, enmity, anger, murder, drunkenness, and many other fearful crimes, all of which we must conquer.[24] But from your body consecrated by religious vows, what an abundant and pure harvest there

---

[22] Matt. xiv. 4.   [23] Galat. vi. 2.
[24] Galat. v. 19—21.

is of admirable works! Those watchings, fastings, disciplines, those numerous austerities, those repulsive actions done for the sick, those wearisome voyages undertaken for the glory of God, that humble and laborious manual labour is like the stigmata of Jesus crucified—divinely imprinted on your body, assimilating it more and more to the Eucharistic Body of Jesus risen again. That which study, meditation, and instruction do for your soul, is done by the exercises of austerity for your body. They secure its perfection, its development, and its transfiguration on earth; they are also the visible pledges of its glorification in heaven.

Nevertheless, as the body belongs to the soul, and is subordinate to it, its works cannot be considered as principal or essential to the regular state. They would be even culpable did they interfere with the free action of the intellectual faculties. Manual labour may certainly be of great service to religious by gaining for them their food, or alms for the needy, or by preventing idleness and the innumerable evils to which it gives birth. It serves to suppress sensual passions, to stifle vainglory and its daughter, disobedience, by the humiliation naturally attaching to servile work. It expiates faults and negligences, draws down the divine mercy upon a terribly impious world, and lastly, as the Apostle teaches us, edifies people by the example of a laborious and disinterested life which is a burden to none, and of service to all.[25] Labour actuated by these motives is truly noble, and the sweat which then covers the face of the workman is like a dew of grace which embellishes, ennobles, and gives to his humiliated features an exact resemblance with Him whose popular name was for a long time "the son of a carpenter."

Notwithstanding their many advantages, these labours might by their excess occasion disgust and weariness, discourage the soul, trouble the heart, and deprive the religious of that just and precious esteem which should make him attractive to those to whom he preaches the gospel. Cannot the body be mortified by other austerities? Is not idleness equally banished by the study of sacred letters, and by the chant of the divine praises?

---

[25] I. Cor. ix. 12; II. Cor. xi. 12, xii. 13; II. Thess. iii. 8.

Are humility, alms-giving, and good example absolutely dependent on this method? Must the corporal life necessarily destroy that of the spirit. "It would be," says St. Thomas, "gross hypocrisy and deadly craft on the part of our enemies, to condemn the religious to a life of perpetual manual labour. The body cannot be overworked without the soul suffering a proportionate loss in the perfection proper to it." [26]

The same principles apply to that absolute poverty, which renounces every permanent possession to live solely on alms, and which we see authorized by the Church in spite of the false delicacy of the world, which is pleased to take scandal at the sight of

---

[26] The general law of bodily labour is obligatory on the religious only in the measure common to all men; that is to say, when such labour is necessary to the life of the body or soul, or to our neighbour. Apart from these cases of necessity, the religious should keep to his rule, and never exaggerate either the merit or obligation of his manual labour. For the acquisition of the food indispensable for him, a religious has need of little time or care; he is not condemned, like the worldly workman, to great anxiety, and he may, more easily than they, preserve sufficient freedom of soul to think of God and to praise Him, even whilst working.

a man humbly begging from door to door the mite, or the bread of public pity. This is indeed a work of perfection! neither the Angel of the School, nor his seraphic friend, St. Bonaventure, nor the greatest men of those Christian ages, were ashamed of it. In exchange for temporal goods, which in some cases were considerable, and even princely, all of which they abandoned on the day of their religious profession; in return for the spiritual blessings which they diffused so generously on the earth by study and the teaching of the most sublime sciences, by evangelical preaching and the administration of the sacraments, by all the works of mercy, by prayer and the divine worship—in return for all that, they humbly sought that little which would prevent their perishing from hunger. And, with God's help, their successors, even to the last day, will follow that noble example. They will ask alms piously, simply, and without arrogance; exacting nothing—complaining neither of refusal, nor of injuries, repressing in their hearts, by this excess of abjection, all natural feelings of haughtiness or pride. And if the shame, for can we deny that this humiliation is a source of great confusion?—if the shame which we can see in their face seems to tarnish their appearance, at any rate, true honour, real beauty, and imperishable glory, will ultimately crown them with a sparkling diadem. Admirable, in truth, and the most victorious of kings is this mendicant, who overcomes so thoroughly the lusts of the senses, who upholds so proudly the standard of faith and reason, and who, triumphing over the ridicule of the world and the repugnance of nature, traces so faithfully in his own person the likeness of Him of whom it is written, "As for me, I am a beggar and poor." [27]

But has not this glorious mendicity sometimes concealed an interior of detestable sloth, gross idleness, cupidity, or avarice? Were all the alms confided to him by charity devoted to their proposed end? Does not

[27] Ps. xxxix. 18 ; lxix. 6. Our Lord has said, "It is more blessed to give than to receive;" but remarks St. Thomas, this is true, all things being equal. For it is certainly better to give or abandon all that one possesses for the love of Jesus Christ, save the things absolutely necessary to life, than simply to give alms to the poor and preserve one's own goods. (See ch. 3, *On Religious Poverty*.)

the religious who is voluntarily poor and a mendicant, ever despise and offend the poor who begs from necessity, whilst he ought rather to succour, console, and assist him? The writings of our Angelic Doctor point out to us the possible abuse of this institution, so excellent in itself, and urges that it should be constantly animated by deep feelings of humility, charity, strength, and prudence, avoiding even the appearance of everything which spiritual wisdom would consider as being in any way indecorous, and thus protecting the sacred liberty of the cloister against any injurious influence, which the fear of temporal loss, or a feeling of false gratitude against encroaching benefactors, might suggest to weak and timorous souls.

We may clearly see that religious life is not unprofitable to the human race, and that Judas could not apply to *it*, any more than to the perfumes of Mary Magdalen, his well-known reproach: " Wherefore this profusion, to what purpose is this waste." [28] The vocation of *active* orders leads them to God through the labyrinth of the miseries and darkness of the world; their mission is to love our Lord

[28] John xii. 4, 5.

by loving those poor souls whom He has created and redeemed with His Blood; their spirit is to honour the sovereign majesty of the Most High in performing by the state of religion, with a religious spirit, the multitudinous works of spiritual and corporal mercy. When he mixes in the crowd, and partakes of the works, anxieties and cares of men, does not then the religious instruct them in the rules of wisdom and Christian prudence? When he preaches the Divine Word, when he administers the sacraments, and when he enlightens and directs consciences, does he not fulfil the most necessary and the highest function belonging to us—the function of the Church, the function even of Jesus Christ the Saviour of the world? Does he not create a current of wholesome ideas, of living affection and salutary action, in the midst of that chaos of fatal errors and corrupt passions which is called the world?

It is assuredly not with a view to attempt the eulogy or the justification of regular orders that we here bring to mind the utility of their works. Ascetic theology has other designs; it only exhibits their excellence to the Christian in order that his duties may be the better understood. The religious should not be content with blindly putting forth, and as by instinct, these great and efficacious acts. He is not an inanimate body, destitute of self-action. To act without intention is the imperfection of an animal, or, rather, it is the moral debasement of man. Let the vivid but redeeming thought of the sins, afflictions and ignorance of the world follow you to the foot of the altar, where, after the distractions and struggles of the outside world, you once more find peace and refreshment for your hearts, you, who under the standard of religion a thousand times victorious combat against the eternal enemy of all that is good. Let our groans, let the echoes of our cries of sorrow penetrate even to the depths of your blessed solitudes. Did Moses on the mountain cease to pray for the people who were fighting in the valley below? The happiness of the cloister consists not in forgetfulness of the world, but in a more distinct insight into its evils, and greater compassion for its woes; in the joy of being freed from its snares, and in the power of rescuing others from them.

The *contemplative* religious is not exempt

from this law. His existence is not fruitless. He cannot say, with a feeling of discouragement or egotism, "I am alone; around me men lament, move, and fall beneath the weight of grief and labour—what is it to me? can they presume to trouble my retreat by their importunate complaints? do they imagine that to my own grief, I am going to add their anguish, and mingle in the cup of my joy the gall of their afflictions?" Catholic tradition does not authorize such unpitying hardness of heart. The Hermits of the desert, the Stylites on their columns, the Carthusians in their solitudes, the Carmelites from the interior of their impenetrable cloisters, are all members of the one great Catholic family; each day they say "our Father, give us this day our daily bread," and not "my Father," nor "my daily bread." They are not above the communion of saints in which they profess to believe when reciting the Creed. The Church prays for them in her liturgy; she has a right to demand their prayers for her, for her head, for her pastors, for the entire flock, for the just who nobly resist the assaults of the enemy, and for sinners who lie fatally wounded by the poisonous sword of hell! And how many generous and pure souls are there whom divine Providence has retained in the midst of the world in order that they may be its light and savour, and who bear in the depths of their hearts, as an ever-gaping wound, the sorrow of being unable to participate in the vows and sacred exercises of the religious life? Have *they* not a special right to the remembrance, to the charity and intercessions of those happier souls, who have been permitted to take the wings of the dove and are resting on the mountain of the Lord?

Sacrifice, too, is always an element of fecundity in the order of grace, and it was when Jesus was raised on the cross that He attracted all to Him. The holocaust made by religious should participate in this glorious efficacy. God bestows on them a new power, in return for each of the three renouncements which are exacted from them. One might say that this threefold effusion of love and life, which constitutes the religious profession, is immediately transformed into a heavenly dew which refreshes and fertilizes the parched earth. Maladies occasioned by excessive heat are counteracted by an excess of cold. Thus the desire of earthly goods, the ambition of honours, the greed of gain, kindle in our veins a burning fever which consumes the world. But to this devouring fire the Church opposes the voluntary poverty inflamed with a holy and, so to speak, excessive enthusiasm of her religious congregations, and more particularly of her mendicant orders. And in this moral atmosphere which each age breathes, there is created—a commingling of disinterestedness and avarice, of highmindedness and meanness, of enjoyment and expiation, in which the supernatural element neutralizes the homicidal action of the human ingredients. The ill-disposed who know this so well have nothing so much at heart as the suppression, or at the least the relaxation and corruption of religious communities. It is a well-established fact, and one might even term it a law of social economy, that the cupidity of the mob increase, yea even to excesses of the most cruel barbarity, in proportion as the exercise of voluntary poverty diminishes. And this should be an incitement to religious of every age, but more especially of our own, to attach themselves more strongly to the vow of poverty: for the salvation of nations depends thereon in no slight degree.

In the treasury wherein God stores up the merits, intercessions, and expiations of the saints, each of these good works preserves its own character, and its distinct efficacy. It is not a confused mass of spiritual riches distributed at hap-hazard, having no specific destination; on the contrary, a perfect order rules their dispensation. The austerities of religious poverty counterbalance the guilty delights of worldlings; the mortifications and the triumphs of virginity appease eternal justice incensed by lust, and procure the strength of the Holy Ghost to souls tempted by impurity; the humiliations of obedience prevent or repair the damage caused by pride.

Besides, however contradictory our language may appear, religious chastity is not less one of the most admirable participations of that sovereign Paternity of God, always fruitful and inexhaustible, and from which all paternity, both supernatural and natural, derives its origin. Who is so active, so creative, or so benevolent as God? or who is so pure or immaterial as He? The angels, whose very name reminds one of perfect innocence and absolute virginity—are they not gifted with a powerful and widely-spread influence, and that in proportion as they are the farthest removed from material things, and from all that imitates the imperfection thereof? And are they not in the same proportion greater sanctifiers and enlighteners of souls as they approach more closely to the infinite spirituality of God? Matter is indeed opposed to real fecundity, because in the moral sphere, as in the physical world, every being composed or defiled with matter is necessarily localised in a narrow space, from which it cannot escape: folded up in itself, concentrated in its miserable essence, and consequently egotistical. Who loves himself more basely or more exclusively than a voluptuous man? But who is so materialized and so useless to others as he? In spiritualizing, therefore, the religious, holy virginity ennobles and develops him—gives him an admirable energy for good, communicates to him a singular aptitude to receive the lights of heaven and to transmit them to men, even as a well-cut crystal appears to multiply the rays of the sun instead of obscuring them. Obedience doubles and increases twofold the fruitfulness of regular life, for it places that soul who is faithful to his vow in direct communication with the adorable element of all light and holiness. Established in this hierarchical current of grace, in the flood of life which we spoke of above,[29] how is it possible not to be inundated by its waters; or how could we remain sterile when impregnated by that grace which is the true mover of the supernatural world?

Oh, the strength, fertility, living and extensive power of the monastic state! How wonderfully true are the words of St. Augustine and of his disciple St. Thomas, when they assure us that even in the desert religious are most useful to the human race. "These men, who are contented with the little bread which they occasionally receive, and who are satisfied with the water which flows from the rocks; men who live in the most secluded places, solely to enjoy the contemplation of God, whom they love with all the purity of their hearts—such men, according to the world, are considered to have abandoned more than was necessary; but in thus

---

[29] Chapter 7, *On Religious Obedience.* See also for the entire teaching on the fecundity of the monastic life, chapters 4 and 6.

blaming them, the world shows that it does not understand how necessary these holy souls are to us by their prayers, and how precious their life is by its example. We cannot discover this with the eyes of our bodies."[30]

The imperfect and rapid sketch which we wished to give of the religious state is now finished. In the acts of this privileged life, in the study of sciences profane and sacred, in teaching and preaching, in the sanctification of the people, and even in its bodily toils, we have recognised the twofold character of perfection and fecundity, which is the true sign of God's works. But who are the souls predestined to such high things, to whom the gates of this mystic Jerusalem fly open; who will ascend these blessed heights and dwell in this holy place?

CHAPTER XIII.

The Entrance into Religion.

IT is certain that God desires both the sanctification and salvation of all men; and that

[30] *The Works of the Church*, ch. 31.

among the means of attaining sanctity in this world and glory in the next, the most efficacious is the faithful observance of the three evangelical counsels of poverty, chastity, and obedience.

It is still more certain that everyone is not capable of walking in so narrow a way, and that it is practically better for the greater number to live in the world and to observe the commandments of the divine law without contracting any obligation by vow to live a life of higher perfection. This inferiority among Christians, this impossibility for the larger number to understand and practise the sublime counsels of the Lord,[1] proceeds sometimes from previous faults—from animal passions or grievous vices, which have weakened and, as it were, limited the freedom of the soul. But more often it is involuntary, and God alone possesses the secret thereof, because it is He alone who has predestined us to this particular grace; to this special condition; to this employment, and to this mission. Why was Mary Magdalen called to the contemplative life, and Martha to an active life; Agnes to martyrdom, and Clare to the re-

[1] St. Matt. xix. 11.

ligious state? God alone knows. It would be vain to reply that Mary's soul had a singular fitness for relishing the delicacy and sweetness of charity: the query would be unsolved, since we have yet to discover the reason why Heaven had endowed her with that heart and these qualities. O! unfathomable abyss of the Divine Wisdom, who may gain from you the knowledge of this mystery! Here, one can but adore, bless, and lovingly follow the guidance of Providence; neither exulting in the heights to which It calls you, nor being discouraged by the obscurity through which It leads you, nor envying nor contemning the vocation of others. Who has selected you? And if God alone has chosen you, if no merit on your part has dictated His desire, wherefore should you glory in being a vessel of election, whereas your brother, although made of the same clay, is but a vessel having neither beauty nor value? However, if we fail to discover the *reason* of our destiny, and if it be to man an insoluble enigma, still the *fact* of his vocation is plainly manifested to him, and distinctly brought before his mind. We can resist it, because we are free, and are unhappily capable of rebelling against the divine plan; but our neglect of it can never be excused on the plea of ignorance, for the voice of the Lord speaks clearly to those who will hear Him; and if it is not heard in a sincere, calm, and attentive conscience; if it excite within it no remorse for the past, disgust of the present, or any inspiration towards a better future, this silence alone is a vocation, since it authorizes, at any rate for the time being, the actual state of the soul; God perhaps reserving to Himself the right of giving it at a later period greater light and a new impulse.

Is it then necessary for you to see at a glance the entire length and all the windings of the road which Providence has marked out for you? What need have you to know what God designs for you in a year's time, provided you know what He now requires of you? If it be the divine will that you should immediately leave the world and shelter your weakness under the shadow of the cloister, ought not that to be sufficient for a generous soul to make her at once courageously obey His call? You are ignorant, you say, whether, after the trials of the noviciate, our Lord will establish you in the regular life, or whether, on the contrary, He may call you to less favoured regions. But this uncertainty should by no means detain you: for the noviciate is precisely instituted to examine seriously the desire, and to settle finally the question of religious profession, so that before entering it is not necessary for you to know the future, or to be completely certain of your definitive vocation, or to have positively decided to take upon yourself the sacred burden of the religious vows. On this point God will enlighten you when the day comes, and then neither His strength nor His light will be wanting to you. He now invites you to make trial of His light and easy yoke, do not therefore require of Him any further knowledge. Do not weary yourself with the rash and impossible desire of looking beyond this horizon. The Church herself is more patient, for to wish to regulate what we have not yet studied is to treat divine things with carnal prudence; and it is a want of confidence in the divine goodness to desire to anticipate Its decrees and arrangements.

If it happens, says St. Thomas, that many enter the noviciate, and then return to the world, we are not thence permitted to conclude that their first resolution was not inspired by grace. It is indeed a fallacy to pretend that everything coming from God is immutable and incorruptible. For then we should have to conclude with the Manicheans that all creatures subject to corruption cannot have been created by the Lord; or agree with the heretics who maintain that those who have once received heavenly grace can never lose it—inferences which are manifestly absurd, and which exhibit the absurdity of their premises. That which is unchangeable is the eternal act of the Divine Will, even when it produces things which are both transitory and changeable. It may therefore happen that a vocation is temporary, and that the Holy Spirit leads a soul into a religious order, not that it may make profession, but that it may derive from this trial of its vocation abundant graces of strength, piety, and self-denial. During these days of recollection which it spends in solitude, it might perhaps have been subjected in the world to such fearful temptations and such terrible trials that it would have succumbed to the struggle.

But do we not give a bad example by abandoning the cloister where we hoped to be permanently fixed by religious vows, and after a certain trial of the regular state, returning to the occupations and less perfect works of ordinary life? Is not this a scandal which may deter many of the faithful from entering religion, finding from their experience of others that they may be afterwards tempted to leave it. Is not this truly putting one's hand to the plough and then looking back, and so rendering oneself unworthy of the kingdom of heaven? would it not be better to await more absolute certainty, more complete evidence, or a divine call which would render all mistakes impossible, rather than to follow the first attraction one experiences, and to be thus exposed to a fatal return.

The admirable St. Thomas is far from applauding such human prudence. While he is far from wishing that we should make an imprudent decision, he maintains that it is better to enter religion with the intention of making a trial of oneself, than not to enter it at all from the fear of leaving it. Is it not preferable to prepare oneself to live perpetually in this state of perfection, than to remain absolutely indifferent to a serious vocation, which may, perhaps, turn out to be definitive? To leave the noviciate for solid reasons, is not to look back and leave the plough; those only fall into that fault, who neglect a positive obligation; otherwise, any good action which we had once begun, would, in itself, incapacitate us for the possession of eternal happiness, from the simple fact of our having afterwards discontinued it! which is a palpable error! Follow, therefore, with confidence that inspiration which attracts you to religion; and if a reasonable cause, such as illness or weakness, obliges you to return, you will give neither scandal nor bad example. You will do that which is permitted to you, and which is even advantageous to you. God and your conscience approve your step, and what more would you have? Having shown sufficient strength of mind to overcome the hindrance the world opposed to your departure, why should you fear the raillery with which it may please it to greet your return?

The problem of religious vocation being thus reduced within its proper limits, now becomes clear and easy to solve; for could we admit that Providence, so maternal in its dealings with us, would leave us without any means of knowing what it both actually and immediately requires of our will, would it not by that very fact cease to govern us, and abandon us to ourselves like a disabled ship on a starless night? Is this credible? God, then, manifests this Will with sufficient clearness for our minds to be cognisant of the eternal designs of His mercy in our regard. To whatsoever state He calls us, for whatever duties He destines us, He either shows them to us Himself, or by such natural or supernatural secondary causes as gently incline us towards our true centre.

Direct or formal revelations are rare; miraculous vocations are not vouchsafed to all as they were to St. Paul and St. Augustine. By always desiring these evident and irresistible impressions, which our Lord bestows *sometimes* on certain souls, we would in vain presume upon exceptional graces, and at the same time expose ourselves to inevitable illusions. For the Holy Ghost usually guides us by very gentle inspirations, which move our heart without bearing it away violently, which enlighten our reason without dazzling it; in order to show a scrupulous respect for our freedom of will. These influences are often imperceptible; we receive them in the depths of our heart and are not aware of their entrance. It is sufficient for God that the mind be more clear-sighted, that principles become more evident, and the will more energetic. A calm conscience is here of greater use than an imagination overheated by the excitement of false mysticism. The Christian is above all a man of faith and reason : his vocation will, therefore, be a matter of prudence and reflexion, and, if I may use the expression, of a syllogism.

Amongst the secondary causes which reveal to us our special end, and lead us to the term to which God who is our first cause summons us, St. Thomas reckons first of all the Angels. They are the chief agents of infinite Wisdom in the government of the world; they strengthen man's mind by their secret, but powerful influence; they furnish him in an imperceptible manner with the matter and occasion of a multitude of good thoughts and useful reasoning; they regulate his passions, and direct him in the vocation marked out for him; and although they cannot change our will, they can at least influence and persuade it. Hence, it appears to us certain, that in every circumstance we should have recourse to the protection of the holy angels, and more especially when there is a question of choosing a new state, or when we have grounds for supposing that we are called to the angelic life of the cloister. With the diminution of catholic sentiment, devotion towards those blessed spirits who surround the throne of God has singularly diminished; it therefore behoves religious orders to strengthen it amongst themselves and to revive it in others.

After our Lord and His angels, it is to your fellow men that you should turn to seek light and strength regarding your entrance into religion. Holy Church, her Pontiffs, her doctors, her priests, her teaching, her books of piety, will enlighten you, dispel your doubts, calm your fears and strengthen your weakness against the importunity of a world which would retain you for itself. They are the echos of heaven; open your soul to them with confidence.

Our incomparable Master developes in favour of this proposition a doctrine so much the more precious as it is strongly opposed to the views of the present day. From the Christian and supernatural point of view, in which we would have our reader place himself, he will readily perceive the truth of this theory. St. Thomas says that it is praiseworthy and highly meritorious to persuade anyone to embrace the regular life. If, in so doing, we are actuated by charity and an upright intention, not only we do not sin, but deserve great reward; for "he," says the Apostle St. James, "that causeth a sinner to be converted from the error of his way, shall save his soul from death, and shall cover a multitude of sins";[2] and in the prophecy of Daniel it is written: "They that instruct many unto justice, shall shine like the stars for all eternity."[3] And, says the Angel of the School, as the sacred veils which covered the tabernacle in the Old Law were fastened together, that they might one draw the other,[4] so men, who are the royal canopy of the divine tabernacle, that is to say the Catholic Church, should mutually draw each other to the service of the Lord.

Disorder would certainly steal in if one were to have recourse to violence, simony or falsehood, in order to lead a soul to religious life; but can we censure those who frankly

---

[2] James v. 20.   [3] Daniel xii. 3.
[4] Exodus xxxvi. 12.

and honestly induce the faithful to enter religion. Is this monastic state dangerous, pernicious, or impracticable? At any rate, we know now what to think about it. Even should the counsel to adopt such a life be imprudent or rash, we have, before taking the final vows, the time of probation or the noviciate, intended for the express purpose of weighing the difficulties as well as the advantages of this new kind of life to which one aspires.

The most holy Scriptural personages—Nehemias, Job, and the great Apostle [5]—show us that they feared not to commend themselves and the state which they had embraced, when they had thus to exhort and encourage souls to the practice of a like perfection. "The just and the perfect," says the Pope St. Gregory, "boast at times of their virtues, and relate the blessings they have

---

[5] II. Esdras v. 18, 19; Job xxix. 14—17; II. Cor. xi. xii., etc. We see further, that the saints sometimes exhibited their own virtues, either to refute thereby the calumnies brought against them by men, or to fortify themselves against the attacks of discouragement or despair by calling to mind their past good works.

received from God, not for the purpose of deriving honour from them before men, but rather, that they may, by their own example, attract towards true life those to whom they preach the Gospel, imitating herein Almighty God Who has manifested His praises to men, in order that they might know Him."[6] Thus it is permitted to religious to extol the privileges of their state, and the spiritual advantages of their order, that by so doing, they may lead others to share in them. If it is allowable for a missionary to proclaim with enthusiasm before infidels the marvels of the religion of Jesus Christ, in order to convert them to the faith, wherefore may not a religious expatiate upon the advantages of perfection? Is it not even an excellent fruit of charity to draw one's brethren after oneself into the paths of divine love? And did not St. Paul say to King Agrippa, "I would to God that both in a little and in much, not only thou, but also all that hear me this day, should become such as I also am, except these bands."[7]

But yet, if the counsels of the wise are very useful to the soul who seeks to discover its

---

[6] *IX Homily on Ezechiel.*   [7] Acts xxvi. 29.

vocation, and if the Holy Ghost has Himself advised us to treat with our friends of those affairs most important to us[8] (amongst which we naturally place the choice of a state of life) let us not exaggerate this truth by wasting too much time in asking advice, or in taking advice of a great many. Did Peter and Andrew, when called by our Lord, go first to confer with their friends? Did James and John deliberate with their father upon the advisability of following Jesus? Did the publican who was afterwards St. Matthew make known his new mission to the princes of the people before he had devoted himself thereto? The divine Master invited them to come with Him, and they came without delay. He did not permit them to go first and bury their dead, or to bid adieu to their homes, however short, easy, and even necessary these works might have appeared to them. Delay is dangerous in those grave moments when the voice of God speaks to the heart. The devil is then more than ever eager to find an entrance into your soul, and if he is able to take advantage of a single act of negligence he will fill you with great pusillanimity.

[8] Prov. xxv. 9.

"The splendours of the East attract you, and yet you look at the darkness of the West."[9] He in whom are all the treasures of wisdom gives you an infallible counsel, and you ask a mortal man his opinion on it! You doubt, you hesitate, you draw back from the plough the hand you had at first so generously put to it. Say not that you would obey more promptly if the Lord Himself had directly called you. This excuse is to your condemnation, for it was precisely to you that He spoke when He addressed His Apostles; it was for you that the Holy Spirit inspired those pages of Holy Writ. The Evangelical Counsels are the same for every age, and apply to all souls of good will; and therefore that interior voice which speaks within you, that grace which inclines you to religious life, should not have less authority than the exterior voice of the Word Incarnate. Nay, it is even more efficacious, more noble, and more precious, because without it, material words or syllables would fall uselessly on the ear.

This spiritual flame, which the Apostle exhorts us not to extinguish [10]—this inspira-

[9] *On our Lord's Words*, Sermon vii. [10] I. Thess. v. 19.

tion of the Holy Ghost, which urges the sons of God[11]—permits neither delay nor slothfulness. It instantaneously changed the hearts of the apostles on the day of Pentecost; and St. Gregory, with good reason, exclaims: " What an admirable workman is the Spirit of God! It needs but an instant to instruct souls in whatsoever It pleases! Hardly has It touched them but they are taught; and this mysterious contact is in itself a perfect teaching, for It changes the human mind at the same moment that It enlightens it—It makes it immediately abandon all that it was, and instantaneously transforms it into what it was not."[12] Hence it is only through ignorance of the power of the Holy Ghost, or from a desire to resist It, that we fetter the divine impetuosity of Its influence by endless consultations.

Would we only took the advice of those who are truly wise and really our friends! But most frequently we address ourselves to our neighbours, or to men whose prudence is wholly worldly; as if the flesh lusteth not against the spirit,[13] and as if a man's enemies

---

[11] Rom. viii. 14.   [12] *Homily on Pentecost.*
[13] Galat. v. 17.

are not chiefly those of his own household,[14] and this because they are nearly always ignorant of the nature of the religious state, and that they are too frequently blinded by the double influence of affection and personal interest. Should not the love of God reign supreme over that of men, and our eternal welfare outweigh temporal interests? The Angelic Doctor exposes with so much energy the imprudence of those who leave the question of their spiritual progress, and of their religious vocation, to be decided by their families, that St. Alphonsus of Liguori shrinks not from thus summing up his teaching: "Not only do we commit no sin in embracing the regular state without having consulted our parents, but we may even affirm, as a general rule, that it is a grievous error to acquaint them with our vocation, on account of the danger we thus incur of being dissuaded by them."[15]

[14] Mich. vii. 6.

[15] *Moral Theology*, Book I. ch. i. v. 68. Many theologians, and amongst them St. Alphonsus, consider the efforts made by parents to prevent their children from entering religion to be a grievous sin. As to souls called to this state, and who neglect their vocation, it is difficult to believe that they do not commit sin by putting themselves out of the providential position in which

Man having sought from our Lord, from His angels, and from His earthly representatives the light necessary to solve this important problem, he should then look into himself. He should examine his capabilities, his moral and physical powers, his weakness, and the dangers to which he is exposed. He should successively compare them with the world and with the cloister; and if the result of this examination is a vivid attraction of the heart, or a serious propension of the reason to the regular state, let him no longer hesitate to burst his fetters and follow the counsels of the Lord.

In these sad times in which we live, the religious vocation (although it begins again to

God designs to place them, and thus imperilling their salvation, particularly when they clearly see that they are bound to fly from the world under pain of living in it in a state of mortal sin. The same may probably be said of such persons as being morally certain of their religious vocation, would persuade themselves that they can be saved just as easily in the world. St. Thomas says that if we should find ourselves in danger and liable to sin mortally by remaining in the world, we are bound to enter religion, even should our parents be in great need of us; because we must ever prefer the salvation of our own *soul* to the temporal relief of our parents.

be of more frequent occurrence) still forms the rare exception, and is, so to speak, an anomaly. We have, consequently, some difficulty in understanding its astounding propagation in the age of the hermits and cenobites of the Eastern Church, in the days of the Benedictines of the West, and, since then, at the rise of the mendicant orders and clerks regular. We are surprised at these migrations of young men and maidens, who went forth in thousands to people the deserts in Egypt, the monasteries of St. Benedict, the colleges of St. Ignatius, or the cloisters of St. Theresa; and many now ask themselves if there was not in this prodigious movement too much enthusiasm, too little reflection and prudence, and an imperfect understanding of this manner of life. Did not these novices of fifteen and sixteen years of age (who were so numerous and so illustrious in the old religious orders) obey a blind instinct, or indulge in an excessive taste for premature self-denial? Are we not right in doing quite the contrary? May we not claim praise for those hesitations, scruples, long deliberations, and even experiments which follow for a long time the first call we think we have received, and which end in showing us clearly that it was either a divine reality or a human delusion? Is not this hesitation and delay useful to calm the imagination, and to prevent our taking an imprudent step? Will not, on the other hand, too great an eagerness drive many souls into religious life who have no vocation for it?

Did not the voice of God speak more clearly and more frequently in the ages of faith? Does not the natural—or rather, pagan—life, led by Christians of the present day, prevent, in some measure, the out-pouring of those privileged graces? Perhaps we are less docile to our Lord, and more than ever attached to the frivolities of this world, even when the call from God is most precise and unmistakable? Finally, does not the extreme rarity of religious vocations spring from the numerous drawbacks and obstacles opposed to it by the spirit of the age? For how is it possible for this heavenly seed to be otherwise than choked, when it falls only amongst thorns which check its growth?

All this is, unfortunately, indisputable. The ill use which we make of our liberty, the levity of our sentiments, the horror with which we regard every sacrifice, the persecutions and difficulties which the world opposes to the practice of these divine counsels, already sufficiently accounts for the diminution and difficult re-organization of religious orders for the last hundred years. But to these lamentable causes, we must add that false prudence with which we so often examine our vocation, and which, after dangerous delays, ends sometimes in extinguishing this saving light. The fervour of bygone ages was in no wise indiscreet, nor was the promptitude with which they followed Francis of Assisi and Dominic de Guzman unreasonable; and even in our days the principles that then held sway have lost none of their truth.

Certainly, says St. Thomas, long deliberation is necessary when there is question of taking a resolution which is both important and doubtful. But in things which are, and which have been already determined by a superior and infallible wisdom, it is absurd to lose oneself in long discussions, and it is, moreover, highly injurious to the sovereign authority, whose judgments we would verify before accepting them. And when God Himself affirms that this spirit is His own, that this impulse comes from Him, and that this tendency is good—shall we still dare to test them?

Four considerations present themselves to the soul which feels drawn to the religious life. *Firstly*, is the state of religion, considered in itself, independently of circumstances of time or place, good, is it better than the ordinary life of Christians in the world? Now of this it is impossible for us to doubt; and it would be impious after the solemn affirmations of our Lord, even to wish to dwell upon the examination of so evident a truth. All dispute and all delay in this regard is, therefore, superfluous.

Secondly, should we give up this state of perfection to spare our friends great sorrow, or to shirk the heavy burden of self-denial and self-sacrifice? But what doubt can there be on this point? Can we hesitate, when there is question of choosing between God and man, eternity and time, and perhaps even between heaven and hell?

Thirdly, is not religious life beyond the strength of him who is called to it by an interior grace? and after having yielded to his heart's desire, may he not be crushed under the weight of his vows and rules? What fear is this, is it worthy of one moment's attention from a man of faith? If he were obliged to rely upon his own resources, his energy, or constancy, he might indeed be alarmed, and remain in a state of great perplexity. But it is in the assistance of divine grace that he trusts, and as the prophet Isaias says: he is assured that "he will renew his strength in the Lord, he will take wings as of eagles, he will run and not be weary, he will walk and not faint."[16] Do not, therefore, be terrified at the thought of the long duration of your evil habits, of the great number of your sins, or at the ardour of your passions. The simple but deep conviction of your insufficiency to accomplish anything good without the Almighty power of that grace which will never fail you, should inspire you with a confidence your own unassisted nature can never give you. Alas! how many poor souls would have found in the cloister peace and consolation for their wounded hearts, had they possessed this conviction, and if, instead of tormenting themselves with fruitless reflections, they had leaped as with one bound to-

---

[16] Isaias xl. 31.

wards those altars where God invited them to partake of the supernatural delights of the holocaust.

Fourthly, and lastly, what order is it better to enter, and what means must we take for so doing? Is there no impediment in us, such as ill health or incapacity which might prevent the execution of this intention? Here, and here alone, are we permitted to deliberate, and consult persons who are disinterested and truly pious. But still this examination should not be too prolonged, for this point is not difficult to determine; whereas, in neglecting to bring it to a close, we expose ourselves to dangerous temptations, and may sometimes have to encounter new and often more formidable difficulties, we are losing time which might be highly useful from spiritual progress; and divine Providence, which now and then gets weary of our continued resistance, may abandon us to the miserable dictates of our own mind. When called by our Saviour, St. Peter and St. Andrew instantly left their nets and followed Him; thus teaching us, says St. John, Chrysostom, "that Jesus Christ requires from us an obedience which will not permit of a moment's hesitation."[17] "Hasten, I pray thee," wrote St. Jerome, "and cut rather than unfasten the cable which moors thy bark to the shore."[18]

In the days even of our Angelic Doctor, his teaching, opposed as it was to all hesitation and delay in the important affair of religious vocation, provoked more than one strong objection. Thus, for instance, it was objected to him that we are frequently ignorant of the source from which our interior inspirations spring, for Satan transforms himself into an angel of light, often suggesting good works with the intention of deceiving us, and of thus profiting by our error to draw us into sin. Hence was it said, the devil may persuade us to embrace the regular state, notwithstanding our frailty and vices, and afterwards he will cast us headlong into pride, lust, sacrilege, and finally into the abyss of despair. But St. Thomas, on the authority of Christian tradition, replied even could the devil allure anyone to attach himself to our Lord, either by faith, or yet more intimately by religious

---

[17] *Homily on St. Matthew*, iv. 22.
[18] *Letter to Paulinus.*

vows, this suggestion would have no efficacy until the Holy Ghost Himself—who knows how to turn to our advantage the artifices of the devil—calls, and draws this soul to Him. No one, in fact, comes really to God, unless led to Him by grace.

Besides, the devil is not to be feared so long as he tries to persuade us to the performance of that which is really good; the danger begins when, by means of this good, he tempts our faith or our virtues. A strict watchfulness is therefore necessary to us; but we have also the certainty that help will not be wanting to us, and that if we faithfully co-operate with grace, the wiles of satan will only increase our glory and his own shame. The precept which the Apostle St. John gives us to try the spirits, refers then to regular superiors who do not know whether novices are drawn to them by the Spirit of God, or by the evil one; and this is why they should carefully study their dispositions, and seek to discover if the steps they have taken are not instigated by culpable motives, which they may possibly conceal. But for you who desire to consecrate yourselves to the Lord, and to Whom your conscience bears sincere witness of the purity of your intentions, it is not necessary to waste time in examining from what quarter the wind blows which leads you to the threshold of the monastic life, nor are you justified in resisting it until such times as its nature shall be clearly revealed to you. At this rate you might deliberate for several years; and by seeking to escape a very questionable danger, and which is at the same time most easy to avoid, you might run the more certain and serious risk of losing a divine vocation. Enter with confidence, as did the Psalmist, "into this right land where the good spirit shall lead you." [19]

The opponents of St. Thomas further objected: the Lord has blamed him who would erect a tower, that is to say religious perfection, without first calculating if he could meet the necessary outlay, which is, says St.

---

[19] Psalm cxlii. 10. It would be useless to endeavour to justify these interminable deliberations by the fear of those dangers which we may incur by making an evil use of religious life, or of our forsaking it altogether; these dangers entirely depend on our will, and it suffices for their avoidance to have a sincere resolution to watch and pray. (See chapter x.) They should engage our attention no longer than if they were the ordinary result of the religious state.

Augustine, self-denial and the renouncement of all personal goods.[20] Now, many souls are as incapable of bearing up under the observances of the cloister, as David was of bearing the armour of Saul. In order to avoid throwing oneself at haphazard into this snare, and also to escape the rebuke of Eternal Wisdom, is it not necessary to remain long in silence, and reflect most attentively on the difficulties of so lofty a construction? Yes, says the Angel of the School, your understanding of the signification of this parable is perfect, but you draw from it a false inference. Why must you take so much time for deliberation? Is it not quite evident, *firstly*, that he who would build, must also wish to possess, and possess in reality the material indispensable for such a work? Is it not then manifest, that to attain perfection one must renounce all earthly goods and joys? On this point all discussion is vain. Is it not certain, *secondly*, that with sufficient resources, we can bring our undertaking to a successful issue, and has not Jesus Christ Himself declared that the three counsels of poverty, chastity and obedience are the infallible means of being perfect?

[20] *XXXVIII Letter to Lætus.*

What is there here that is obscure, or that needs any long discussion? It remains then, *thirdly*, to determine whether the resources indispensable for such a work are forthcoming. In the material order, this question may require some time to decide; but in the spiritual order, it is clearly solved by the supreme authority of the Church, which approves of the religious state as faithfully fulfilling the conditions of true progress, and as containing all things necessary for the construction of this mystic tower. Once more, God has deliberated for you; all is clear, all is sharply defined. The Holy Ghost, Who is the Spirit of wisdom and counsel, has put into your heart this good thought which before being yours was His own. Would you say it was rash on the part of this infinite mind? And if it be not rash in God, how can it be so for you? Embrace, therefore, generously one of those rules which are the very code of laws wherein the sacred art of building up one's sanctity is safely set forth; and if you are fearful lest the weight of this religious armour should overpower you, apply to yourself the encouragement which heavenly chastity gave to St. Augustine: " Wherefore do you lean on yourself, when I can sustain thee? Cast thyself upon God; fear not, He will not withdraw and allow thee to fall. Cast thyself with confidence into His arms, He will receive and save thee." [21] "How can He be said to lay a heavy burden on our shoulders asks St. Gregory, when He urges us to escape the wearisome burdens of this world?" [22]

There is another error, very current in the world, and yet more fatal than this false persuasion of the necessity of a long deliberation of one's vocation to the regular state. It is to consider a monastery as a dwelling open exclusively to perfect souls. Such a theory would, if put in practice, bar access to Christians who are not exercised in the observances

[21] *Confessions*, Book VIII. ch. 11.

[22] *Morals*, Book V. Conformably with these principles, St. Thomas advises souls who feel drawn to the religious life to engage themselves by vow to enter it, thus putting a stop to all reflexion and all superfluous hesitation. We have seen in chapter VIII., and especially in chapter IX., the reasons which secure additional excellence to actions done in virtue of a vow. These reasons apply perfectly to the entrance into religion, which will be so much the more meritorious, as it is the result of a promise made to God in a spirit of piety.

of the ordinary commandments; and consequently to exclude from the path of perfection children, sinners, or too recent converts. St. Thomas compares this doctrine to a plague which makes desolate the Church. For he plainly affirms that entrance into religion is useful to persons already faithful to the law of the Lord, in that it facilitates a greater perfection; and to persons who have not yet attained this virtuous habit, for it affords them better means of avoiding sin, and quickly raises them to a certain degree of perfection.

In truth, the regular state consists essentially in vows and observances, destined to destroy the obstacles opposed to the increase of charity. It is then eminently favourable to souls burning with this heavenly fire, and will purify and excite still more within them this celestial flame. Less attached to riches, less enslaved to the flesh and to their own self-will, they are united more closely and more nearly with our Lord.

Still, the fetters from which religious life frees us, are not only pernicious to the perfection of charity, but they frequently form an impediment to its actual existence, because they degrade our hearts by bringing them down to a level with the mire of earth, and sometimes cause them, by means of this dangerous contact, to forget the Supreme Good in their attachment to perishable goods, wherein the soul will find both death and corruption. Wherefore monastic exercises, by rescuing and freeing man from these evils, withdraw him from the occasions of sin, and make the path of God's commandments easy to him. Not only do they make persons perfect, but they also make Christians of them.

There is nothing more simple or more solidly grand than this teaching. It shows us how admirable is the divine mercy in the foundation of these cloisters, where we may find the full satisfaction of every holy desire, and consolation of every pious sorrow. The ambition of good and the hatred of evil; eagerness after high perfection, and the fear of eternal punishments, the love of virtue and the abhorrence of vice, the delights of innocence and the expiation of sin, are all to be found here in delightful harmony, reminding us that the religious life is not yet a paradise, where one is established in grace, and dispensed from the efforts of the conflict and the labours of penance. It is not yet a glorious repose and a triumphant peace. Tears are not banished from this dwelling; we still require prudence, humility, and prayer; and whatever degree of contemplation we may attain, we must continually bear in mind that we profess a state marked with the twofold character of perfection to be realized, and of imperfection to be avoided.

The sinner, far from being driven away from the threshold of religious life, may then enter in: for our Lord, from whom all regular congregations derive their origin and rule, called to follow Him not only the young man who had fulfilled all His commandments from his childhood, but also Levi the unjust publican. The Divine Master even allowed that he should obey His call by forthwith forsaking all created things, whereas the young man disobeyed through his love of riches; whence we may learn that sinners can devote themselves more generously to His service than those just, who are presumptuous and proud of their merit. "Amen, I say to you, that the publicans and the harlots shall go into the kingdom of God before you," [23] said He to the priests and

[23] St. Matthew xxi. 31.

elders of Jerusalem. And did He not admit His Apostles to the practice of the most sublime counsels at the very moment of their conversion? Were Peter and Andrew first tried in the world? Did Paul observe the commandments before entering on the road of perfection?

The light of reason shows us that it is most wise to secure the treasure of grace the moment one recovers it, whether by returning to the Catholic faith, or by penance. And who can point out to us a safer refuge against the attacks of the enemy than this spiritual fortress of the religious state? By sanctifying us, Jesus Christ clothes us, so to speak, with His whole being; He is in us, and we in Him; He dwells in our regenerated heart; and when a God deigns to be so closely united to a soul which merited formerly His abhorrence and infinite anger, would you still dare to despise that soul and keep it away from its Redeemer by barring to it the entrance to the religious life? Do you not know that this soul wishes to repair it's ruin and regain the time it has squandered; that it has a claim to a special light; and that, weak as yet and unsteady, it requires a constant support? When one would straighten a tree bent towards the ground, do we not pull it violently towards the opposite side, so as to make it grow in its proper position? Instead of allowing great liberty to children under the pretext of their age, do we not subject them to a strict and severe discipline, which will alone form them to virtue? Thus the religious life is particularly fitted to the sinner who wishes to be converted and remain faithful to the commandments of God.

This truth is a powerful preservative against the pride which might take possession of religious when they contemplate the celestial heights to which the Divine Master leads them in His train. Their vocation by no means indicates that they have had the sole and exclusive monopoly of virtue and piety in their secular life; they should even accept without murmuring, and as a salutary humiliation, our ignorance of their past life, which allows us to conjecture that they have perhaps grievously offended God, and that they are living proofs of His immense mercy. And how can they prefer themselves to Christians in the world, or even to the members of a less austere congregation? Their entrance into a holier and more excellent state proves absolutely nothing in favour of their personal merit, or against the virtue of those who have not been so called.

It is equally impossible in monasteries to foster either contempt or dislike for souls formerly sinful, and who are now consecrated by the religious vows: for are they not in their true vocation? and who would dare to grieve them when Jesus Christ with His adorable hands dresses their wounds and dries their tears?

And you poor sinners, once seduced by the illusions of the age, and now undeceived by their frightful emptiness, do not lose the confidence of finding once more real joys and solid happiness. Do not think that God condemns you to groan under the weight of your chains, or to wander for ever as outcasts among those who have undone you, who now perhaps insult you in your sorrow. These sacred refuges and blessed solitudes will never be wanting in the Church, where you may mourn with a sweet bitterness over your years of error and vanity, where you may meditate before God on eternity, and where finally, like the publican who became an Apostle, and like the sinner who became Mary the contemplative, you will carry out the great work of religious perfection.

If the regular state is a state of perfection founded upon the practice of the noblest counsels, ought we not, before entering it, to be formed to the practice of ordinary virtues, and to the exact observance of the laws common to all? No one can become excellent by a sudden act, or by an unexpected chance. In order to ascend to the summit of science or justice, we must patiently climb up the lower grades as the Church prescribes regarding sacred orders, which she confers only after she has made severe trial of the vocation. Thus thinks human wisdom, but the Angelic Doctor formally condemns this theory. When there is question, says he, of attaining the highest degree in the state in which we live, is it necessary for us to advance by the lowest grade? On the contrary, nothing obliges us to enter an inferior state before we embrace a more exalted one. It is not necessary to remain long a layman before becoming one of the clergy. And although the active life be a good preparation for that of the contemplative, one is not obliged to pass through a teaching order to be afterwards received into an order which is principally contemplative. The evangelical counsels are not the summit of this mystic mountain of perfection; they are but its easy and commodious ascent. And, further, what can hinder Divine Providence from assigning to a soul, for its starting-point in this earthly pilgrimage, a state of perfection or a degree of religion to which other souls, after years of labour, would scarcely attain in the end? Were not SS. Benedict and Aloysius Gonzaga, from their infancy, far superior in perfection to numbers of religious grown grey in the observances of regular life?

Sacred orders pre-suppose sanctity; they require it as a preliminary condition. It is, therefore, not surprising that the Church only bestows them upon men who are proved and tried. But religious life is precisely a series of efforts—a continual tendency towards this sanctity—in such a manner, says our admirable Master, that the Pope St. Gregory had good grounds for refusing holy orders to those who would not support them better than walls newly built can support the weight of the beams and roof; yet one may, nevertheless, even though steeped in imperfection, bind himself to the religious state, because of itself it dries the edifice upon which it rests, and draws from the heart the ruinous moisture of its vices. You see, to your sorrow, the unwholesome humidity of sin trickling down the walls of the temple you are raising to the Lord. Do not therefore conclude that the cloister is forbidden you. Provided that your walls stand upright in the sight of God, provided that the cement of a sincere faith ensure the holding together of your materials—you may fearlessly place on them the roof of religious life; and under the influence of fervour and charity, all will close, all will be rendered wholesome, and the tempests raised by the world or by hell will not overturn your work. Neither the weakness nor the languor of these souls will impede the workings of the Holy Ghost. When He breathes, man becomes strong, energetic, and capable of the greatest actions and of the most cruel sufferings.

Why do men seek to banish from religious orders Christians who are still imperfect? It is because three essential things are overlooked. People forget that supernatural perfection consists in charity; that charity in all its degrees, and with the virtues springing from it, is the object of positive precepts, and consequently the counsels, though ever so sublime, are only the instruments, and by no means the essence of perfection. With the counsels, but without the commandments, you are neither in the path of sanctity nor in the way of salvation; but with the commandments and without the counsels you may be saved. And as every means is inspired by the end to which it leads, the faithful observation of the counsels is impossible without the will of obeying God, of loving Him, and of being perfect. The counsels, therefore, hold but a secondary rank in the magnificent work of our sanctification and of our spiritual progress.

It is thus absolutely illogical to require that a person should keep the commandments ere we allow him to follow the counsels of our Lord. It would be to reverse the order of the object and its means; it would be to wish for the end before the instruments, or the effect before the cause.

And not only is this unreasonable—it is also tyrannical and cruel. For although I may be able to keep the commandments of

God and of His Church in an imperfect way, without having recourse to the precious facilities afforded me in the evangelical counsels, yet it is almost impossible for me to be entirely and constantly faithful to those necessary laws, unless I can avail myself of the help of free discretionary practices. Is it to be supposed that in the midst of riches, pleasure, and independence, I can attain to a perfect love of God and my neighbour? If, then, you impose this condition on me before opening to me the doors of the cloister, I find myself condemned to realize an impossibility, or else to become poor, absolutely chaste and obedient in the midst of the world—that is to say, live as a religious without either the advantages or helps of the religious life. What could be more unjust, or more pitiless than such a requirement?

But let us suppose that I succeed, what will be the result. I wanted to love God with my whole soul, and you oblige me to moderate my love for Him. My ambition is to enter forthwith on the career of perfection, and you tie me down to worldly vanity. Am I so certain of the future that I can hope to compensate for the loss of the present time?

And would to God this were but a delay? But how can it be admitted that the prolonged possession of riches is an efficacious preparation for voluntary poverty; that ordinary chastity is a useful noviciate for virginity; or that the freedom to follow the fancies of one's own will must naturally lead to profound obedience? All this is but an empty dream! The observance of the commandments alone is not so onerous as that of the commandments and counsels together. This is an ordinary saying, which is at least as gratuitous as it is common. At least, let us not conclude therefrom that weak souls, and but little exercised in virtue, must not be allowed to take upon themselves this double burden. This would be but to ignore the power of God, the wondrous workings of His grace, the numerous obstacles in the path of virtue in the world, and the succour they will find in the religious life. Such views, as St. Thomas energetically expresses it, remind us of the stupidity of a general who would expose all his young and inexperienced soldiers to the most dangerous combats in order to train them for unimportant skirmishes; or to the absurdity of a philosopher who would maintain that it is necessary to be an ass before being a man; or that a workman should prepare himself by a very rough trade before taking to one that seems much easier. But if Christians accustomed to live in a state of grace in this world become religious, they will increase greatly in virtue from the moment they embrace the evangelical counsels; while life in the world is a grievous impediment to the acceptance and practice of these counsels.

"It is good for a man," says Jeremias, "to have borne the yoke of the Lord from his youth, for he will know how to live in solitude, and will raise himself above himself."[24] "Behold a proverb," adds Solomon: "a young man according to his way, even when he is old he will not depart from it."[25] This is why our Lord gives to His Apostles this striking command: "Suffer little children, and forbid them not to come to Me."[26] And how can they better go to Jesus than by hearkening obediently to His word and even to His counsels? Let not your wisdom and imaginary greatness lead you to despise

---

[24] Chronicles iii. 27. [25] Proverbs xxii. 6.
[26] St. Matthew xix. 14.

those little ones : they are themselves called to the inner School of Eternal Wisdom! What matter if it costs you somewhat perhaps, to have to hear this strange doctrine? It is both permitted and praiseworthy, says the admirable St. Thomas, to receive children into monasteries, to educate them for the religious life, so as to initiate them at a tender age into that sacred art, which they will profess later in their lives when they come to the use of their entire free will, and when the rules of the Church authorize them to do so. Blessed are those parents who conduct to the altar these new Samuels, these John the Baptists, in order that they may grow and be "strengthened in spirit,"[27] under the good influence of solitude.

From the cradle little children are taught those futile arts from which they derive but passing and material advantages, often accompanied by a thousand temptations and a thousand dangers. Would it not be far better to fashion them to the observances of the religious state, and to these virtuous habits which they would then so easily learn. And if in the case of children the penance observed in the

[27] Luke i. 80.

cloister is not requisite for their purification from sin, will it not be of immense advantage in shielding them from so many passions as yet unknown to them, and from so many combats and falls which generally make up the sum of human life? A religious practising from his childhood the sublime art of perfection will succeed better than any other man. Others may become excellent men; such a one will become an angel. Alas! how far removed are we from this magnificent ideal. We hesitate not to sacrifice to profane education the ingenious joys and sweet happiness of childhood. College life, the routine of a military school, the discipline of a public school do not alarm you for these dear little ones. But when their eternal welfare, their eternal destiny, and even their real happiness on earth, their purity, their fortitude and their greatness are in question, you immediately tremble, you fear the shade of the cloister, the hymns of the Church and the voice of religious! The possibility of a religious profession seems to terrify you! And your fears will be respected; your children will behold but from afar, and, as it were, from behind a veil, the monastic life, with all its beauty and delights. I cannot assure you that this vision, fleeting and indistinct as it may be, will not have stirred up some emotion in their hearts, and will not leave behind it some deep regret. But they will return to you to be delivered up by your own hands to the nameless sorrows of modern life. They only will escape them whom God will have transformed into heroes, or perhaps into martyrs to religious life. Exult therefore, your sons will be neither Jesuits, nor Benedictines, nor disciples of St. Francis of Assisi; your daughters will be neither Carmelites nor Sisters of Charity; you have other riches to bequeath them, viz., the luxury, turmoil, sorrows and scandals of the world!

But the day is close at hand when society, rent in its inmost parts, will cry despairingly towards the Holy Roman Church, imploring it to receive once more into its bosom the rising generation, and train it to religious perfection, so that it may no longer grow up in crime. Oh, Angelic Master, inspire these youthful souls, by your writings and by your example, with this precocious taste for the monastic life! From the age of five years, you were entrusted to the monks of Monte Cassino, and there, on those blessed heights where one seems to view God more closely, and to love Him more fervently, you opened your mind to light and your heart to sanctity. At the age of fifteen we behold you clothed in the white robe of St. Dominic, as a true soldier of poverty, chastity and obedience. Yes, give back to us these vocations bright as the day-dawn and sweet as the dew on the lilies, that they may rejoice heaven, reanimate the monastic orders, and give to the Church more mighty servants, more holy intercessors and more learned doctors. And above aught else, give back once more to us that religious education which preserves to childhood its purity, and to Christian youth its quickening strength.

In this mysterious question of vocation would that I had clearly explained your holy and learned doctrine! that I had clearly set forth the tokens by which we may acknowledge the Will of God in our regard; how the angels and men manifest it to us; how it is imprinted on us, without our being condemned to discover it by long and arduous study; and lastly, how religious life is open to all—to sinners converted to God, to beginners who desire to be better, to the just who aspire to higher sanctity, and to children who desire to be brought up to the fulness of the manhood and the perfection of our Lord Jesus Christ.

CHAPTER XIV.

CONCLUSION.

The Religious.

THE nature of beings is the basis of their obligations. The moral law, and the duties which it imposes, are founded upon the intimate relation of creatures with their Creator. That which I must do results from what I am; and the knowledge of my state, condition, and destiny is the starting point of the good I perform of my own free will. So, too, the idea that a religious forms to himself of his own personality is of extreme importance for the work of his perfection; the clearer and more complete this idea is, the more fruit will it bear. Let us now gather up the elements which this idea contains, and which this book has distinguished, analysed, and then separately explained. This closing work, although it be purely theoretical in appearance, may nevertheless inspire souls with a holy desire for their own reformation, with ardent zeal for higher perfection, and with a generous yearning after our Lord, who is their supreme model and Master.

But the better to understand what a religious should be, we must gaze into the depths of the heavens; we must penetrate the infinite essence, and amongst the eternal modes of created beings contemplate that grand Ideal, that severe, yet sweet form, on which, during the space of fifteen centuries, the founders of so many illustrious orders have been moulded. It is a prodigy of privileged graces gathered together by God, who desired to show forth in them the most dazzling proofs of His exterior glory, a likeness of Himself; and why should I not say it?—His consolation for the forgetfulness and the offences by which the world repays his love.

In every soul regenerated by the waters of

Baptism our Lord has, it is true, sown those supernatural virtues, out of which perfection may grow. But the thorn of riches, the poisoned exhalations of sensuality, the burning wind of pride, would soon crush these heavenly plants, or at least in the greater number of cases would stunt their growth, if the Divine Redeemer, Who wishes to propagate His work, and enrich His Church with wondrous sanctity, did not give to the men chosen by Him sufficient means to enable them to overcome every attack of the enemy. To some He accords the grace of living in possession of temporal goods without being affected by any dangerous love for them; of preserving an entire freedom without ever abusing it; of supporting even the burden of an earthly family without being overwhelmed by the charge. In this last case the superabundance of interior grace compensates for the defect of exterior liberty; and both St. Lewis of France on his throne, and St. Elizabeth of Hungary in her domestic life, present to us miraculous examples of most sublime perfection, in spite of innumerable obstacles. But the royal road of sanctity, the normal manner of attaining to the complete imitation of Jesus

Christ will always be the renouncement of the riches, joys, and independence of the world. Our Lord never ceases to say, "If any one would be perfect, let him follow Me;" and where does he lead those who leave the company of men and attach themselves to Him? Where does He conduct these—just men and sinners—these beginners, and the perfect in virtue—these mere children, and these advanced in years—who have been moved by His words? It is into the dwelling of poverty, chastity, and obedience—it is to the silence of the monastery that He calls them. The just already enjoyed a happy freedom of the soul, which they had gained even in the midst of the world; the others, on the contrary, had been embarrassed by a thousand cares; but *all* are now definitely released; "they go out of Egypt," says St. Gregory, "and go forth to offer sacrifice in the desert."[1] The religious vows deliver them from a crushing yoke, from cruel fetters —more cruel, more crushing, to some than to others; but it communicates to all an equal impulse towards heaven, and an equal capability of attaining to perfect charity. On the

[1] *Homily XX. on Ezechiel.*

great day of religious profession their virtues receive a Baptism, gain a new vigour, and a wondrous growth. Our Lord deigns to strengthen them, in reward for their love, and to hasten the perfection of His disciples.

Listen for a moment to the echos of the earth. In the midst of the confused noise of wailing, cries of senseless joy, of impious blasphemies, of frivolous discourses, do you not distinguish a voice pure as the angels' hymns, ardent as the *Sanctus* of the seraphim, and harmonious as the Psalmist's harp, which ceases not to repeat night and day that our God is holy, infinitely good and merciful, worthy of all glory, and of all our love? This faithful voice, that neither suffering, weariness, nor persecution can stifle, is the voice of the religious.

Whilst men rush in crowds to the temple of idols, do you not see that perpetual adorer of the holy Eucharist, himself a victim, and who is unceasingly devoured by the flames of the holocaust, neither thinking, speaking, nor acting save by the inspiration of the virtue of religion—directing all his works and even his perfection to his one and sovereign object, to the glory of God? Again it is a religious.

Innumerable legions of slaves cover the earth, laden with chains (though their fetters are sometimes hidden beneath flowers), of sensuality, avarice, and pride, disgraceful however concealed they may be, their degraded heads have forgotten how to look upwards towards heaven; and their debased hearts have lost all affection save for dust and mire. But there is a man, absolutely free from all perishable ties, who stands proudly erect in the midst of so much human ruin, and who cares not to breathe other than the fresh and strong air of heaven—and that man is the religious.

By an astounding but necessary contrast, the slave of creatures is a rebel against God— a hateful and powerless enemy of the order established by Providence, the adversary of all that is good, of all truth, and of all light; he is already stamped with the hideous seal of reprobation. Such is the being who pretends to be noble, perfect, and truly a man! Blessed be the grace which opposes to this monstrous rebel the joyous and peaceful servant of our Lord, the truly obedient creature whose will is wholly governed by eternal law and justice, the man who is entirely attached to his Beginning and his last End—in a word, a religious. And from that dark mass of matter wherein so many shameful passions are fermenting, which is called the human race—do you not see even there, standing out, portions transfigured and, one might say, spiritualized by the angelic virtue? These are the virgins, pure as light, empurpled as charity; their sacred phalanx, says St. Thomas of Aquino, is like a heavenly flower-bed, enamelled with the variegated colours of all the other virtues, for Jesus, like a divine artist, is pleased to adorn them each day with His graces, in return for the glory they procure Him in their feeble and tempted flesh. They are the virgins, pure lilies, and clothed in splendour; immortal flowers which the breath of earthly prosperity has not parched, nor the winter of adversity withered; white corollas where He loves to dwell, like the morning's dew, until they shall bear to heaven a fragrance of incomparable sweetness, God Himself being present in them for all eternity. These are the virgin souls, the royal spouses of the King of Kings, receiving from Him the sceptre by which they govern so absolutely all the passions of the body. They possess an inestimable treasure, which is more dazzling than the treasures of snow spoken of in Scripture;[2] and having bought it at a great price, they hide it carefully in the sacred field of the monastic life.[3]

To be led only by caprice, to live as one likes, to lighten as much as we can the yoke of authority, even though we do not entirely shake it off, such appears the chief aim of *our* days. But the religious remains immoveable in his love of abnegation, of humility, and obedience. He never thinks that he can be submissive enough, or that he has sufficiently conquered himself, since his God and his Model was obedient, even unto the death of the cross.

Two worlds struggle for our souls—the invisible and lasting world, which is the richest, and, alas! the least attractive to our foolish hearts, and this transitory world, which fascinates the eye, without being able really to satisfy the heart. There are sinful Christians who desire to see nothing beyond this earth, and so condemn themselves to perish with it. There are others who are divided between the two; and their happiness is diminished

[2] Job xxxviii. 22. [3] St. Matthew xiii. 44.

both in this world and in the world to come. But there is one, the religious, who is happier than any of these, because he belongs entirely to the Supreme Good, because he scrupulously consecrates to his true country all that he is, and all the strength, activity, and energy that he possesses, because he is a heavenly man, living for the only reality, a man of God.

He even deprives himself of the power of changing his views or aspirations, making himself immoveable in the midst of an ever-changing world; he imposes on himself the holy obligation of vows, perseverance in his sacrifice, and thus constancy in true happiness, in the midst of those fools whose whole lives are nothing but violent passions, anxieties, and excitement. The religious has but one Guide, that of the Holy Spirit, which leads him to heaven. He overcomes the tedium of monotony and the temptations to weariness or disgust, which so regular a life might bring with it. He has precipitated into the fire of the holocaust his entire being; he would not recall his sacrifice even for an instant. Although the Church permits him under certain circumstances to change his order and rule, he knows that it is better to remain immoveably fixed in his own congregation, even should it be less severe, and less fervent than others; for unity in spiritual exercises is more useful to perfection than a change of spirit and observances. We have on this point the authority of a holy abbot, who says that "it is impossible for one and the same man to excel at one and the same time in every virtue. Should he, therefore, pretend to acquire and profess them altogether, as a natural consequence it would come to pass that he would fail to attain to the perfection of even one. Let him then follow with a real zeal and great application the rule which he has once deliberately chosen, and never forsake it."[4]

The monastic habit, of itself, is an eloquent protest against that unbridled luxury which is the symbol, as well as the origin, of all social corruption. It reminds the world and the religious that this earth is but a valley of tears, an abode of sadness and of penance;

[4] The Abbot Nesteros in the *Conferences of the Fathers*; Conf. xiv. The Angelic Doctor adds, that these changes are, in the greater number of cases, a scandal to the brethren whom we abandon.

that the glory of this world is nothing, and deserves nought but the contempt of the spiritual man. For it is not out of ostentation, nor vanity, nor the love of singularity and novelty; nor out of negligence nor avarice, that the monk appears before us in so miserable an exterior. His coarse habit and his poor cloak humiliate his soul, even as rich clothes fill other people with pride. If the dark veil of the religious is dearer to him than the most brilliant dress, it is because it hides from his gaze the frivolity of the world, and so permits him uninterruptedly to contemplate the adorable beauty alone of his divine Spouse.

The religious is, therefore, more than all other Christians, a living contrast with the world; he is the solemn denial which God opposes to the senseless affirmatives of man; the permanent answer which heaven gives to earth, eternity to time, the spirit to the flesh, grace to sin, light to darkness, and Jesus Christ to Bélial.

To each one of us the religious recalls that "life is not life;" that the soul is infinitely above the body, that we are merely pilgrims and travellers, and that our country is beyond the grave. He teaches the family that its end is not to enjoy the pleasures of earth; that the son is not placed in his father's hands as the object of his vanity, neither as a means of attaining a fortune, nor as a slave or debtor perpetually doomed to pay off by his work an ever-renewed debt. The religious teaches that the obedience due by children to their parents is not universal, but limited to the concerns of education and the maintenance of good domestic order; that the divine commandment to honour one's father and mother does not exclusively extend to temporal services, but also regards the soul and spiritual services, which are far superior to purely exterior assistance; and that even in the depths of the cloister one may be more useful to one's family than by remaining under the paternal roof.

Even to civil society monastic bodies teach that not only man in his individual capacity, but also public men, cities, and kingdoms, are obliged to adore and glorify God, to procure for all consciences efficacious means for the avoidance of evil and performance of good, to subordinate material progress to the advance of spiritual progress, grace to nature, and that the spirit of sacrifice is necessary to the existence of empires; that abnegation is the virtue especially necessary for those who govern the people; and that real authority coming from God is always obeyed.

It is therefore with good reason that our Angelic Master calls religious teaching orders (and are not all orders teachers in one manner or another?) "architects of morality;" indefatigable workmen placed in the centre of paganism, in order to erect new Christian communities; who are sent into the heart of cities desolated by heresy, in order to restore their ruins; and who come to us lukewarm Catholics, so forgetful of our great dignity, to repair our shortcomings, and to arrest the thunder-bolt which threatens to crush Sodom and Gomorrah. They pray and they work, they intercede, they labour, and fight. For if they build up with one hand, in the other they carry the sword to defend Holy Church. They are but simple soldiers, under the authority of princes, and more especially of the King of the New Jerusalem; but no one is more ardent for this spiritual warfare, none is better armed with good weapons and is more free in all his movements. It is a picked band, always prepared for the fight, and, if needs be, for martyrdom. It darts forward at the first alarm to the extremities of the earth, because it is withheld neither by temporal cares, family duties, nor even by the charge of souls. Having nothing to lose, what can it fear, save not to be able entirely to sacrifice itself for the triumph of our Lord Jesus Christ, of His Vicar, His bishops, and His whole flock.

When the day of the last judgment and the great regeneration shall arrive, the religious will reap the hundredfold for all the riches and joys that he has abandoned here below; and not only will God render him this hundredfold—that is to say, the infinite delights of eternal life—but He will call him to the honour of sitting as judge near the Son of Man, upon a throne raised in the face of all the tribes of the earth.[5]

Three chief reasons will assure this privilege to the religious who has become poor of his own will! *Firstly*, in despising and in quitting all temporal riches to attach himself wholly to Jesus Christ, he has stripped himself of all that would darken his intelligence and impede

[5] St. Matthew xix. 28, 29.

his right judgment; he has thus acquired a particular capacity for this solemn judgeship, which will determine the fate of mankind; having loved what is true, what is beautiful and just, above all created things, he will apply these laws, so long violated, but which are at length triumphant. *Secondly*, our Lord is bound to compensate the merit of humility by a glory proportionate to the degree of his free and spontaneous abjection. Now, amongst all the causes which can disgrace us, without rendering us guilty, poverty is certainly one of the most powerful. Is it therefore surprising that God should exalt such a one, even so far as to give to him the inestimable dignity of Judge in this universal assize? *Thirdly* and lastly, even as terrestial goods prevent the increase of the heavenly seed in souls,[6] so the spirit of poverty forms the first and most effectual condition of the growth of knowledge of spiritual things in us. Now, it is according to the principles of this knowledge that the trial of this world will be conducted and the sentence passed. The catholic religious will then be as a sacred book, as the inflexible code manifesting the decrees of

[6] Luke viii. 14.

divine justice. Do not contemn and proudly disdain him now ye rich and powerful and worldly wise, for he will some day be your Judge. He will reign eternally at the right hand of Jesus Christ, the Conqueror; he will bear upon his forehead, so lately humiliated, the crown of the elect and the aureola of virgins; he will hold in his hand the sceptre of obedience, and he will taste of the sweet fruits of monastic chastity—the good ground bringing forth fruit, and yielding thirty-fold, sixty-fold, and even a hundred fold:[7] and as the labourer rejoices not only in his abundant harvest, but also in happy and fruitful tillage, so, also, the good disposition which these souls had to bring forth fruits during this life, will procure to them in the next a special blessing, which the disciples of St. Thomas style "*celestial fruit.*" And because this good disposition consists in the *spirituality*, which is the result of ordinary chastity, but more especially of the chastity of Christian widows, and above all of virginity, the religious who is faithful to his engagements will rejoice in a most precious fruit, and will be as the hundred-fold, whereas the Christians who are less pure

[7] St. Matthew xiii. 23.

and less spiritual will be as the less fertile soil which will render only thirty or sixty-fold.

How true then, oh Angelic Master, are the consoling words which, in your *Summa* of theology, you place at the end of this treatise on the religious state: "It is a sweet yoke, and those who bear it on their shoulders have the promise to be one day consoled by the delightful possession of God, and by the eternal repose of the soul. May Jesus Christ our Lord the most High, God, worthy of all honour to the end of the world, and Who has given us this promise, may He by His Divine Hand lead us to that state!"

We have begun this book by joining with the sacred liturgy in begging of heaven the favour rightly to understand the teaching of the Angel of the School. Let us now complete the pious and maternal prayer of the Holy Roman Church: "Grant us, O God, the grace to accomplish the works which this great Doctor has left us for our imitation."

FINIS.

ALPHABETICAL AND ANALYTICAL INDEX.

ADORATION OF GOD : necessary for a perfect consecration, and fully realized by the religious vows 186.

ANGELS : their share in the direction of men, and the devotion we owe to them 318.

ASCETICISM : a real science XIII. ;—how it should be studied XIII.-XIV. ;—its end 301.

AUREOLA : its definition 128 ;—due to religious for their virginity *idem* ;—may also be accorded to Doctors and Martyrs 291.

BEATITUDE : the first is voluntary poverty 38 *note*, 57.

BEAUTY : its definition 124 ;—conditions of moral beauty 125-127.

CHARITY : its perfection the object of the religious state 23-4 ;—prompts the religious vows 25 ;—its two principal acts are the sources of the distinction between religious orders 235.

CHASTITY : its definition 112 ;—counselled by our Lord 19, 87-9 ;—has no limits 83 ;—a principle of purity, and consequently of perfection 86 ;—the reason it was not observed by the

Patriarchs of the old Testament 88;—its necessity to perfection *idem*;—it emancipates and spiritualizes human nature 91-98;—its various degrees *idem*;—three conditions of *religious* chastity 98-100;—*ordinary* chastity is less noble, less happy, and maintained with more difficulty 97, 115, 117;—it does not destroy all discord in man 105;—it does not completely fortify him 113;—does not deliver him from all shame 128;—*religious* chastity excels in all these points *idem*;—it is a principle of spiritual fecundity 110, 306-9;—it is, however, not the highest of the virtues 125;—in what mystical or spiritual chastity consists 101.

CHILDREN: may be admitted to the practice of the evangelical counsels 353;—and be brought up in monasteries to become eventually religious 354;—thus they attain to a higher perfection 354;—their duties towards their parents 368.

COMMANDMENTS OF GOD: need not necessarily be observed before we practise the counsels; nor even can they be kept perfectly before the counsels are followed 349-352.

COMMUNITIES, RELIGIOUS: should not possess excessive riches 63, 70-1.

CONSECRATION: the religious is a person consecrated to God 5;—and for that three things are requisite 183, 188, 217;—religious life is a perfect consecration 188.

CONSOLATIONS OF THE RELIGIOUS LIFE 25, 163-4, 193.

CONSTANCY IN THE DIVINE SERVICE: is necessary for a true consecration, and is secured by religious vows 186;—the religious must be faithful to his state 107.

CONTEMPT OF THE LAW: its terrible effects 207, 209, 217.

CONTINENCE, RELIGIOUS: its definition 107;—cannot be violated without a horrible adultery 109.

CORRUPTION, MORAL: its three causes 118-120;—they are most to be feared in a sensual man 120.

COUNSELS, EVANGELICAL: their definition 16, 27;—they are both essential and secondary to the religious state 20, 21;—their bearing on perfection 348;—secular life does not prepare one for their practice 351-53;—they are the normal means of attaining perfection 359;—it is lawful and even praiseworthy to advise anyone to embrace religious life 320;—even by praising one's own community 322.

CREATURES, VISIBLE: are symbolical of the invisible world 130.

DEVIL: cannot really lead us to God, even when he would do so in order to gain us to himself in the end 334;—is not to be feared so long as he restricts himself to good suggestions 335.

DISOBEDIENCE: its results 132;—grievousness of this sin 144-218 *note*.

END OF THE RELIGIOUS STATE 9, 15, 167;—chief and secondary ends 232, 242, 248, 254.

FORMS OF THE REGULAR LIFE: the reason why there are several 229;—do not lead to confusion in the Church 230-32;—cannot create dissension between various orders 232;—how important it is to know their classification 228, 234, 272;—the principal grounds of this distinction 235-40;—secondary grounds 246-250;—modern congregations and Third orders 252;—manner of appreciating and comparing the excellence of these various forms 252-257, 263;—each possesses an excellence peculiar to itself 271.

FRANCIS OF ASSISI (Saint): an admirable type of religious poverty 58, 75, 82.

HABIT, RELIGIOUS: its symbolism, and the spirit in which it is to be worn 366-7.

HAPPINESS: where it is to be found 39;—the fruit of perfection 40;—its various degrees 41;—happiness of the active and contemplative life 46-47;—not dependent on riches 49.

HOLOCAUST: its definition 171, 175;—its symbolical signification 179-182;—the religious offers himself as a holocaust 3;—and this is his distinctive character 6, 174-179.

HONOUR: in what it consists 125;—is due to religious 177 *note*.

IMPERFECTION: not necessarily culpable in a religious 9, 216, 221-24.

IMPURITY: its offspring 91;—is a principle of dissolution in man 103, 108 *note*;—reduces the soul to a state of perpetual childhood 111;—is a source of corruption 120;—is the most frightful of all the passions 123.

LEAH AND RACHEL: their allegorical character 242-44, 262.

LIFE (RELIGIOUS): is not dangerous 203, 210, 225;—assistance it affords against sin 211, 214;—is not suited to everyone 310;—is not meant exclusively for the perfect 339;—though highly beneficial to them 340;—and though they are specially fitted to profit by it 352;—it is also very profitable to sinners, and to the imperfect 340-48;—*active* life has its own special character 46, 236-40, 245;—it makes use of exterior goods, and in what manner 47, 66;—the definition of the *contemplative* life 48;—the need it has of worldly riches 47, 66-69.

MAN: his excellence and two principal acts 238-9.

MANUAL LABOUR: the degree in which it is suited to religious life 290.

MARTHA AND MARY 48, 242-3, 257, 262, 276, 310;—their symbolical character.

MENDICITY (CHRISTIAN): mendicant orders 250;—rules to observe in its regard 298.

MONK: definition of the word and character of perfect unity 109, 250-1, 258.

NAZARENES: prefigurative of Catholic religious 153.

NOVICIATE: its object 313-14;—its utility even for persons who will never be professed 314-15.

OBEDIENCE: counselled and practised by our Lord 19, 135;—its general necessity 131-133; —is an act of true self-love 133;—its happy effects 135-36;—especially necessary for religious 136;—its nobility 137;—is a principle of true liberty 137;—its excellence compared with other virtues 139;—its limits 141;—religious obedience is more perfect than that of other Christians 143;—it is indispensable to perfect souls, and is in itself a mark of perfection 144-5;—defects to be avoided 146;—it should be especially practised towards the Sovereign Pontiff and the Episcopacy 147;—obedience is the most excellent of the three religious vows 197.

ORDERS: the active ones inferior to the contemplative 257-262;—Apostolic orders the most perfect 259;—they all stand in need of study 276;—contemplative orders 235-46;—should not forget the interests of the Church 303;— mixed orders 246;—degree of poverty suitable to each order 66-9.

PENANCE: is not the distinctive character of the religious state 12;—but very suitable to it 13;

—and is then more perfect than when practised in the world 14, 195;—is useful even to children 354;—is not a positive mark of excellence in religious orders 257.

PERFECTION: how it is to be obtained 40;—its various degrees 41-2;—is the cause of happiness 40;—how it is expressed in human language 2;—in what *Christian* perfection consists 8;—*religious* perfection 8, 22, 349-50;—it demands a close following of Jesus Christ 24;—threefold impediment to perfection 17-19;—does not consist in the religious virtues, which serve only as its means 22, 346;—a high degree of perfection can be allied with an ordinary life 46;—the religious is not bound actually to possess perfection, but to tend towards it 9-10;—it is not an object of the vows 167;—one is not bound to employ all the existing means for its attainment 21, 223, 228;—in what manner God and man unite for its development 150;—three things to be considered in it 221-24;—Jesus Christ is its type, measure, and Judge 102;—the perfection of a state is different from that of an individual 89;—in order to attain to a state of perfection it is not necessary to pass through a state of imperfection 346.

POVERTY: counselled by Jesus Christ 20;—practised by Him 70;—is a beatitude 28 *note*, 57;—was embraced by certain philosophers of antiquity 33-4;—facilitates perfect charity 30, 50;—and the contemplation of wisdom 35, 50;—frees us from many cares and anxieties 32, 49, 62;—is better than almsgiving 35;—is a real holocaust 37;—its dangers when it is compulsory 38, 51;—is not perfection of itself 50;—its disadvantages 51;—should not be pushed too far, nor be productive of idleness 52;—when it is most perfect 52, 68;—the poverty of communities 59, 60;—should have divers degrees 65, 250;—exaggerations to be avoided 53, 67 *note*, 68;—religious poverty is an Apostolic state 58-69, 81;—procures us riches for the soul 78;—is a mark of disinterestedness and divine power 78, 81;—renders us like unto our Lord 76;—gives us the privilege of judging men at the last day 371.

PREACHER: the virtues necessary for him 74, 80;—excellence of his function 259;—he must study 282;—every religious is in some measure a preacher of the Gospel 271;—what he teaches individuals, families, and human societies 368.

PROFESSION (RELIGIOUS): the religious does not make profession of being actually perfect 9;—what profession is 151;—it subsists in virtue of the vows 163;—its excellence 182;—its three effects for the advancement of the soul 191-3;—is like another Baptism 195.

PROMISES MADE TO GOD: very different from those made to men 194.

PURITY OF BODY AND SOUL: necessary for perfection 85, 185;—realized in the highest degree by religious vows, *idem*.

RELIGIOUS: divers meanings of the word 3;—definition of a religious 5;—he is in a more perfect state than that of the Patriarchs or Prophets 90;—he is fully spiritualized 100;—he is the true Nazarene 153;—what his obligation is of tending to perfection 9, 20, 220-225;—he is not in a supreme or active state of perfection 8, 231 *note*;—he is, however, an Apostle 76;—his part in the divine plan 359;—like our Lord, he is both priest and victim 174;—what he is with regard to the world 360-8;—his militant character, he will judge the world 370.

RELIGION: its definition 2 *note*, 6 *note*;—its highest degree 3;—it may constitute a state in the Church 4;—its twofold function 236;—its influence over the other virtues, and the entire regular life 4-6, 188.

RETREAT: its advantages, 265, 269.

RICHES: attachment to them is injurious to the love of God 29;—the possession of them is more dangerous than the desire of them, *idem*; indifferent in themselves 39;—they cannot directly affect our happiness 40;—are good only in relation to an end, *idem*;—their advantages and dangers 43-4; useful to the active life they are pernicious to the contemplative 47-8; —when possessed in common are less injurious 62-4;—precautions to be taken against them in this case 70-2.

RULE, RELIGIOUS: its nature 214-17; the nature and extent of the obligation it imposes 215-20.

SANCTITY: its definition, and the means to attain it 239.

SIN: its essential opposition to the religious state 202;—is sometimes, but not always a real sacrilege 206-7;—may be more grievous than in secular life 207-11;—but often less grievous 211-14; St. Thomas' theory on venial sin 211 *note*, 218 *note*.

SINNERS: when repentant may enter religion 341-6;—and are better suited than the presumptuous just 343;—should not be despised in the communities into which they have entered 345.

SOLITUDE: its importance 249, 265;—its dangers 265-8.

SOLICITUDE OCCASIONED BY WORLDLY GOODS: is not necessarily injurious 52-7;—may even further charity 64, 70;—two antagonistic anxieties in religious life 66.

SPIRIT OF RELIGION: in what it consists 6, 24.

STATE: meaning of the word 154;—its source 156-58;—nature of the religious state 4-6;—

state of perfection 8-9 ;—what is essential to it, or merely secondary 21 ;—the religious state is the school of our Lord 135.

STUDY : suitable to regulars of every order 276-80, 282, 287 ;—what we must think of its dangers 280-82 ;—it is of great help to the fulfilment of religious vows 284-86 ;—and is, in its turn, helped by a religious life, *idem* ;—in what spirit we should study 288.

SUPERIORS: in what light we should consider them 145.

THOMAS OF AQUINO (Saint): importance of his teaching at the present time, more particularly as regards the religious state v-vi ;—he was a martyr to religious life ix ;—feeling of the Church respecting his doctrine 1 ;—how we have expounded and developed it viii-xii ;—his knowledge produced by virginity 85 ;—manner in which he treats of chastity 86 ;—he is a beautiful model of a religious vocation 356.

TUITION GIVEN BY RELIGIOUS: is very meritorious 288 ;—they can succeed better than others 288-91.

UNION WITH GOD: necessary to the intimate unity of man 109 ;—is a mystical marriage of the soul with God, *idem*.

UNITY IN MAN: is equivalent to perfection 107-10 ;—is diminished by sensual pleasures 103-5 ;—there is one which is essential, and another of counsel 108;—preserved and augmented by the virginal union of the soul with God 109;—beautiful unity of the religious life 4 *note*, 15, 175 *note*, 258 *note*;—unity of the divine plan 130.

UTILITY OF THE RELIGIOUS STATE: for the world and for the whole Church 299-308.

VIRGINITY: a very reasonable virtue 93;—a grand and magnificent virtue 96;—which governs all human powers, even sensitive ones 94;—it is necessarily consecrated and perpetual 95;—makes us like to the angels 98, 108;—may be restored to the soul 95;—a principle of perfect *unity* in us 108;—is a mystic marriage with God 109;—powerful means of religion 110;—its spiritual fruitfulness, *idem*;—principle of an admirable strength in us 114-15;—and, consequently, the source of peace 116;—facility with which it overcomes temptation 117-18;—its definition 121;—preserves us from the causes of corruption 122;—supreme source of honour and moral beauty 124-28;—crowned with an aureola in heaven 129;—sings the new canticle of virgins 129; —is a perfect imitation of our Lord 129;—praise given to it by St. Thomas 363;—it will bear the heavenly fruit a hundred-fold 372.

VIRTUES: their mutual subordination 4;—they are essential and secondary in the regular state 22;—they are dispositions, effect and signs with regard to perfection 22-5, 103;—the reason of their being and their origin 27-8;—supernatural virtues find their best development in the religious life 359-61;—interior virtues are not the matter of vows 167;—difference between a virtue and a state 153.

VOCATION: is a mystery 310;—but speaks distinctly to sincere souls 312;—we should only wish to know it so far as God wills 313;—is sometimes transitory, and may change 314-15;—must not expect miraculous revelations concerning it 317;—means of knowing one's vocation 318-20, 326;—we should not consult tóo many persons 322;—especially worldlings 325;—what must be said of parents who oppose their children's vocation 326;—is one obliged to follow one's vocation? 326 *note*;—the reason why religious vocations are more rare now than they used to be 329-30;—four questions which must not be examined too long a time with regard to vocation 331-34;—it needs no long deliberation 336-9;—is not a proof that one was holy in the world 352.

VOWS: their definition 151 *note*;—necessary to religious life 153-6;—are at once a deliverance and a new obligation 156;—distinguish states and conditions in the Church 160;—give to religious life the stability necessary for it, in order to be the School of our Lord and the foreshadowing of heaven 160;—they render our acts stable and perpetual 161;—their relations with human liberty 160-61 *note*, 165;—sources of joy, *idem*;—are the centre of all religious observances 165;—are an excellent spiritual sacrifice 171;—in honour of God, our Beginning 173;—and our last End 173;—Vows are a true holocaust 175;—immolating both man and his powers of action 176;—his passions, *idem*;—his future even 179;—they constitute a permanent sacrifice 184;—and a sublime consecration 144-5;—their violation is a sacrilege 179.

WORKS: necessary to glorify God 274-5;—particularly for religious, *idem*;—even secular business may be useful to religious 292;—bodily labours of religious life 294-5.

WORSHIP DIVINE: its importance and character in the religious state 6-7.

www.ingramcontent.com/pod-product-compliance
Lightning Source LLC
Chambersburg PA
CBHW022123290426
44112CB00008B/789